T0257031

THIRD EDITION

PostgreSQL: Up and Running

A Practical Guide to the Advanced Open Source Database

Regina O. Obe and Leo S. Hsu

Beijing · Boston · Farnham · Sebastopol · Tokyo

PostgreSQL: Up and Running

by Regina O. Obe and Leo S. Hsu

Copyright © 2018 Regina Obe, Leo Hsu. All rights reserved.

Printed in the United States of America.

Published by O'Reilly Media, Inc., 1005 Gravenstein Highway North, Sebastopol, CA 95472.

O'Reilly books may be purchased for educational, business, or sales promotional use. Online editions are also available for most titles (*http://oreilly.com/safari*). For more information, contact our corporate/institutional sales department: 800-998-9938 or *corporate@oreilly.com*.

Editor: Andy Oram	**Indexer:** Lucie Haskins
Production Editor: Melanie Yarbrough	**Interior Designer:** David Futato
Copyeditor: Kim Cofer	**Cover Designer:** Karen Montgomery
Proofreader: Christina Edwards	**Illustrator:** Rebecca Demarest

October 2017:   Third Edition

Revision History for the Third Edition
2017-10-10:   First Release

See *http://oreilly.com/catalog/errata.csp?isbn=9781491963418* for release details.

978-1-491-96341-8

[LSI]

Table of Contents

Preface

PostgreSQL bills itself as the world's most advanced open source database. We couldn't agree more.

What we hope to accomplish in this book is to give you a firm grounding in the concepts and features that make PostgreSQL so impressive. Along the way, we should convince you that PostgreSQL does indeed stand up to its claim to fame. Because the database is advanced, no book short of the 3500 pages of documentation can bring out all its glory. But then again, most users don't need to delve into the most abstruse features that PostgreSQL has to offer. So in our shorter 300-pager, we hope to get you, as the subtitle proclaims, *Up and Running*.

Each topic is presented with some context so you understand when to use it and what it offers. We assume you have prior experience with some other database so that we can jump right to the key points of PostgreSQL. We generously litter the pages of this book with links to references so you can dig deeper into topics of interest. These links lead to sections in the manual, to helpful articles, to blog posts of PostgreSQL vanguards. We also link to our own site at Postgres OnLine Journal (*http://www.postgresonline.com*), where we have collected many pieces that we have written on PostgreSQL and its interoperability with other applications.

This book focuses on PostgreSQL versions 9.5, 9.6, and 10, but we will cover some unique and advanced features that are also present in prior versions.

Audience

For migrants from other database engines, we'll point out parallels that PostgreSQL shares with other leading products. Perhaps more importantly, we highlight feats you can achieve with PostgreSQL that are difficult or impossible to do in other databases.

We stop short of teaching you SQL, as you'll find many excellent sources for that. SQL is much like chess—a few hours to learn, a lifetime to master. You have wisely chosen PostgreSQL. You'll be greatly rewarded.

If you're currently a savvy PostgreSQL user or a weather-beaten DBA, much of the material in this book should be familiar terrain, but you'll be sure to pick up some pointers and shortcuts introduced in newer versions of PostgreSQL. Perhaps you'll even find the hidden gem that eluded you. If nothing else, this book is at least ten times lighter than the PostgreSQL manual.

Not using PostgreSQL yet? This book is propaganda—the good kind. Each day you continue to use a database with limited SQL capabilities, you handicap yourself. Each day that you're wedded to a proprietary system, you're bleeding dollars.

Finally, if your work has nothing to do with databases or IT, or if you've just graduated from kindergarten, the cute picture of the elephant shrew on the cover should be worthy of the price alone.

For More Information on PostgreSQL

PostgreSQL has a well-maintained set of online documentation: PostgreSQL manuals (*http://www.postgresql.org/docs/manuals*). We encourage you to bookmark it. The manual is available both as HTML and as a PDF. Hardcopy collector editions are available for purchase.

Other PostgreSQL resources include:

- *Planet PostgreSQL* (*http://planet.postgresql.org*) is an aggregator of PostgreSQL blogs. You'll find PostgreSQL core developers and general users showcasing new features, novel ways to use existing ones, and reporting of bugs that have yet to be patched.

- *PostgreSQL Wiki* (*http://wiki.postgresql.org*) provides tips and tricks for managing various facets of the database and migrating from other databases.

- *PostgreSQL Books* (*http://www.postgresql.org/docs/books/*) is a list of books about PostgreSQL.

- *PostGIS in Action Books* (*http://www.postgis.us*) is the website for the books we've written on PostGIS, the spatial extender for PostgreSQL, and more recently pgRouting, another PostgreSQL extension that provides network routing capabilities useful for building driving apps.

Code and Output Formatting

For elements in parentheses, we gravitate toward placing the open parenthesis on the same line as the preceding element and the closing parenthesis on a line by itself. This is a classic C formatting style that we like because it cuts down on the number of blank lines:

```
function(
        Welcome to PostgreSQL
);
```

We also remove gratuitous spaces in screen output, so if the formatting of your results doesn't match ours exactly, don't fret.

We omit the space after a serial comma for short elements. For example, ('a','b','c').

The SQL interpreter treats tabs, newlines, and carriage returns as whitespace. In our code, we generally use whitespaces for indentation, not tabs. Make sure that your editor doesn't automatically remove tabs, newlines, and carriage returns or convert them to something other than spaces.

After copying and pasting, if you find your code not working, check the copied code to make sure it looks like what we have in the listing.

We use examples based on both Linux and Windows. Path notations differ between the two, namely the use of solidus (/) versus reverse solidus (\). While on Windows, use the Linux solidus, always! /, not \. You may see a path such as */postgresql_book/somefile.csv*. These are always relative to the root of your server. If you are on Windows, you must include the drive letter: *C:/postgresql_book/somefile.csv*.

Conventions Used in This Book

The following typographical conventions are used in this book:

Italic

Indicates new terms, URLs, email addresses, filenames, and file extensions.

`Constant width`

Used for program listings. Used within paragraphs, where needed for clarity, to refer to programming elements such as variables, functions, databases, data types, environment variables, statements, and keywords.

`Constant width bold`

Shows commands or other text that should be typed literally by the user.

`Constant width italic`

Shows text that should be replaced with user-supplied values or by values determined by context.

 This icon signifies a tip, suggestion, or general note.

This icon indicates a warning or caution.

Using Code Examples

Code and data examples are available for download at *http://www.postgresonline.com/downloads/postgresql_book_3e.zip*.

This book is here to help you get your job done. In general, you may use the code in this book in your programs and documentation. You do not need to contact us for permission unless you're reproducing a significant portion of the code. For example, writing a program that uses several chunks of code from this book does not require permission. Selling or distributing a CD-ROM of examples from O'Reilly books does require permission. Answering a question by citing this book and quoting example code does not require permission. Incorporating a significant amount of example code from this book into your product's documentation does require permission.

We appreciate, but do not require, attribution. An attribution usually includes the title, author, publisher, and ISBN. For example: "*PostgreSQL: Up and Running, Third Edition* by Regina Obe and Leo Hsu (O'Reilly). Copyright 2018 Regina Obe and Leo Hsu, 978-1-491-96341-8."

If you feel your use of code examples falls outside fair use or the permission given above, feel free to contact us at *permissions@oreilly.com*.

O'Reilly Safari

 Safari (formerly Safari Books Online) is a membership-based training and reference platform for enterprise, government, educators, and individuals.

Members have access to thousands of books, training videos, Learning Paths, interactive tutorials, and curated playlists from over 250 publishers, including O'Reilly Media, Harvard Business Review, Prentice Hall Professional, Addison-Wesley Professional, Microsoft Press, Sams, Que, Peachpit Press, Adobe, Focal Press, Cisco Press, John Wiley & Sons, Syngress, Morgan Kaufmann, IBM Redbooks, Packt, Adobe Press, FT Press, Apress, Manning, New Riders, McGraw-Hill, Jones & Bartlett, and Course Technology, among others.

For more information, please visit *http://oreilly.com/safari*.

How to Contact Us

Please address comments and questions concerning this book to the publisher:

O'Reilly Media, Inc.
1005 Gravenstein Highway North
Sebastopol, CA 95472
800-998-9938 (in the United States or Canada)
707-829-0515 (international or local)
707-829-0104 (fax)

Please submit errata using the book's errata page (*http://bit.ly/postgresql-up-and-running-3e*).

The companion site for this book is at *http://bit.ly/postgresql-up-and-running-3e*.

To contact the authors, send email to *lr@pcorp.us*.

To comment or ask technical questions to the publisher, send email to *bookquestions@oreilly.com*.

For more information about our books, courses, conferences, and news, see our website at *http://www.oreilly.com*.

Find us on Facebook: *http://facebook.com/oreilly*

Follow us on Twitter: *http://twitter.com/oreillymedia*

Watch us on YouTube: *http://www.youtube.com/oreillymedia*

## CHAPTER 1

The Basics

PostgreSQL is an extremely powerful piece of software that introduces features you may not have seen before. Some of the features are also present in other well-known database engines, but under different names. This chapter lays out the main concepts you should know when starting to attack PostgreSQL documentation, and mentions some related terms in other databases.

We begin by pointing you to resources for downloading and installing PostgreSQL. Next, we provide an overview of indispensable administration tools followed by a review of PostgreSQL nomenclature. PostgreSQL 10 was recently released. We'll highlight some of the new features therein. We close with resources to turn to when you need additional guidance and to submit bug reports.

Why PostgreSQL?

PostgreSQL is an enterprise-class relational database management system, on par with the very best proprietary database systems: Oracle, Microsoft SQL Server, and IBM DB2, just to name a few. PostgreSQL is special because it's not just a database: it's also an application platform, and an impressive one at that.

PostgreSQL is fast. In benchmarks, PostgreSQL either exceeds or matches the performance of many other databases, both open source and proprietary.

PostgreSQL invites you to write stored procedures and functions in numerous programming languages. In addition to the prepackaged languages of C, SQL, and PL/pgSQL, you can easily enable support for additional languages such as PL/Perl, PL/Python, PL/V8 (aka PL/JavaScript), PL/Ruby, and PL/R. This support for a wide variety of languages allows you to choose the language with constructs that can best solve the problem at hand. For instance, use R for statistics and graphing, Python for calling web services, the Python SciPy library for scientific computing, and PL/V8 for validating data, processing strings, and wrangling with JSON data. Easier yet, find a freely available function that you need, find out the language that it's written in, enable that specific language in PostgreSQL, and copy the code. No one will think less of you.

Most database products limit you to a predefined set of data types: integers, texts, Booleans, etc. Not only does PostgreSQL come with a larger built-in set than most, but you can define additional data types to suit your needs. Need complex numbers? Create a composite type made up of two floats. Have a triangle fetish? Create a coordinate type, then create a triangle type made up of three coordinate pairs. A dozenal activist? Create your own duodecimal type. Innovative types are useful insofar as the operators and functions that support them. So once you've created your special number types, don't forget to define basic arithmetic operations for them. Yes, PostgreSQL will let you customize the meaning of the symbols (+,-,/,*). Whenever you create a type, PostgreSQL automatically creates a companion array type for you. If you created a complex number type, arrays of complex numbers are available to you without additional work.

PostgreSQL also automatically creates types from any tables you define. For instance, create a table of dogs with columns such as breed, cuteness, and barkiness. Behind the scenes, PostgreSQL maintains a dogs data type for you. This amazingly useful bridge between the relational world and the object world means that you can treat data elements in a way that's convenient for the task at hand. You can create functions that work on one object at a time or functions that work on sets of objects at a time. Many third-party extensions for PostgreSQL leverage custom types to achieve performance gains, provide domain-specific constructs for shorter and more maintainable code, and accomplish feats you can only fantasize about with other database products.

Our principal advice is this: don't treat databases as dumb storage. A database such as PostgreSQL can be a full-fledged application platform. With a robust database, everything else is eye candy. Once you're versant in SQL, you'll be able to accomplish in seconds what would take a casual programmer hours, both in coding and running time.

In recent years, we've witnessed an upsurge of NoSQL movements (though much of it could be hype). Although PostgreSQL is fundamentally relational, you'll find plenty of facilities to handle nonrelational data. The ltree extension to PostgreSQL has been around since time immemorial and provides support for graphs. The hstore extensions let you store key-value pairs. JSON and JSONB types allow storage of documents similar to MongoDb. In many ways, PostgreSQL accommodated NoSQL before the term was even coined!

PostgreSQL just celebrated its 20th birthday, dating from its christening to PostgreSQL from Postgres95. The beginnings of the PostgreSQL code-base began well before that in 1986. PostgreSQL is supported on all major operating systems: Linux, Unix, Windows, and Mac. Every year brings a new major release, offering enhanced performance along with features that push the envelope of what's possible in a database offering.

Finally, PostgreSQL is open source with a generous licensing policy (*https://open source.org/licenses/postgresql*). PostgreSQL is supported by a community of developers and users where profit maximization is not the ultimate pursuit. If you want features, you're free to contribute, or at least vocalize. If you want to customize and experiment, no one is going to sue you. You, the mighty user, make PostgreSQL what it is.

In the end, you will wonder why you ever used any other database, because PostgreSQL does everything you could hope for and does it for free. No more reading the licensing cost fineprint of those other databases to figure out how many dollars you need to spend if you have eight cores on your virtualized servers with X number of concurrent connections. No more fretting about how much more the next upgrade will cost you.

Why Not PostgreSQL?

Given all the proselytizing thus far, it's only fair that we point out situations when PostgreSQL might not be suitable.

The typical installation size of PostgreSQL without any extensions is more than 100 MB. This rules out PostgreSQL for a database on a small device or as a simple cache store. Many lightweight databases abound that could better serve your needs without the larger footprint.

Given its enterprise stature, PostgreSQL doesn't take security lightly. If you're developing lightweight applications where you're managing security at the application level, PostgreSQL security with its sophisticated role and permission management could be overkill. You might consider a single-user database such as SQLite or a database such as Firebird that can be run either as a client server or in single-user embedded mode.

All that said, it is a common practice to combine PostgreSQL with other database types. One common combination you will find is using Redis or Memcache to cache PostgreSQL query results. As another example, SQLite can be used to store a disconnected set of data for offline querying when PostgreSQL is the main database backend for an application.

Finally, many hosting companies don't offer PostgreSQL on a shared hosting environment, or they offer an outdated version. Most still gravitate toward the impotent MySQL. To a web designer, for whom the database is an afterthought, MySQL might suffice. But as soon as you learn to write any SQL beyond a single-table select and simple joins, you'll begin to sense the shortcomings of MySQL. Since the first edition of this book, virtualization has resown the landscape of commerical hosting, so having your own dedicated server is no longer a luxury, but the norm. And when you have your own server, you're free to choose what you wish to have installed. PostgreSQL bodes well with the popularity of cloud computing such as Platform as a Service (PaaS) and Database as a Service (DbaaS). Most of the major PaaS and DbaaS providers offer PostgreSQL, notably Heroku, Engine Yard, Red Hat OpenShift, Amazon RDS for PostgreSQL, Google Cloud SQL for PostgreSQL, Amazon Aurora for PostgreSQL, and Microsoft Azure for PostgreSQL.

Where to Get PostgreSQL

Years ago, if you wanted PostgreSQL, you had to compile it from source. Thankfully, those days are long gone. Granted, you can still compile from source, but using packaged installers won't make you any less cool. A few clicks or keystrokes, and you're on your way.

If you're installing PostgreSQL for the first time and have no existing database to upgrade, you should install the latest stable release version for your OS. The downloads page for the PostgreSQL core distribution (*https://www.postgresql.org/down load*) maintains a listing of places where you can download PostgreSQL binaries for various OSes. In Appendix A, you'll find useful installation instructions and links to additional custom distributions.

Administration Tools

Four tools widely used with PostgreSQL are psql, pgAdmin, phpPgAdmin, and Adminer. PostgreSQL core developers actively maintain the first three; therefore, they tend to stay in sync with PostgreSQL releases. Adminer, while not specific to PostgreSQL, is useful if you also need to manage other relational databases: SQLite, MySQL, SQL Server, or Oracle. Beyond the four that we mentioned, you can find plenty of other excellent administration tools, both open source and proprietary.

psql

psql is a command-line interface for running queries and is included in all distributions of PostgreSQL (see "psql Interactive Commands" on page 276). psql has some unusual features, such as an import and export command for delimited files (CSV or tab), and a minimalistic report writer that can generate HTML output. psql has been around since the introduction of PostgreSQL and is the tool of choice for many expert users, for people working in consoles without a GUI, or for running common tasks in shell scripts. Newer converts favor GUI tools and wonder why the older generation still clings to the command line.

pgAdmin

pgAdmin (*http://www.pgadmin.org*) is a popular, free GUI tool for PostgreSQL. Download it separately from PostgreSQL if it isn't already packaged with your installer. pgAdmin runs on all OSes supported by PostgreSQL.

Even if your database lives on a console-only Linux server, go ahead and install pgAdmin on your workstation, and you'll find yourself armed with a fantastic GUI tool.

pgAdmin recently entered its fourth release, dubbed pgAdmin4. pgAdmin4 is a complete rewrite of pgAdmin3 that sports a desktop as well as a web server application version utilizing Python. pgAdmin4 is currently at version 1.5. It made its debut at the same time as PostgreSQL 9.6 and is available as part of several PostgreSQL distributions. You can run pgAdmin4 as a desktop application or via a browser interface.

An example of pgAdmin4 appears in Figure 1-1.

If you're unfamiliar with PostgreSQL, you should definitely start with pgAdmin. You'll get a bird's-eye view and appreciate the richness of PostgreSQL just by exploring everything you see in the main interface. If you're deserting Microsoft SQL Server and are accustomed to Management Studio, you'll feel right at home.

pgAdmin4 still has a couple of pain points compared to pgAdmin3, but its feature set is ramping up quickly and in some ways already surpasses pgAdmin3. That said, if you are a long-time user of pgAdmin3, you might want to go for the pgAdmin3 Long Time support (LTS) (*http://www1.bigsql.org/pgadmin3/*) version supported and distributed by BigSQL, and spend a little time test-driving pgAdmin4 before you fully commit to it. But keep in mind that the pgAdmin project is fully committed to pgAdmin4 and no longer will make changes to pgAdmin3.

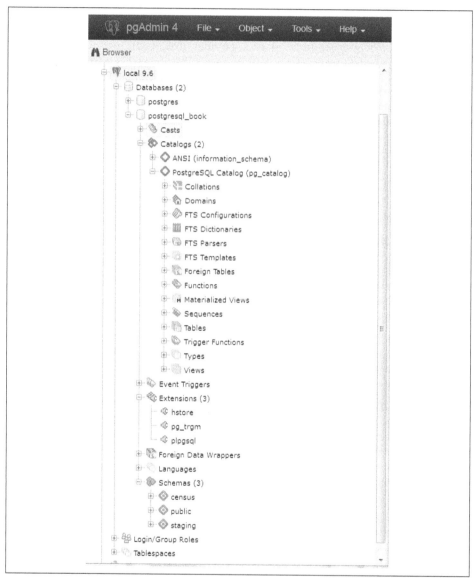

Figure 1-1. pgAdmin4 tree browser

phpPgAdmin

phpPgAdmin (*https://github.com/phppgadmin/phppgadmin*), pictured in Figure 1-2, is a free, web-based administration tool patterned after the popular phpMyAdmin. phpPgAdmin differs from phpMyAdmin by including ways to manage PostgreSQL objects such as schemas, procedural languages, casts, operators, and so on. If you've used phpMyAdmin, you'll find phpPgAdmin to have the same look and feel.

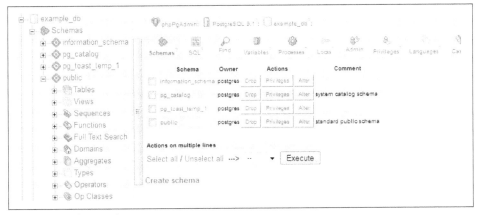

Figure 1-2. phpPgAdmin

Adminer

If you manage other databases besides PostgreSQL and are looking for a unified tool, Adminer (*http://www.adminer.org/*) might fit the bill. Adminer is a lightweight, open source PHP application with options for PostgreSQL, MySQL, SQLite, SQL Server, and Oracle, all delivered through a single interface.

One unique feature of Adminer we're impressed with is the relational diagrammer that can produce a schematic layout of your database schema, along with a linear representation of foreign key relationships. Another hassle-reducing feature is that you can deploy Adminer as a single PHP file.

Figure 1-3 is a screenshot of the login screen and a snippet from the diagrammer output. Many users stumble in the login screen of Adminer because it doesn't include a separate text box for indicating the port number. If PostgreSQL is listening on the standard 5432 port, you need not worry. But if you use some other port, append the port number to the server name with a colon, as shown in Figure 1-3.

Adminer is sufficient for straightforward querying and editing, but because it's tailored to the lowest common denominator among database products, you won't find management applets that are specific to PostgreSQL for such tasks as creating new users, granting rights, or displaying permissions. Adminer also treats each schema as a separate database, which severely reduces the usefulness of the relational diagrammer if your relationships cross schema boundaries. If you're a DBA, stick to pgAdmin or psql.

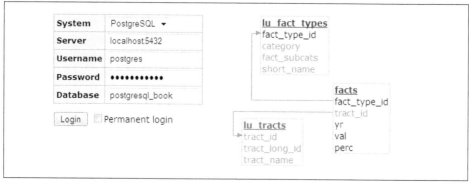

Figure 1-3. Adminer

PostgreSQL Database Objects

So you installed PostgreSQL, fired up pgAdmin, and expanded its browse tree. Before you is a bewildering display of database objects, some familiar and some completely foreign. PostgreSQL has more database objects than most other relational database products (and that's before add-ons). You'll probably never touch many of these objects, but if you dream up something new, more likely than not it's already implemented using one of those esoteric objects. This book is not even going to attempt to describe all that you'll find in a standard PostgreSQL install. With PostgreSQL churning out features at breakneck speed, we can't imagine any book that could possibly do this. We limit our quick overview to those objects that you should be familiar with:

Databases
Each PostgreSQL service houses many individual databases.

Schemas
Schemas are part of the ANSI SQL standard. They are the immediate next level of organization within each database. If you think of the database as a country, schemas would be the individual states (or provinces, prefectures, or departments, depending on the country). Most database objects first belong to a schema, which belongs to a database. When you create a new database, PostgreSQL automatically creates a schema named *public* to store objects that you create. If you have few tables, using public would be fine. But if you have thousands of tables, you should organize them into different schemas.

Tables
Tables are the workhorses of any database. In PostgreSQL, tables are first citizens of their respective schemas, which in turn are citizens of the database.

PostgreSQL tables have two remarkable talents: first, they are inheritable. Table inheritance streamlines your database design and can save you endless lines of looping code when querying tables with nearly identical structures. Second, whenever you create a table, PostgreSQL automatically creates an accompanying custom data type.

Views

Almost all relational database products offer views as a level of abstraction from tables. In a view, you can query multiple tables and present additional derived columns based on complex calculations. Views are generally read-only, but PostgreSQL allows you to update the underlying data by updating the view, provided that the view draws from a single table. To update data from views that join multiple tables, you need to create a trigger against the view. Version 9.3 introduced materialized views, which cache data to speed up commonly used queries at the sacrifice of having the most up-to-date data. See "Materialized Views" on page 169.

Extension

Extensions allow developers to package functions, data types, casts, custom index types, tables, attribute variables, etc., for installation or removal as a unit. Extensions are similar in concept to Oracle packages and have been the preferred method for distributing add-ons since PostgreSQL 9.1. You should follow the developer's instructions on how to install the extension files onto your server, which usually involves copying binaries into your PostgreSQL installation folders and then running a set of scripts. Once done, you must enable the extension for each database separately. You shouldn't enable an extension in your database unless you need it. For example, if you need advanced text search in only one database, enable `fuzzystrmatch` for that one only.

When you enable extensions, you choose the schemas where all constituent objects will reside. Accepting the default will place everything from the extension into the public schema, littering it with potentially thousands of new objects. We recommend that you create a separate schema that will house all extensions. For an extension with many objects, we suggest that you create a separate schema devoted entirely to it. Optionally, you can append the name of any schemas you add to the search_path variable of the database so you can refer to the function without having to prepend the schema name. Some extensions, especially ones that install a new procedural language (PL), will dictate the installation schema. For example, PL/V8 must be installed the pg_catalog schema.

Extensions may depend on other extensions. Prior to PostgreSQL 9.6, you had to know all dependent extensions and install them first. With 9.6, you simply need to add the CASCADE option and PostgreSQL will take care of the rest. For example:

```
CREATE EXTENSION postgis_tiger_geocoder CASCADE;
```

first installs the dependent extensions postgis and fuzzystrmatch, if not present.

Functions

You can program your own custom functions to handle data manipulation, perform complex calculations, or wrap similar functionality. Create functions using PLs. PostgreSQL comes stocked with thousands of functions, which you can view in the postgres database that is part of every install. PostgreSQL functions can return scalar values, arrays, single records, or sets of records. Other database products refer to functions that manipulate data as stored procedures. PostgreSQL does not make this distinction.

Languages

Create functions using a PL. PostgreSQL installs three by default: SQL, PL/pgSQL, and C. You can easily install additional languages using the extension framework or the CREATE PRODCEDURAL LANGUAGE command. Languages currently in vogue are PL/Python, PL/V8 (JavaScript), and PL/R. We'll show you plenty of examples in Chapter 8.

Operators

Operators are nothing more than symbolically named aliases such as = or && for functions. In PostgreSQL, you can invent your own. This is often the case when you create custom data types. For example, if you create a custom data type of complex numbers, you'd probably want to also create addition operators (+,-,*,/) to handle arithmetic on them.

Foreign tables and foreign data wrappers

Foreign tables are virtual tables linked to data outside a PostgreSQL database. Once you've configured the link, you can query them like any other tables. Foreign tables can link to CSV files, a PostgreSQL table on another server, a table in a different product such as SQL Server or Oracle, a NoSQL database such as Redis, or even a web service such as Twitter or Salesforce.

Foreign data wrappers (FDWs) facilitate the magic handshake between PostgreSQL and external data sources. FDW implementations in PostgreSQL follow the SQL/Management of External Data (MED) standard (*http://en.wikipedia.org/wiki/SQL/MED*).

Many charitable programmers have already developed FDWs for popular data sources. You can try your hand at creating your own FDWs as well. (Be sure to publicize your success so the community can reap the fruits of your toil.) Install FDWs using the extension framework. Once installed, pgAdmin lists them under a node called Foreign Data Wrappers.

Triggers and trigger functions

You will find triggers in all enterprise-level databases; triggers detect data-change events. When PostgreSQL fires a trigger, you have the opportunity to execute trigger functions in response. A trigger can run in response to particular types of statements or in response to changes to particular rows, and can fire before or after a data-change event.

In pgAdmin, to see which table triggers, drill down to the table level. Pick the table of interest and look under *triggers*.

Create trigger functions to respond to firing of triggers. Trigger functions differ from regular functions in that they have access to special variables that store the data both before and after the triggering event. This allows you to reverse data changes made by the event during the execution of the trigger function. Because of this, trigger functions are often used to write complex validation routines that are beyond what can be implemented using check constraints.

Trigger technology is evolving rapidly in PostgreSQL. Starting in 9.0, a WITH clause lets you specify a boolean WHEN condition, which is tested to see whether the trigger should be fired. Version 9.0 also introduced the UPDATE OF clause, which allows you to specify which column(s) to monitor for changes. When data in monitored columns changes, the trigger fires. In 9.1, a data change in a view can fire a trigger. Since 9.3, data definition language (DDL) events can fire triggers. For a list of triggerable DDL events, refer to the Event Trigger Firing Matrix (*http://bit.ly/12sbQI8*). pgAdmin lists DDL triggers under the Event Triggers branch. Finally, as of version 9.4, you may place triggers against foreign tables.

Catalogs

Catalogs are system schemas that store PostgreSQL builtin functions and metadata. Every database contains two catalogs: *pg_catalog*, which holds all functions, tables, system views, casts, and types packaged with PostgreSQL; and *information_schema*, which offers views exposing metadata in a format dictated by the ANSI SQL standard.

PostgreSQL practices what it preaches. You will find that PostgreSQL itself is built atop a self-replicating structure. All settings to finetune servers are kept in system tables that you're free to query and modify. This gives PostgreSQL a level of extensibility (read hackability) impossible to attain by proprietary database products. Go ahead and take a close look inside the pg_catalog schema. You'll get a sense of how PostgreSQL is put together. If you have superuser privileges, you are at liberty to make updates to the pg_catalog directly (and screw things up royally).

The information_schema catalog is one you'll find in MySQL and SQL Server as well. The most commonly used views in the PostgreSQL information_schema are *columns*, which list all table columns in a database; *tables*, which list all tables (including views) in a database; and *views*, which list all views and the associated SQL to rebuild the view.

Types

Type is short for data type. Every database product and every programming language has a set of types that it understands: integers, characters, arrays, blobs, etc. PostgreSQL has composite types, which are made up of other types. Think of complex numbers, polar coordinates, vectors, or tensors as examples.

Whenever you create a new table, PostgreSQL automatically creates a composite type based on the structure of the table. This allows you to treat table rows as objects in their own right. You'll appreciate this automatic type creation when you write functions that loop through tables. pgAdmin doesn't make the automatic type creation obvious because it does not list them under the types node, but rest assured that they are there.

Full text search

Full text search (FTS) is a natural language–based search. This kind of search has some "intelligence" built in. Unlike regular expression search, FTS can match based on the semantics of an expression, not just its syntactical makeup. For example, if you're searching for the word *running* in a long piece of text, you may end up with run, running, ran, runner, jog, sprint, dash, and so on. Three objects in PostgreSQL together support FTS: FTS configurations, FTS dictionaries, and FTS parsers. These objects exist to support the built-in Full Text Search engine packaged with PostgreSQL. For general use cases, the configurations, dictionaries, and parsers packaged with PostgreSQL are sufficient. But should you be working in a specific industry with specialized vocabulary and syntax rules such as pharmacology or organized crime, you can swap out the packaged FTS objects with your own. We cover FTS in detail in "Full Text Search" on page 130.

Casts

Casts prescribe how to convert from one data type to another. They are backed by functions that actually perform the conversion. In PostgreSQL, you can create your own casts and override or enhance the default casting behavior. For example, imagine you're converting zip codes (which are five digits long in the US) to character from integer. You can define a custom cast that automatically prepends a zero when the zip is between 1000 and 9999.

Casting can be implicit or explicit. Implicit casts are automatic and usually expand from a more specific to a more generic type. When an implicit cast is not offered, you must cast explicitly.

Sequences

A sequence controls the autoincrementation of a serial data type. PostgresSQL automatically creates sequences when you define a serial column, but you can easily change the initial value, step, and next available value. Because sequences are objects in their own right, more than one table can share the same sequence object. This allows you to create a unique key value that can span tables. Both

SQL Server and Oracle have sequence objects, but you must create them manually.

Rules

Rules are instructions to rewrite an SQL prior to execution. We're not going to cover rules as they've fallen out of favor because triggers can accomplish the same things.

For each object, PostgreSQL makes available many attribute variables that you can set. You can set variables at the server level, at the database level, at the function level, and so on. You may encounter the fancy term *GUC*, which stands for grand unified configuration, but it means nothing more than configuration settings in PostgreSQL.

What's New in Latest Versions of PostgreSQL?

Every September a new PostgreSQL is released. With each new release comes greater stability, heightened security, better performance—and avant-garde features. The upgrade process itself gets easier with each new version. The lesson here? Upgrade. Upgrade often. For a summary chart of key features added in each release, refer to the PostgreSQL Feature Matrix (*http://www.postgresql.org/about/featurematrix*).

Why Upgrade?

If you're using PostgreSQL 9.1 or below, upgrade now! Version 9.1 retired to end-of-life (EOL) status in September 2016. Details about PostgreSQL EOL policy can be found here: PostgreSQL Release Support Policy (*http://www.postgresql.org/support/versioning/*). EOL is not where you want to be. New security updates and fixes to serious bugs will no longer be available. You'll need to hire specialized PostgreSQL core consultants to patch problems or to implement workarounds—probably not a cheap proposition, assuming you can even locate someone willing to undertake the work.

Regardless of which major version you are running, you should always keep up with the latest micro versions. An upgrade from say, 9.1.17 to 9.1.21, requires no more than a file replacement and a restart. Micro versions only patch bugs. Nothing will stop working after a micro upgrade. Performing a micro upgrade can in fact save you much grief down the road.

Features Introduced in PostgreSQL 10

PostgreSQL 10 is the latest stable release and was released in October 2017. Starting with PostgreSQL 10, the PostgreSQL project adopted a new versioning convention. In prior versions, major versions got a minor version number bump. For example, PostgreSQL 9.6 introduced some major new features that were not in its PostgreSQL 9.5 predecessor. In contrast, starting with PostgreSQL 10, major releases will have the first digit bumped. So major changes to PostgreSQL 10 will be called PostgreSQL 11.

This is more in line with what other database vendors follow, such as SQLite, SQL Server, and Oracle.

Here are the key new features in 10:

Query parallelization improvements
There are new planner strategies for parallel queries: Parallel Bitmap Heap Scan, Parallel Index Scan, and others. These changes allow a wider range of queries to be parallelized for. See "Parallelized Queries" on page 233.

Logical replication
Prior versions of PostgreSQL had streaming replication that replicates the whole server cluster. Slaves in streaming replication were read-only and could be used only for queries that don't change data. Nor could they have tables of their own. Logical replication provides two features that streaming replication did not have. You can now replicate just a table or a database (no need for the whole cluster); since you are replicating only part of the data, the slaves can have their own set of data that is not involved in replication.

Full text support for JSON and JSONB
In prior versions, to_tsvector would work only with plain text when generating a full text vector. Now to_tsvector can understand the json and jsonb types, ignoring the keys in JSON and including only the values in the vector. The ts_headline function for json and jsonb was also introduced. It highlights matches in a json document during a tsquery. Refer to "Full Text Support for JSON and JSONB" on page 141.

ANSI standard XMLTABLE construct
XMLTABLE provides a simpler way of deconstructing XML into a standard table structure. This feature has existed for some time in Oracle and IBM DB2 databases. Refer to Example 5-41.

FDW push down aggregates to remote servers
The FDW API can now run aggregations such as COUNT(*) or SUM(*) on remote queries. postgres_fdw takes advantage of this new feature. Prior to postgres_fdw, any aggregation would require the local server to request all the data that needed aggregation and do the aggregation locally.

Declarative table partitioning
In prior versions, if you had a table you needed to partition but query as a single unit, you would utilize PostgreSQL table inheritance support. Using inheritance was cumbersome in that you had to write triggers to reroute data to a table PARTITION if adding to the parent table. PostgreSQL 10 introduces the PARTITION BY construct. PARTITION BY allows you to create a parent table with no data, but with a defined PARTITION formula. Now you can insert data into the parent

table without the need to define triggers. Refer to "Partitioned Tables" on page 150.

Query execution
Various speedups have been added.

CREATE STATISTICS
New construct for creating statistics on multiple columns. Refer to Example 9-18.

IDENTITY
A new IDENTITY qualifier in DDL table creation and ALTER statements provides a more standards-compliant way to designate a table column as an auto increment. Refer to Example 6-2.

Features Introduced in PostgreSQL 9.6

PostgreSQL 9.6 was released in September 2016. PostgreSQL 9.6 is the last of the PostgreSQL 9+ series:

Query parallelization
Up to now, PostgreSQL could not take advantage of multiple processor cores. In 9.6, the PostgreSQL engine can distribute certain types of queries across multiple cores and processers. Qualified queries include those with sequential scans, some joins, and some aggregates. However, queries that involve changing data such as deletes, inserts, and updates are not parallelizable. Parallelization is a work in progress with the eventual hope that all queries will take advantage of multiple processor cores. See "Parallelized Queries" on page 233.

Phrase full text search
Use the distance operator <-> in a full text search query to indicate how far two words can be apart from each other and still be considered a match. In prior versions you could indicate only which words should be searched; now you can control the sequence of the words. See "Full Text Search" on page 130.

psql \gexec options
These read an SQL statement from a query and execute it. See "Dynamic SQL Execution" on page 67.

postgres_fdw
Updates, inserts, and deletes are all much faster for simple cases. See *Depesz: Directly Modify Foreign Table (http://bit.ly/2kD8DnN)* for details.

Pushed-down FDW joins
This is now supported by some FDWs. postgres_fdw supports this feature. When you join foreign tables, instead of retrieving the data from the foreign server and performing the join locally, FDW will perform the join remotely if foreign tables

involved in the join are from the same foreign server and then retrieve the result set. This could lower the number of rows that have to come over from the foreign server, dramatically improving performance when joins eliminate many rows.

Features Introduced in PostgreSQL 9.5

Version 9.5 came out in January of 2016. Notable new features are as follows:

Improvements to foreign table architecture

A new IMPORT FOREIGN SCHEMA command allows for bulk creation of foreign tables from a foreign server. Foreign table inheritance means that a local table can inherit from foreign tables; foreign tables can inherit from local tables; and foreign tables can inherit from other foreign tables. You can also add constraints to foreign tables. See "Foreign Data Wrappers" on page 254 and "Querying Other PostgreSQL Servers" on page 257.

Using unlogged tables as a fast way to populate new tables

The downside is that unlogged tables would get truncated during a crash. In prior versions, promoting an unlogged table to a logged table could not be done without creating a new table and repopulating the records. In 9.5, just use the ALTER TABLE ... SET UNLOGGED command.

Arrays in array_agg

The array_agg function accepts a set of values and combines them into a single array. Prior to 9.5, passing in arrays would throw an error. With 9.5, array_agg is smart enough to automatically construct multidimensional arrays for you. See Example 5-17.

Block range indexes (BRIN)

A new kind of index with smaller footprint than B-Tree and GIN. Under some circumstances BRIN can outperform the former two. See "Indexes" on page 157.

Grouping sets, ROLLUP, AND CUBE SQL predicates

This feature is used in conjunction with aggregate queries to return additional subtotal rows. See "GROUPING SETS, CUBE, ROLLUP" on page 195 for examples.

Index-only scans

These now support GiST indexes.

Insert and update conflict handling

Prior to 9.5, any inserts or updates that conflicted with primary key and check constraints would automatically fail. Now you have an opportunity to catch the exception and offer an alternative course, or to skip the records causing the conflict. See "UPSERTs: INSERT ON CONFLICT UPDATE" on page 176.

Update lock failures

If you want to select and lock rows with the intent of updating the data, you can use `SELECT ... FOR UPDATE`. If you're unable to obtain the lock, prior to 9.5, you'd receive an error. With 9.5, you can add the `SKIP LOCKED` option to bypass rows for which you're unable to obtain locks.

Row-level security

You now have the ability to set visibility and updatability on rows of a table using policies. This is especially useful for multitenant databases or situations where security cannot be easily isolated by segmenting data into different tables.

Features Introduced in PostgreSQL 9.4

Version 9.4 came out in September 2014. Notable new features are as follows:

Materialized view enhancements

In 9.3, materialized views are inaccessible during a refresh, which could be a long time. This makes their deployment in a production undesirable. 9.4 eliminated the lock provided for materizalized views with a unique index.

New analytic functions to compute percentiles

percentile_disc (percentile discrete) and percentile_cont (percentile continuous) were added. They must be used with the special `WITHIN GROUP (ORDER BY ...)` construct. PostgreSQL vanguard Hubert Lubaczewski described their use in *Ordered Set Within Group Aggregates (http://bit.ly/12sbTnq)*. If you've ever looked for an aggregate median function in PostgreSQL, you didn't find it. Recall from your introduction to medians that the algorithm has an extra tie-breaker step at the end, making it difficult to program as an aggregate function. The new percentile functions approximate the true median with a "fast" median. We cover these two functions in more detail in "Percentiles and Mode" on page 182.

Protection against updates in views

`WITH CHECK OPTION` clause added to the `CREATE VIEW` statement will block, update, or insert on the view if the resulting data would no longer be visible in the view. We demonstrate this feature in Example 7-3.

A new data type, JSONB

The JavaScript object notation binary type allows you to index a full JSON document and expedite retrieval of subelements. For details, see "JSON" on page 120 and check out these blog posts: *Introduce jsonb: A Structured Format for Storing JSON (http://bit.ly/1yo0Tp9)* and *JSONB: Wildcard Query (http://bit.ly/12sbZv4)*.

Improved Generalized Inverted Index (GIN)

GIN was designed with FTS, trigrams, hstores, and JSONB in mind. Under many circumstances, you may choose GIN with its smaller footprint over B-Tree without loss in performance. Version 9.5 improved its query speed. Check out *GIN as a Substitute for Bitmap Indexes (http://hlinnaka.iki.fi/2014/03/28/gin-as-a-substitute-for-bitmap-indexes)*.

More JSON functions
These are json_build_array, json_build_object, json_object, json_to_record, and json_to_recordset.

Expedited moves between tablespaces
You can now move all database objects from one tablespace to another by using the syntax `ALTER TABLESPACE old_space MOVE ALL TO new_space;`.

Row numbers in returned sets
You can add a row number for set-returning functions with the system column ordinality. This is particularly handy when converting denormalized data stored in arrays, hstores, and composite types to records. Here is an example using hstore:

```
SELECT ordinality, key, value
  FROM EACH('breed=>pug,cuteness=>high'::hstore) WITH ordinality;
```

Using SQL to alter system-configuration settings
The `ALTER system SET ...` construct allows you to set global system settings without editing the *postgresql.conf*, as detailed in "The postgresql.conf File" on page 25. This also means you can now programmatically change system settings, but keep in mind that PostgreSQL may require a restart for new settings to take effect.

Triggers
Version 9.4 lets you place triggers on foreign tables.

Better handling of unnesting
The unnest function predictably allocates arrays of different sizes into columns. Prior to 9.4, unnesting arrays of different sizes resulted in shuffling of columns in unexpected ways.

ROWS FROM
This construct allows the use of multiple set-returning functions in a series, even if they have an unbalanced number of elements in each set:

```
SELECT *
FROM ROWS FROM ( jsonb_each('{"a":"foo1","b":"bar"}'::jsonb),
                 jsonb_each('{"c":"foo2"}'::jsonb) )
                 x (a1,a1_val,a2,a2_val);
```

Dynamic background workers

You can code these in C to do work that is not available through SQL or functions. A trivial example is available in the 9.4 source code in the *contrib/worker_spi* directory.

Database Drivers

Chances are that you're not using PostgreSQL in a vacuum. You need a database driver to interact with applications and other databases. PostgreSQL works with free drivers for many programming languages and tools. Moreover, various commercial organizations provide drivers with extra bells and whistles at modest prices. Here are some of the notable open source drivers:

- PHP is a popular language for web development, and most PHP distributions include at least one PostgreSQL driver: the old pgsql driver or the newer pdo_pgsql. You may need to enable them in your *php.ini*.

- For Java developers, the JDBC driver keeps up with latest PostgreSQL versions. Download it from PostgreSQL (*http://jdbc.postgresql.org*).

- For .NET (both Microsoft or Mono), you can use the Npgsql (*http://www.npgsql.org/*) driver. Both the source code and the binary are available for .NET Framework, Microsoft Entity Framework, and Mono.NET.

- If you need to connect from Microsoft Access, Excel, or any other products that support Open Database Connectivity (ODBC), download drivers from the PostgreSQL ODBC drivers (*http://www.postgresql.org/ftp/odbc/versions/msi*) site. You'll have your choice of 32-bit or 64-bit.

- LibreOffice 3.5 and later comes packaged with a native PostgreSQL driver. For OpenOffice and older versions of LibreOffice, you can use the JDBC driver or the SDBC driver. Learn more details from our article *OO Base and PostgreSQL* (*http://www.postgresonline.com/journal/categories/23-oobase*).

- Python has support for PostgreSQL via many database drivers (*http://wiki.postgresql.org/wiki/Python*). At the moment, psycopg2 (*http://initd.org/psycopg/*) is the most popular. Rich support for PostgreSQL is also available in the Django (*http://bit.ly/1w5GbtX*) web framework. If you are looking for an object-relational mapper, SQL Alchemy (*http://www.sqlalchemy.org/*) is the most popular and is used internally by the Multicorn Foreign Data Wrapper (*http://multicorn.org*).

- If you use Ruby, connect to PostgreSQL using rubygems pg (*http://bit.ly/1vXsUSk*).

- You'll find Perl's connectivity to PostgreSQL in the DBI and the DBD::Pg drivers. Alternatively, there's the pure Perl DBD::PgPP driver from CPAN (*http://search.cpan.org*).
- Node.js is a JavaScript framework for running scalable network programs. There are two PostgreSQL drivers currently: Node Postgres (*https://github.com/brianc/node-postgres*) with optional native libpq bindings and pure JS (no compilation required) and Node-DBI (*https://github.com/DrBenton/Node-DBI*).

Where to Get Help

There will come a day when you need help. That day always arrives early; we want to point you to some resources now rather than later. Our favorite is the lively mailing list designed for helping new and old users with technical issues. First, visit PostgreSQL Help Mailing Lists (*http://www.postgresql.org/community/lists/*). If you are new to PostgreSQL, the best list to start with is the PGSQL General Mailing List (*http://archives.postgresql.org/pgsql-general*). If you run into what appears to be a bug in PostgreSQL, report it at PostgreSQL Bug Reporting (*http://www.postgresql.org/docs/current/interactive/bug-reporting.html*).

Notable PostgreSQL Forks

The MIT/BSD-style licensing of PostgreSQL makes it a great candidate for forking. Various groups have done exactly that over the years. Some have contributed their changes back to the original project or funded PostgreSQL work. For list of forks, refer to PostgreSQL-derived databases (*http://bit.ly/2kCW8bU*).

Many popular forks are proprietary and closed source. Netezza (*http://www.netezza.com*), a popular database choice for data warehousing, was a PostgreSQL fork at inception. Similarly, the Amazon Redshift (*http://aws.amazon.com/redshift/*) data warehouse is a fork of a fork of PostgreSQL. Amazon has two other offerings that are closer to standard PostgreSQL: Amazon RDS for PostgreSQL and Amazon Aurora for PostgreSQL. These stay in line with PostgreSQL versions in SQL syntax but with more management and speed features.

PostgreSQL Advanced Plus by EnterpriseDB (*http://enterprisedb.com*) is a fork that adds Oracle syntax and compatibility features to woo Oracle users. EnterpriseDB ploughs funding and development support back to the PostgreSQL community. For this, we're grateful. Its Postgres Plus Advanced Server is fairly close to the most recent stable version of PostgreSQL.

Postgres-X2 (*http://postgres-x2.github.io/*), Postgres-XL (*http://www.postgres-xl.org/*), and GreenPlum (*http://greenplum.org/*) are three budding forks with open source licensing (although GreenPlum was closed source for a period). These three target large-scale data analytics and replication.

Part of the reason for forking is to advance ahead of the PostgreSQL release cycle and try out new features that may or may not be of general interest. Many of the new features developed this way do find their way back into a later PostgreSQL core release. Such is the case with the multi-master bi-directional replication (BDR) (*http:// 2ndquadrant.com/en/resources/bdr/*) fork developed by 2nd Quadrant (*http://2ndqua drant.com*). Pieces of BDR, such as the logical replication support, are beefing up the built-in replication functionality in PostgreSQL proper. Some of the parallelization work of Postgres-XL will also likely make it into future versions of PostgreSQL.

Citus (*https://www.citusdata.com/*) is a project that started as a fork of PostgreSQL to support real-time big data and parallel queries. It has since been incorporated back and can be installed in PostgreSQL 9.5 as an extension.

Google Cloud SQL for PostgreSQL (*https://cloud.google.com/sql/docs/postgres/*) is a fairly recent addition by Google and is currently in beta.

## CHAPTER 2

Database Administration

This chapter covers what we consider basic administration of a PostgreSQL server: managing roles and permissions, creating databases, installing extensions, and backing up and restoring data. Before continuing, you should have already installed PostgreSQL and have administration tools at your disposal.

Configuration Files

Three main configuration files control operations of a PostgreSQL server:

postgresql.conf
Controls general settings, such as memory allocation, default storage location for new databases, the IP addresses that PostgreSQL listens on, location of logs, and plenty more.

pg_hba.conf
Controls access to the server, dictating which users can log in to which databases, which IP addresses can connect, and which authentication scheme to accept.

pg_ident.conf
If present, this file maps an authenticated OS login to a PostgreSQL user. People sometimes map the OS root account to the PostgresSQL superuser account, *postgres*.

PostgreSQL officially refers to users as *roles*. Not all roles need to have login privileges. For example, group roles often do not. We use the term *user* to refer to a role with login privileges.

If you accepted default installation options, you will find these configuration files in the main PostgreSQL data folder. You can edit them using any text editor or the Admin Pack in pgAdmin. Instructions for editing with pgAdmin are in "Editing postgresql.conf and pg_hba.conf from pgAdmin3" on page 81. If you are unable to find the physical location of these files, run the Example 2-1 query as a superuser while connected to any database.

Example 2-1. Location of configuration files

```
SELECT name, setting FROM pg_settings WHERE category = 'File Locations';
       name        |                  setting
-------------------+-------------------------------------------
 config_file       | /etc/postgresql/9.6/main/postgresql.conf
 data_directory    | /var/lib/postgresql/9.6/main
 external_pid_file | /var/run/postgresql/9.6-main.pid
 hba_file          | /etc/postgresql/9.6/main/pg_hba.conf
 ident_file        | /etc/postgresql/9.6/main/pg_ident.conf
(5 rows)
```

Making Configurations Take Effect

Some configuration changes require a PostgreSQL service restart, which closes any active connections from clients. Other changes require just a reload. New users connecting after a reload will receive the new setting. Extant users with active connections will not be affected during a reload. If you're not sure whether a configuration change requires a reload or restart, look under the context setting associated with a configuration. If the context is `postmaster`, you'll need a restart. If the context is `user`, a reload will suffice.

Reloading

A reload can be done in several ways. One way is to open a console window and run this command:

```
pg_ctl reload -D your_data_directory_here
```

If you have PostgreSQL installed as a service in RedHat Enterprise Linux, CentOS, or Ubuntu, enter instead:

```
service postgresql-9.5 reload
```

postgresql-9.5 is the name of your service. (For older versions of PostgreSQL, the service is sometimes called *postgresql* sans version number.)

You can also log in as a superuser to any database and execute the following SQL:

```
SELECT pg_reload_conf();
```

Finally, you can reload from pgAdmin; see "Editing postgresql.conf and pg_hba.conf from pgAdmin3" on page 81.

Restarting

More fundamental configuration changes require a restart. You can perform a restart by stopping and restarting the postgres service (daemon). Yes, power cycling will do the trick as well.

You can't restart with a PostgreSQL command, but you can trigger a restart from the operating system shell. On Linux/Unix with a service, enter:

```
service postgresql-9.6 restart
```

For any PostgreSQL instance not installed as a service:

```
pg_ctl restart -D your_data_directory_here
```

On Windows you can also just click Restart on the PostgreSQL service in the Services Manager.

The postgresql.conf File

postgresql.conf controls the life-sustaining settings of the PostgreSQL server. You can override many settings at the database, role, session, and even function levels. You'll find many details on how to finetune your server by tweaking settings in the article Tuning Your PostgreSQL Server (*http://bit.ly/2kDH2Tq*).

Version 9.4 introduced an important change: instead of editing *postgresql.conf* directly, you should override settings using an additional file called *postgresql.auto.conf*. We further recommend that you don't touch the *postgresql.conf* and place any custom settings in *postgresql.auto.conf*.

Checking postgresql.conf settings

An easy way to read the current settings without opening the configuration files is to query the view named *pg_settings*. We demonstrate in Example 2-2.

Example 2-2. Key settings

```
SELECT
    name,
    context ❶,
    unit ❷,
    setting, boot_val, reset_val ❸
FROM pg_settings
WHERE name IN ('listen_addresses','deadlock_timeout','shared_buffers',
    'effective_cache_size','work_mem','maintenance_work_mem')
ORDER BY context, name;
```

```
name                    | context    | unit | setting | boot_val   | reset_val
------------------------+------------+------+---------+------------+----------
listen_addresses        | postmaster |      | *       | localhost  | *
shared_buffers          | postmaster | 8kB  | 131584  | 1024       | 131584
deadlock_timeout        | superuser  | ms   | 1000    | 1000       | 1000
effective_cache_size    | user       | 8kB  | 16384   | 16384      | 16384
maintenance_work_mem    | user       | kB   | 16384   | 16384      | 16384
work_mem                | user       | kB   | 5120    | 1024       | 5120
```

❶ The context is the scope of the setting. Some settings have a wider effect than others, depending on their context.

User settings can be changed by each user to affect just that user's sessions. If set by the superuser, the setting becomes a default for all users who connect after a reload.

Superuser settings can be changed only by a superuser, and will apply to all users who connect after a reload. Users cannot individually override the setting.

Postmaster settings affect the entire server (postmaster represents the PostgreSQL service) and take effect only after a restart.

Settings with user or superuser context can be set for a specific database, user, session, and function level. For example, you might want to set work_mem higher for an SQL guru-level user who writes mind-boggling queries. Similarly, if you have one function that is sort-intensive, you could raise work_mem just for it. Settings set at database, user, session, and function levels do not require a reload. Settings set at the database level take effect on the next connect to the database. Settings set for the session or function take effect right away.

❷ Be careful checking the units of measurement used for memory. As you can see in Example 2-2, some are reported in 8-KB blocks and some just in kilobytes. Regardless of how a setting displays, you can use any unit of choice when setting; 128 MB is a versatile choice for most memory settings.

Showing units as 8 KB is annoying at best and is destabilizing at worst. The SHOW command in SQL offers display settings in labeled and more intuitive units. For example, running:

```
SHOW shared_buffers;
```

returns 1028MB. Similarly, running:

```
SHOW deadlock_timeout;
```

returns 1s. If you want to see the units for all settings, enter SHOW ALL.

❸ setting is the current setting; boot_val is the default setting; reset_val is the new setting if you were to restart or reload the server. Make sure that setting

---

and `reset_val` match after you make a change. If not, the server needs a restart or reload.

New in version 9.5 is a system view called *pg_file_settings*, which you can use to query settings. Its output lists the source file where the settings can be found. The *applied* tells you whether the setting is in effect; if the setting has an f in that column you need to reload or restart to make it take effect. In cases where a particular setting is present in both *postgresql.conf* and *postgresql.auto.conf*, the *postgresql.auto.conf* one will take precedent and you'll see the other files with applied set to false (f). The applied is shown in Example 2-3.

Example 2-3. Querying pg_file_settings

```
SELECT name, sourcefile, sourceline, setting, applied
FROM pg_file_settings
WHERE name IN ('listen_addresses','deadlock_timeout','shared_buffers',
    'effective_cache_size','work_mem','maintenance_work_mem')
ORDER BY name;

name                  | sourcefile                      | sourceline | setting | applied
----------------------+---------------------------------+------------+---------+--------
effective_cache_size  | E:/data96/postgresql.auto.conf|         11 | 8GB     | t
listen_addresses      | E:/data96/postgresql.conf     |         59 | *       | t
maintenance_work_mem  | E:/data96/postgresql.auto.conf|          3 | 16MB    | t
shared_buffers        | E:/data96/postgresql.conf     |        115 | 128MB   | f
shared_buffers        | E:/data96/postgresql.auto.conf|          5 | 131584  | t
```

Pay special attention to the following network settings in *postgresql.conf* or *postgresql.auto.conf*, because an incorrect entry here will prevent clients from connecting. Changing their values requires a service restart:

listen_addresses
> Informs PostgreSQL which IP addresses to listen on. This usually defaults to local (meaning a socket on the local system), or localhost, meaning the IPv6 or IPv4 localhost IP address. But many people change the setting to *, meaning all available IP addresses.

port
> Defaults to 5432. You may wish to change this *well-known port* to something else for security or if you are running multiple PostgreSQL services on the same server.

max_connections
> The maximum number of concurrent connections allowed.

log_destination
> This setting is somewhat a misnomer. It specifies the format of the logfiles rather than their physical location. The default is *stderr*. If you intend to perform exten-

sive analysis on your logs, we suggest changing it to *csvlog*, which is easier to export to third-party analytic tools. Make sure you have the logging_collection set to on if you want logging.

The following settings affect performance. Defaults are rarely the optimal value for your installation. As soon as you gain enough confidence to tweak configuration settings, you should tune these values:

shared_buffers
Allocated amount of memory shared among all connections to store recently accessed pages. This setting profoundly affects the speed of your queries. You want this setting to be fairly high, probably as much as 25% of your RAM. However, you'll generally see diminishing returns after more than 8 GB. Changes require a restart.

effective_cache_size
An estimate of how much memory PostgreSQL expects the operating system to devote to it. This setting has no effect on actual allocation, but the query planner figures in this setting to guess whether intermediate steps and query output would fit in RAM. If you set this much lower than available RAM, the planner may forgo using indexes. With a dedicated server, setting the value to half of your RAM is a good starting point. Changes require a reload.

work_mem
Controls the maximum amount of memory allocated for each operation such as sorting, hash join, and table scans. The optimal setting depends on how you're using the database, how much memory you have to spare, and whether your server is dedicated to PostgreSQL. If you have many users running simple queries, you want this setting to be relatively low to be democratic; otherwise, the first user may hog all the memory. How high you set this also depends on how much RAM you have to begin with. A good article to read for guidance is Understanding work_mem (*http://bit.ly/15SWsHh*). Changes require a reload.

maintenance_work_mem
The total memory allocated for housekeeping activities such as vacuuming (pruning records marked for deletion). You shouldn't set it higher than about 1 GB. Reload after changes.

max_parallel_workers_per_gather
This is a new setting introduced in 9.6 for parallelism. The setting determines the maximum parallel worker threads that can be spawned for each gather operation. The default setting is 0, which means parallelism is completely turned off. If you have more than one CPU core, you will want to elevate this. Parallel processing is new in version 9.6, so you may have to experiment with this setting to find what works best for your server. Also note that the number you have here should be

less than `max_worker_processes`, which defaults to 8 because the parallel background worker processes are a subset of the maximum allowed processes.

In version 10, there is an additional setting called `max_parallel_workers`, which controls the subset of max_worker_processes allocated for parallelization.

Changing the postgresql.conf settings

PostgreSQL 9.4 introduced the ability to change settings using the *ALTER SYSTEM* SQL command. For example, to set the work_mem globally, enter the following:

```
ALTER SYSTEM SET work_mem = '500MB';
```

This command is wise enough to not directly edit *postgres.conf* but will make the change in *postgres.auto.conf*.

Depending on the particular setting changed, you may need to restart the service. If you just need to reload it, here's a convenient command:

```
SELECT pg_reload_conf();
```

If you have to track many settings, consider organizing them into multiple configuration files and then linking them back using the *include* or *include_if_exists* directive within the *postgresql.conf*. The exact syntax is as follows:

```
include 'filename'
```

The filename argument can be an absolute path or a relative path from the *postgresql.conf* file.

"I edited my postgresql.conf and now my server won't start."

The easiest way to figure out what you screwed up is to look at the logfile, located at the root of the data folder, or in the *pg_log* subfolder. Open the latest file and read what the last line says. The error raised is usually self-explanatory.

A common culprit is setting shared_buffers too high. Another suspect is an old *postmaster.pid* left over from a failed shutdown. You can safely delete this file, located in the data cluster folder, and try restarting again.

The pg_hba.conf File

The *pg_hba.conf* file controls which IP addresses and users can connect to the database. Furthermore, it dictates the authentication protocol that the client must follow. Changes to the file require at least a reload to take effect. A typical *pg_hba.conf* looks like Example 2-4.

Example 2-4. Sample pg_hba.conf

```
# TYPE  DATABASE USER ADDRESS          METHOD
host    all      all  127.0.0.1/32     ident  ❶
host    all      all  ::1/128          trust  ❷
host    all      all  192.168.54.0/24  md5    ❸
hostssl all      all  0.0.0.0/0        md5    ❹

# TYPE DATABASE    USER      ADDRESS       METHOD
# Allow replication connections from localhost,
# by a user with replication privilege.  ❺
#host  replication postgres 127.0.0.1/32 trust
#host  replication postgres ::1/128       trust
```

❶ Authentication method. The usual choices are ident, trust, md5, peer, and password.

❷ IPv6 syntax for defining network range. This applies only to servers with IPv6 support and may prevent *pg_hba.conf* from loading if you add this section without actually having IPv6 networking enabled on the server.

❸ IPv4 syntax for defining network range. The first part is the network address followed by the bit mask; for instance: 192.168.54.0/24. PostgreSQL will accept connection requests from any IP address within the range.

❹ SSL connection rule. In our example, we allow anyone to connect to our server outside of the allowed IP range as long as they can connect using SSL.

SSL configuration settings can be found in *postgres.conf* or *postgres.auto.conf*: `ssl`, `ssl_cert_file`, `ssl_key_file`. Once the server confirms that the client is able to support SSL, it will honor the connection request and all transmissions will be encrypted using the key information.

❺ Range of IP addresses allowed to replicate with this server.

For each connection request, *pg_hba.conf* is checked from the top down. As soon as a rule granting access is encountered, a connection is allowed and the server reads no further in the file. As soon as a rule rejecting access is encountered, the connection is denied and the server reads no further in the file. If the end of the file is reached without any matching rules, the connection is denied. A common mistake people make is to put the rules in the wrong order. For example, if you added 0.0.0.0/0 reject before 127.0.0.1/32 trust, local users won't be able to connect, even though a rule is in place allowing them to.

New in version 10 is the `pg_hba_file_rules` system view that lists all the contents of the *pg_hba.conf* file.

"I edited my pg_hba.conf and now my server is broken."

Don't worry. This happens quite often, but is easy to recover from. This error is generally caused by typos or by adding an unavailable authentication scheme. When the postgres service can't parse *pg_hba.conf*, it blocks all access just to be safe. Sometimes, it won't even start up. The easiest way to figure out what you did wrong is to read the logfile located in the root of the data folder or in the *pg_log* subfolder. Open the latest file and read the last line. The error message is usually self-explanatory. If you're prone to slippery fingers, back up the file prior to editing.

Authentication methods

PostgreSQL gives you many choices for authenticating users—probably more than any other database product. Most people are content with the popular ones: trust, peer, ident, md5, and password. And don't forget about reject, which immediately denies access. Also keep in mind that *pg_hba.conf* offers settings at many other levels as the gatekeeper to the entire PostgreSQL server. Users or devices must still satisfy role and database access restrictions after being admitted by *pg_hba.conf*.

We describe the common authentication methods here:

trust
> This is the least secure authentication, essentially no password is needed. As long as the user and database exist in the system and the request comes from an IP within the allowed range, the user can connect. You should implement trust only for local connections or private network connections. Even then it's possible for someone to spoof IP addresses, so the more security-minded among us discourage its use entirely. Nevertheless, it's the most common for PostgreSQL installed on a desktop for single-user local access where security is not a concern.

md5
> Very common, requires an md5-encrypted password to connect.

password
> Uses clear-text password authentication.

ident
> Uses *pg_ident.conf* to check whether the OS account of the user trying to connect has a mapping to a PostgreSQL account. The password is not checked. ident is not available on Windows.

peer
> Uses the OS name of the user from the kernel. It is available only for Linux, BSD, macOS, and Solaris, and only for local connections on these systems.

cert

> Stipulates that connections use SSL. The client must have a registered certificate. cert uses an ident file such as *pg_ident* to map the certificate to a PostgreSQL user and is available on all platforms where SSL connection is enabled.

More esoteric options abound, such as gss, radius, ldap, and pam. Some may not always be installed by default.

You can elect more than one authentication method, even for the same database. Keep in mind that *pg_hba.conf* is processed from top to bottom.

Managing Connections

More often than not, someone else (never you, of course) will execute an inefficient query that ends up hogging resources. They could also run a query that's taking much longer than what they have patience for. Cancelling the query, terminating the connection, or both will put an end to the offending query.

Cancelling and terminating are far from graceful and should be used sparingly. Your client application should prevent queries from going haywire in the first place. Out of politeness, you probably should alert the connected role that you're about to terminate its connection, or wait until after hours to do the dirty deed.

There are few scenarios where you should cancel all active update queries: before backing up the database and before restoring the database.

To cancel running queries and terminate connections, follow these steps:

1. Retrieve a listing of recent connections and process IDs (PIDs):

   ```
   SELECT * FROM pg_stat_activity;
   ```

   pg_stat_activity is a view that lists the last query running on each connection, the connected user (usename), the database (datname) in use, and the start times of the queries. Review the list to identify the PIDs of connections you wish to terminate.

2. Cancel active queries on a connection with PID *1234*:

   ```
   SELECT pg_cancel_backend(1234);
   ```

   This does not terminate the connection itself, though.

3. Terminate the connection:

   ```
   SELECT pg_terminate_backend(1234);
   ```

   You may need to take the additional step of terminating the client connection. This is especially important prior to a database restore. If you don't terminate the connection, the client may immediately reconnect after restore and run the offending query anew. If you did not already cancel the queries on the connection, terminating the connection will cancel all of its queries.

PostgreSQL lets you embed functions within a regular SELECT statement. Even though pg_terminate_backend and pg_cancel_backend act on only one connection at a time, you can kill multiple connections by wrapping them in a SELECT. For example, let's suppose you want to kill all connections belonging to a role with a single blow. Run this SQL command:

```
SELECT pg_terminate_backend(pid) FROM pg_stat_activity
WHERE usename = 'some_role';
```

You can set certain operational parameters at the server, database, user, session, or function level. Any queries that exceed the parameter will automatically be cancelled by the server. Setting a parameter to 0 disables the parameter:

deadlock_timeout

This is the amount of time a deadlocked query should wait before giving up. This defaults to 1000 ms. If your application performs a lot of updates, you may want to increase this value to minimize contention.

Instead of relying on this setting, you can include a NOWAIT clause in your update SQL: SELECT FOR UPDATE NOWAIT ... .

The query will be automatically cancelled upon encountering a deadlock.

In PostgreSQL 9.5, you have another choice: SELECT FOR UPDATE SKIP LOCKED will skip over locked rows.

statement_timeout

This is the amount of time a query can run before it is forced to cancel. This defaults to 0, meaning no time limit. If you have long-running functions that you want cancelled if they exceed a certain time, set this value in the definition of the function rather than globally. Cancelling a function cancels the query and the transaction that's calling it.

lock_timeout

This is the amount of time a query should wait for a lock before giving up, and is most applicable to update queries. Before data updates, the query must obtain an exclusive lock on affected records. The default is 0, meaning that the query will wait infinitely. This setting is generally used at the function or session level. lock_timeout should be lower than statement_timeout, otherwise statement_timeout will always occur first, making lock_timeout irrelevant.

idle_in_transaction_session_timeout

This is the amount of time a transaction can stay in an idle state before it is terminated. This defaults to 0, meaning it can stay alive infinitely. This setting is new in PostgreSQL 9.6. It's useful for preventing queries from holding on to locks on data indefinitely or eating up a connection.

Check for Queries Being Blocked

The `pg_stat_activity` view has changed considerably since version 9.1 with the renaming, dropping, and addition of new columns. Starting from version 9.2, `proc pid` was renamed to `pid`.

`pg_stat_activity` changed in PostgreSQL 9.6 to provide more detail about waiting queries. In prior versions of PostgreSQL, there was a field called `waiting` that could take the value `true` or `false`. `true` denoted a query that was being blocked waiting some resource, but the resource being waited for was never stated. In PostgreSQL 9.6, `waiting` was removed and replaced with `wait_event_type` and `wait_event` to provide more information about what resource a query was waiting for. Therefore, prior to PostgreSQL 9.6, use `waiting = true` to determine what queries are being blocked. In PostgreSQL 9.6 or higher, use `wait_event IS NOT NULL`.

In addition to the change in structure, PostgreSQL 9.6 will now track additional wait locks that did not get set to `waiting=true` in prior versions. As a result, you may find lighter lock waits being listed for queries than you saw in prior versions. For a list of different wait_event types, refer to PostgreSQL Manual: wait_event names and types. (*http://bit.ly/2kCag53*)

Roles

PostgreSQL handles credentialing using *roles*. Roles that can log in are called *login roles*. Roles can also be members of other roles; the roles that contain other roles are called *group roles*. (And yes, group roles can be members of other group roles and so on, but don't go there unless you have a knack for hierarchical thinking.) Group roles that can log in are called *group login roles*. However, for security, group roles generally cannot log in. A role can be designated as a *superuser*. These roles have unfettered access to the PostgreSQL service and should be assigned with discretion.

 Recent versions of PostgreSQL no longer use the terms *users* and *groups*. You will still run into these terms; just know that they mean login roles and group roles, respectively. For backward compatibility, CREATE USER and CREATE GROUP still work in current versions, but shun them and use CREATE ROLE instead.

Creating Login Roles

When you initialize the data cluster during setup, PostgreSQL creates a single login role with the name *postgres*. (PostgreSQL also creates a namesake database called postgres.) You can bypass the password setting by mapping an OS root user to the new role and using `ident`, `peer`, or `trust` for authentication. After you've installed PostgreSQL, before you do anything else, you should log in as postgres and create other roles. pgAdmin has a graphical section for creating user roles, but if you want to create one using SQL, execute an SQL command like the one shown in Example 2-5.

Example 2-5. Creating login roles

```
CREATE ROLE leo LOGIN PASSWORD 'king' VALID UNTIL 'infinity' CREATEDB;
```

Specifying VALID UNTIL is optional. If omitted, the role remains active indefinitely. CREATEDB grants database creation privilege to the new role.

To create a user with superuser privileges, follow Example 2-6. Naturally, you must be a superuser to create other superusers.

Example 2-6. Creating superuser roles

```
CREATE ROLE regina LOGIN PASSWORD 'queen' VALID UNTIL '2020-1-1 00:00' SUPERUSER;
```

Both of the previous examples create roles that can log in. To create roles that cannot log in, omit the LOGIN PASSWORD clause.

Creating Group Roles

Group roles generally cannot log in. Rather, they serve as containers for other roles. This is merely a best-practice suggestion. Nothing stops you from creating a role that can log in as well as contain other roles.

Create a group role using the following SQL:

```
CREATE ROLE royalty INHERIT;
```

Note the use of the modifier *INHERIT*. This means that any member of royalty will automatically inherit privileges of the royalty role, except for the superuser privilege. For security, PostgreSQL never passes down the superuser privilege. INHERIT is the default, but we recommend that you always include the modifier for clarity.

To refrain from passing privileges from the group to its members, create the role with the *NOINHERIT* modifier.

To add members to a group role, you would do:

```
GRANT royalty TO leo;
GRANT royalty TO regina;
```

Some privileges can't be inherited. For example, although you can create a group role that you mark as superuser, this doesn't make its member roles superusers. However, those users can *impersonate* their group role by using the SET ROLE command, thereby gaining superuser privileges for the duration of the session. For example:

Let's give the royalty role superuser rights with the command:

```
ALTER ROLE royalty SUPERUSER;
```

Although leo is a member of the royalty group and he inherits most rights of royalty, when he logs in, he still will not have superuser rights. He can gain superuser rights by doing:

```
SET ROLE royalty;
```

His superuser rights will last only for his current session.

This feature, though peculiar, is useful if you want to prevent yourself from unintentionally doing superuser things while you are logged in.

SET ROLE is a command available to all users, but a more powerful command called SET SESSION AUTHORIZATION is available to people who log in as superusers. In order to understand the differences, we'll first introduce two global variables that PostgreSQL has called: current_user and session_user. You can see these values when you log in by running the SQL statement:

```
SELECT session_user, current_user;
```

When you first log in, the values of these two variables are the same. SET ROLE changes the current_user, while SET SESSION AUTHORIZATION changes both the cur rent_user and session_user variables.

Here are the salient properties of SET ROLE:

- SET ROLE does not require superuser rights.
- SET ROLE changes the current_user variable, but not the session_user variable.
- A session_user that has superuser rights can SET ROLE to any other role.
- Nonsuperusers can SET ROLE only to the role the session_user is or the roles the session_user belongs to.
- When you do SET ROLE you gain all privileges of the impersonated user except for SET SESSION_AUTHORIZATION and SET ROLE.

A more powerful command, SET SESSION AUTHORIZATION, is available as well. Key features of SET SESSION AUTHORIZATION are as follows:

- Only a user that logs in as a superuser has permission to do SET SESSION AUTHORIZATION to another role.
- The SET SESSION AUTHORIZATION privilege is in effect for the life of the session, meaning that even if you SET SESSION AUTHORIZATION to a user that

is not a superuser, you still have the SET SESSION AUTHORIZATION privilege for the life of your session.

- SET SESSION AUTHORIZATION changes the values of the current_user and session_user variables to those of the user being impersonated.
- A session_user that has superuser rights can SET ROLE to any other role.

We'll do a set of exercises that illustrate the differences between `SET ROLE` and `SET SESSION AUTHORIZATION` by first logging in as *leo* and then running the code in Example 2-7.

Example 2-7. SET ROLE and SET AUTHORIZATION

```
SELECT session_user, current_user;

 session_user | current_user
--------------+--------------
 leo          | leo
(1 row)

SET SESSION AUTHORIZATION regina;

ERROR:  permission denied to set session authorization

SET ROLE regina;

ERROR:  permission denied to set role "regina"

ALTER ROLE leo SUPERUSER;

ERROR:  must be superuser to alter superusers

SET ROLE royalty;
SELECT session_user, current_user;

 session_user | current_user
--------------+--------------
 leo          | royalty
(1 row)

SET ROLE regina;

ERROR:  permission denied to set role "regina"

ALTER ROLE leo SUPERUSER;
SET ROLE regina;
SELECT session_user, current_user;

 session_user | current_user
--------------+--------------
 leo          | regina
(1 row)

SET SESSION AUTHORIZATION regina;

ERROR:  permission denied to set session authorization
```

```
-- After ending session and logging back in as leo
SELECT session_user, current_user;
SET SESSION AUTHORIZATION regina;
SELECT session_user, current_user;

session_user | current_user
-------------+-------------
leo | leo
(1 row)
SET SESSION AUTHORIZATION
session_user | current_user
-------------+-------------
regina | regina
(1 row)
```

In Example 2-7 leo was unable to use SET SESSION AUTHORIZATION because he's not a superuser. He was also unable to SET ROLE to regina because he is not in the regina group. However, he was able to SET ROLE royalty since he is a member of the royalty group (he's a king consort). Even though royalty has superuser rights, he still wasn't able to impersonate the queen, regina, because his SET ROLE abilities are still based on being the powerless leo. Since royalty is a group that has superuser rights, he was able to promote his own account leo to be a superuser. Once leo is promoted to power, he can then impersonate regina. He is now able to completely take over her session_user and current_user persona with SET SESSION AUTHORIZATION.

Database Creation

The minimum SQL command to create a database is:

```
CREATE DATABASE mydb;
```

This creates a copy of the template1 database. Any role with CREATEDB privilege can create new databases.

Template Databases

A template database is, as the name suggests, a database that serves as a skeleton for new databases. When you create a new database, PostgreSQL copies all the database settings and data from the template database to the new database.

The default PostgreSQL installation comes with two template databases: *template0* and *template1*. If you don't specify a template database to follow when you create a database, *template1* is used.

You should never alter template0 because it is the immaculate model that you'll need to copy from if you screw up your templates. Make your customizations to template1 or a new template database you create. You can't change the encoding and collation of a database you create from template1 or any other template database you create. So if you need a different encoding or collation from those in template1, create the database from template0.

The basic syntax to create a database modeled after a specific template is:

```
CREATE DATABASE my_db TEMPLATE my_template_db;
```

You can pick any database to serve as the template. This could come in quite handy when making replicas. You can also mark any database as a template database. Once you do, the database is no longer editable and deletable. Any role with the CREATEDB privilege can use a template database. To make any database a template, run the following SQL as a superuser:

```
UPDATE pg_database SET datistemplate = TRUE WHERE datname = 'mydb';
```

If ever you need to edit or drop a template database, first set the *datistemplate* attribute to FALSE. Don't forget to change the value back after you're done with edits.

Using Schemas

Schemas organize your database into logical groups. If you have more than two dozen tables in your database, consider cubbyholing them into schemas. Objects must have unique names within a schema but need not be unique across the database. If you cram all your tables into the default public schema, you'll run into name clashes sooner or later. It's up to you how to organize your schemas. For example, if you are an airline, you can place all tables of planes you own and their maintenance records into a planes schema. Place all your crew and staff into an employees schema and place all passenger-related information into a passengers schema.

Another common way to organize schemas is by roles. We found this to be particularly handy with applications that serve multiple clients whose data must be kept separate.

Suppose that you started a dog beauty management business (doggie spa). You start with a table in public called dogs to track all the dogs you hope to groom. You convince your two best friends to become customers. Whimsical government privacy regulation passes, and now you have to put in iron-clad assurances that one customer cannot see dog information from another. To comply, you set up one schema per customer and create the same dogs table in each as follows:

```
CREATE SCHEMA customer1;
CREATE SCHEMA customer2;
```

You then move the dog records into the schema that corresponds with the client. The final touch is to create different login roles for each schema with the same name as the schema. Dogs are now completely isolated in their respective schemas. When customers log in to your database to make appointments, they will be able to access only information pertaining to their own dogs.

Wait, it gets better. Because we named our roles to match their respective schemas, we're blessed with another useful technique. But we must first introduce the *search_path* database variable.

As we mentioned earlier, object names must be unique within a schema, but you can have same-named objects in different schemas. For example, you have the same table called dogs in all 12 of your schemas. When you execute something like `SELECT * FROM dogs`, how does PostgreSQL know which schema you're referring to? The simple answer is to always prepend the schema name onto the table name with a dot, such as in `SELECT * FROM customer1.dogs`. Another method is to set the search_path variable to be something like `customer1, public`. When the query executes, the planner searches for the dogs table first in the customer1 schema. If not found, it continues to the public schema and stops there.

PostgreSQL has a little-known variable called *user* that retrieves the role currently logged in. `SELECT user` returns this name. `user` is just an alias for `current_user`, so you can use either.

Recall how we named our customers' schemas to be the same as their login roles. We did this so that we can take advantage of the default search path set in *postgresql.conf*:

```
search_path = "$user", public;
```

Now, if role customer1 logs in, all queries will first look in the customer1 schema for the tables before moving to public. Most importantly, the SQL remains the same for all customers. Even if the business grows to have thousands or hundreds of thousands of dog owners, none of the SQL scripts need to change. Commonly shared tables such as common lookup tables can be put in the public schema.

Another practice that we strongly encourage is to create schemas to house extensions ("Step 2: Installing into a database" on page 47). When you install an extension, new tables, functions, data types, and plenty of other relics join your server. If they all swarm into the public schema, it gets cluttered. For example, the entire PostGIS suite of extensions will together add thousands of functions. If you've already created a few tables and functions of your own in the public schema, imagine how maddening it would be to scan a list of tables and functions trying to find your own among the thousands.

Before you install any extensions, create a new schema:

```
CREATE SCHEMA my_extensions;
```

Then add your new schema to the search path:

```
ALTER DATABASE mydb SET search_path='$user', public, my_extensions;
```

When you install extensions, be sure to indicate your new schema as their new home.

ALTER DATABASE .. SET search_path will not take effect for existing connections. You'll need to reconnect.

Privileges

Privileges (often called permissions) can be tricky to administer in PostgreSQL because of the granular control at your disposal. Security can bore down to the column and row level. Yes! You can assign different privileges to each data point of your table, if that ever becomes necessary.

Row-level security (RLS) first appeared in PostgreSQL 9.5. Although RLS is available on all PostgreSQL installations, when used in SELinux, certain advanced features are enabled.

Teaching you all there is to know about privileges could take a few chapters. What we'll aim for in this section instead is to give you enough information to get up and running and to guide you around some of the more nonintuitive land mines that could either lock you out completely or expose your server inappropriately.

Privilege management in PostgreSQL is no cakewalk. The pgAdmin graphical administration tool can ease some of the tasks or, at the very least, paint you a picture of your privilege settings. You can accomplish most, if not all, of your privilege assignment tasks in pgAdmin. If you're saddled with the task of administering privileges and are new to PostgreSQL, start with pgAdmin. Jump to "Creating Database Assets and Setting Privileges" on page 81 if you can't wait.

Types of Privileges

PostgreSQL has a few dozen privileges, some of which you may never need to worry about. The more mundane privileges are SELECT, INSERT, UPDATE, ALTER, EXECUTE, DELETE, and TRUNCATE.

Most privileges must have a context. For example, a role having an ALTER privilege is meaningless unless qualified with a database object such as ALTER privilege on tables1, SELECT privilege on table2, EXECUTE privilege on function1, and so on. Not all privileges apply to all objects: an EXECUTE privilege for a table is nonsense.

Some privileges make sense without a context. CREATEDB and CREATE ROLE are two privileges where context is irrelevant.

 Privileges in other database products might be called rights or permissions.

Getting Started

So you successfully installed PostgreSQL; you should have one superuser, whose password you know by heart. Now you should take the following steps to set up additional roles and assign privileges:

1. PostgreSQL creates one superuser and one database for you at installation, both named postgres. Log in to your server as postgres.

2. Before creating your first database, create a role that will own the database and can log in, such as:

   ```
   CREATE ROLE mydb_admin LOGIN PASSWORD 'something';
   ```

3. Create the database and set the owner:

   ```
   CREATE DATABASE mydb WITH owner = mydb_admin;
   ```

4. Now log in as the mydb_admin user and start setting up additional schemas and tables.

GRANT

The GRANT command is the primary means to assign privileges. Basic usage is:

```
GRANT some_privilege TO some_role;
```

A few things to keep in mind when it comes to GRANT:

- Obviously, you need to have the privilege you're granting. And, you must have the GRANT privilege yourself. You can't give away what you don't have.
- Some privileges always remain with the owner of an object and can never be granted away. These include DROP and ALTER.
- The owner of an object retains all privileges. Granting an owner privilege in what it already owns is unnecessary. Keep in mind, though, that ownership does not

drill down to child objects. For instance, if you own a database, you may not necessarily own all the schemas within it.

- When granting privileges, you can add WITH GRANT OPTION. This means that the grantee can grant her own privileges to others, passing them on:

```
GRANT ALL ON ALL TABLES IN SCHEMA public TO mydb_admin WITH GRANT OPTION;
```

- To grant specific privileges on ALL objects of a specific type use ALL instead of the specific object name, as in:

```
GRANT SELECT, REFERENCES, TRIGGER ON
ALL TABLES IN SCHEMA my_schema TO
PUBLIC;
```

  Note that `ALL TABLES` includes regular tables, foreign tables, and views.

- To grant privileges to all roles, you can use the PUBLIC alias, as in:

```
GRANT USAGE ON SCHEMA my_schema TO PUBLIC;
```

The GRANT command is covered in detail in GRANT (*http://www.postgresql.org/docs/current/interactive/sql-grant.html*). We strongly recommend that you take the time to study this document before you inadvertently knock a big hole in your security wall.

Some privileges are, by default, granted to PUBLIC. These are CONNECT and CREATE TEMP TABLE for databases and EXECUTE for functions. In many cases you might consider revoking some of the defaults with the REVOKE command, as in:

```
REVOKE EXECUTE ON ALL FUNCTIONS IN SCHEMA my_schema FROM PUBLIC;
```

Default Privileges

Default privileges ease privilege management by letting you set privileges before their creation.

Adding or changing default privileges won't affect privilege settings on existing objects.

Let's suppose we want all users of our database to have EXECUTE and SELECT privileges access to any future tables and functions in a particular schema. We can define privileges as shown in Example 2-8. All roles of a PostgreSQL server are members of the group PUBLIC.

Example 2-8. Defining default privileges on a schema

```
GRANT USAGE ON SCHEMA my_schema TO PUBLIC; ❶

ALTER DEFAULT PRIVILEGES IN SCHEMA my_schema
GRANT SELECT, REFERENCES ON TABLES TO PUBLIC; ❷

ALTER DEFAULT PRIVILEGES IN SCHEMA my_schema
GRANT ALL ON TABLES TO mydb_admin WITH GRANT OPTION; ❸

ALTER DEFAULT PRIVILEGES IN SCHEMA my_schema ❹
GRANT SELECT, UPDATE ON SEQUENCES TO public;

ALTER DEFAULT PRIVILEGES IN SCHEMA my_schema ❺
GRANT ALL ON FUNCTIONS TO mydb_admin WITH GRANT OPTION;

ALTER DEFAULT PRIVILEGES IN SCHEMA my_schema ❻
GRANT USAGE ON TYPES TO PUBLIC;
```

❶ Allows all users that can connect to the database to also be able to use and create objects in a schema if they have rights to those objects in the schema. GRANT USAGE on a schema is the first step to granting access to objects in the schema. If a user has rights to select from a table in a schema but no USAGE on the schema, then he will not be able to query the table.

❷ Grant read and reference rights (the ability to create foreign key constraints against columns in a table) for all future tables created in a schema to all users that have USAGE of the schema.

❸ GRANT ALL permissions on future tables to role mydb_admin. In addition, allow members in mydb_admin to be able to grant a subset or all privileges to other users to future tables in this schema. GRANT ALL gives permission to add/update/delete/truncate rows, add triggers, and create constraints on the tables.

❹❺❻ GRANT permissions on future sequences, functions, and types.

To read more about default privileges, see ALTER DEFAULT PRIVILEGES (*http://bit.ly/1vwCs6L*).

Privilege Idiosyncrasies

Before we unleash you to explore privileges on your own, we do want to point out a few quirks that may not be apparent.

Unlike in other database products, being the owner of a PostgreSQL database does not give you access to all objects in the database. Another role could conceivably create a table in your database and deny you access to it! However, the privilege to drop the entire database could never be wrestled away from you.

After granting privileges to tables and functions with a schema, don't forget to grant usage on the schema itself.

Extensions

Extensions, formerly called contribs, are add-ons that you can install in a PostgreSQL database to extend functionality beyond the base offerings. They exemplify the best of open source software: people collaborating, building, and freely sharing new features. Since version 9.1, the new extension model has made adding extensions a cinch.

 Older add-ons outside the extension model are still called contribs, but with an eye toward the future, we'll call them all extensions.

Not all extensions need to be in all databases. You should install extensions to your individual database on an as-needed basis. If you want all your databases to have a certain set of extensions, you can develop a template database, as discussed in "Template Databases" on page 38, with all the extensions installed, and then beget future databases from that template.

Occasionally prune extensions that you no longer need to avoid bloat. Leaving old extensions you don't need may cause problems during an in-place upgrade since all extensions you have installed must be also installed in the new PostgreSQL version you are upgrading to.

To see which extensions you have already installed in a database, connect to the database and run the query in Example 2-9. Your list could vary significantly from ours.

Example 2-9. Extensions installed in a database

```
SELECT name, default_version, installed_version, left(comment,30) As comment
FROM pg_available_extensions
WHERE installed_version IS NOT NULL
ORDER BY name;
```

name	default_version	installed_version	comment
btree_gist	1.5	1.5	support for indexing common da
fuzzystrmatch	1.1	1.1	determine similarities and dis
hstore	1.4	1.4	data type for storing sets of
ogr_fdw	1.0	1.0	foreign-data wrapper for GIS d
pgrouting	2.4.1	2.4.1	pgRouting Extension

```
plpgsql      | 1.0      | 1.0      | PL/pgSQL procedural language
plv8         | 1.4.10   | 1.4.10   | PL/JavaScript (v8) trusted pro
postgis      | 2.4.0dev | 2.4.0dev | PostGIS geometry, geography, a
(8 rows)
```

If you want to see all the extensions installed on the server, regardless of if they are installed in your current database, leave out the `WHERE installed_version IS NOT NULL`.

To get more details about a particular extension already installed in your database, enter the following command from psql:

```
\dx+ fuzzystrmatch
```

Alternatively, execute the following query:

```
SELECT pg_describe_object(D.classid,D.objid,0) AS description
FROM pg_catalog.pg_depend AS D INNER JOIN pg_catalog.pg_extension AS E
ON D.refobjid = E.oid
WHERE
D.refclassid = 'pg_catalog.pg_extension'::pg_catalog.regclass AND
deptype = 'e' AND
E.extname = 'fuzzystrmatch';
```

This shows what's packaged in the extension:

```
description
--------------------------------------------------------------------
function dmetaphone_alt(text)
function dmetaphone(text)
function difference(text,text)
function text_soundex(text)
function soundex(text)
function metaphone(text,integer)
function levenshtein_less_equal(text,text,integer,integer,integer,integer)
function levenshtein_less_equal(text,text,integer)
function levenshtein(text,text,integer,integer,integer)
function levenshtein(text,text)
```

Extensions can include database assets of all types: functions, tables, data types, casts, languages, operators, etc., but functions usually constitute the bulk of the payload.

Installing Extensions

Getting an extension into your database takes two installation steps. First, download the extension and install it onto your server. Second, install the extension into your database.

We'll be using the same term—*install*—to refer to both procedures but distinguish between the installation on the server and the installation into the database when the context is unclear.

We cover both steps in this section as well as how to install on PostgreSQL versions prior to extension support.

Step 1: Installing on the server

The installation of extensions on your server varies by OS. The overall idea is to download binary files and requisite libraries, then copy the respective binaries to the *bin* and *lib* folders and the script files to *share/extension* (versions 9.1 and above) or *share/contrib* (prior to version 9.1). This makes the extension available for the second step.

For smaller popular extensions, many of the requisite libraries come prepackaged with your PostgreSQL installation or can be easily retrieved using yum or apt-get postgresql-contrib. For others, you'll need to compile your own, find installers that someone has already created, or copy the files from another equivalent server setup. Larger extensions, such as PostGIS, can usually be found at the same location where you downloaded PostgreSQL. To view all extension binaries already available on your server, enter:

```
SELECT * FROM pg_available_extensions;
```

Step 2: Installing into a database

The extension support makes installation of added features simple. Use the CREATE EXTENSION command to install extensions into each database. The three big benefits are that you don't have to figure out where the extension files are kept (*share/extension*), you can uninstall them at will using DROP EXTENSION, and you will have a readily available listing of what is installed and what is available.

PostgreSQL installation packages already include the most popular extensions. To retrieve additional extensions, visit the PostgreSQL Extension Network (*http://pgxn.org/*). You'll also find many PostgreSQL extensions on GitHub (*https://github.com*) by searching for postgresql extension.

Here is how we would install the fuzzystrmatch extension using SQL:

```
CREATE EXTENSION fuzzystrmatch;
```

You can still install an extension noninteractively using psql. Make sure you're connected to the database where you need the extension, then run:

```
psql -p 5432 -d mydb -c "CREATE EXTENSION fuzzystrmatch;"
```

C-based extensions must be installed by a superuser. Most extensions fall into this category.

We strongly suggest you create one or more schemas to house extensions to keep them separate from production data. After you create the schema, install extensions into it through a command like the following:

```
CREATE EXTENSION fuzzystrmatch SCHEMA my_extensions;
```

Upgrading to the new extension model

If you've been using a version of PostgreSQL older than 9.1 and restored your old database into version 9.1 or later during a version upgrade, all extensions should continue to function without intervention. For maintainability, you should upgrade your old extensions in the *contrib* folder to use the new approach to extensions. You can upgrade extensions, especially the ones that come packaged with PostgreSQL, from the old contrib model to the new one. Remember that we're referring only to the upgrade in the installation model, not to the extension itself.

For example, suppose you had installed the tablefunc extension (for cross-tab queries) to your PostgreSQL 9.0 in a schema called contrib, and you have just restored your database to a 9.1 server. Run the following command to upgrade:

```
CREATE EXTENSION tablefunc SCHEMA contrib FROM unpackaged;
```

This command searches through contrib schema (assuming this is where you placed all the extensions), retrieves all components of the extension, and repackages them into a new extension object so it appears in the pg_available_extensions list as being installed.

This command leaves the old functions in the contrib schema intact but removes them from being a part of a database backup.

Common Extensions

Many extensions come packaged with PostgreSQL but are not installed by default. Some past extensions have gained enough traction to become part of the PostgreSQL core. If you're upgrading from an ancient version, you may gain functionality without needing any extensions.

Popular extensions

Since version 9.1, PostgreSQL prefers the extension model to deliver all add-ons. These include basic extensions consisting only of functions and types, as well as PLs, index types, and FDWs. In this section we list the most popular extensions (some say, "must-have" extensions) that PostgreSQL doesn't install into your database by default. Depending on your PostgreSQL distribution, you'll find many of these already available on your server:

btree_gist (http://www.postgresql.org/docs/current/interactive/btree-gist.html)
Provides GiST index operator classes that implement B-Tree equivalent behavior for common B-Tree services data types. See "PostgreSQL Stock Indexes" on page 157 for more details.

btree_gin (http://www.postgresql.org/docs/current/interactive/btree-gin.html)
Provides GIN index operator classes that implement B-Tree equivalent behavior for common B-Tree serviced data types. See "PostgreSQL Stock Indexes" on page 157 for more details.

postgis (http://postgis.net)
Elevates PostgreSQL to a state-of-the-art spatial database outrivaling all commercial options. If you deal with standard OGC GIS data, demographic statistics data, or geocoding, 3d data, or even raster data, you don't want to be without this one. You can learn more about PostGIS in our book *PostGIS in Action (http://www.postgis.us)*. PostGIS is a whopper of an extension, weighing in at more than 800 functions, types, and spatial indexes. PostGIS is so big it has extensions that extend it. There exist extensions on top of PostGIS such as those included with PostGIS itself. In addition, there is pgpointcloud for managing point clouds and pgRouting for network routing, which are packaged separately.

fuzzystrmatch (http://www.postgresql.org/docs/current/interactive/fuzzystrmatch.html)
A lightweight extension with functions such as soundex, levenshtein, and metaphone algorithms for fuzzy string matching. We discuss its use in Where is Soundex and Other Fuzzy Things (*http://www.postgresonline.com/journal/archives/ 158-Where-is-soundex-and-other-warm-and-fuzzy-string-things.html*).

hstore (http://www.postgresql.org/docs/current/interactive/hstore.html)
An extension that adds key-value pair storage and index support, well-suited for storing pseudonormalized data. If you are looking for a comfortable medium between a relational database and NoSQL, check out hstore. Usage of hstore in many cases has been replaced with the built-in jsonb type. So this extension isn't as popular as it used to be.

pg_trgm (trigram) (http://www.postgresql.org/docs/current/interactive/pgtrgm.html)
Another fuzzy string search library, used in conjunction with fuzzystrmatch. It includes an operator class, making searches using the `ILIKE` operator indexable. trigram can also allow wildcard searches in the form of `LIKE %something%`' or regular expression searches such as `somefield ~ '(foo|bar)'` to utilize an index. See *Teaching ILIKE and LIKE New Tricks (http://www.postgresonline.com/*

journal/archives/212-PostgreSQL-9.1-Trigrams-teaching-LIKE-and-ILIKE-new-tricks.html) for further discussion.

dblink (http://www.postgresql.org/docs/current/interactive/dblink.html)
   Allows you to query a PostgreSQL database on another server. Prior to the introduction of FDWs in version 9.3, this was the only supported mechanism for
   cross-database interactions. It remains useful for one-time connections or ad hoc
   queries, especially where you need to call functions on the foreign server. Prior to
   PostgreSQL 9.6, postgres_fdw doesn't allow a statement to call functions on the
   foreign server, only local ones. In PostgreSQL 9.6 you can call functions defined
   in an extension if you denote in the foreign server that the server has that extension installed.

pgcrypto (http://www.postgresql.org/docs/current/interactive/pgcrypto.html)
   Provides encryption tools, including the popular PGP. It's handy for encrypting
   top-secret information stored in the database. See our quick primer on it at
   Encrypting Data with pgcrypto (*http://bit.ly/12scJQW*).

Classic extensions

Here are a few venerable ex-extensions that have gained enough of a following to
make it into official PostgreSQL releases. We call them out here because you could
still run into them as separate extensions on older servers:

tsearch (http://www.postgresql.org/docs/current/interactive/textsearch-intro.html)
   A suite of indexes, operators, custom dictionaries, and functions that enhance
   FTSs. It is now part of PostgreSQL proper. If you're still relying on behavior from
   the old extension, you can install tsearch2 (*http://bit.ly/12scNQD*). A better tactic
   would be just to update servers where you're using the old functions, because
   compatibility could end at any time.

xml (http://www.postgresql.org/docs/current/interactive/functions-xml.html)
   An extension that added an XML data type, related functions, and operators. The
   XML data type is now an integral part of PostgreSQL, in part to meet the ANSI
   SQL XML standard. The old extension, now dubbed xml2 (*http://bit.ly/12scKV7*),
   can still be installed and contains functions that didn't make it into the core. In
   particular, you need this extension if you relied on the xlst_process function for
   processing XSL templates. There are also a couple of old XPath functions only
   found in xml2.

Backup and Restore

PostgreSQL ships with three utilities for backup: *pg_dump*, *pg_dumpall*, and *pg_base-backup*. You'll find all of them in the PostgreSQL *bin* folder.

Use *pg_dump* to back up specific databases. To back up all databases in plain text along with server globals, use *pg_dumpall*, which needs to run under a superuser account so that it back up all databases. Use *pg_basebackup* to do system-level disk backup of all databases.

For the rest of this section, we'll focus our discussion on using *pg_dump* and *pg_dumpall*. *pg_basebackup* is the most efficient way of doing a full postgresql server cluster backup. If you have a reasonably sized database, as in 500 GB or more, you should be using pg_basebackup as part of your backup strategy. pg_basebackup, however, requires enabling of features that are often turned off, but that are also needed for replication, so we'll save discussion of *pg_basebackup* for "Setting Up Full Server Replication" on page 249.

Most of the command-line options for these tools exist both in GNU style (two hyphens plus a word) and the traditional single-letter style (one hyphen plus an alphabetic character). You can use both styles interchangeably, even in the same command. We'll be covering just the basics here; for a more in-depth discussion, see the PostgreSQL documentation Backup and Restore (*http://bit.ly/12scOUX*).

In this section we will not discuss third-party tools that are often used for PostgreSQL backup and restore. Two popular open source ones you might want to consider are pgBackRest (*http://www.pgbackrest.org/*) and Barman (*http://www.pgbarman.org/*). These offer additional features like backup scheduling, multiserver support, and restore shortcuts.

As you wade through this section, you'll find that we often specify the port and host in our examples. This is because we often run backups for a different server as scheduled jobs using pgAgent, as discussed in "Job Scheduling with pgAgent" on page 94. We often have multiple instances of PostgreSQL running on the same machine, on different ports as well. Sometimes specifying the host can cause problems if your service is set to listen only on localhost. You can safely leave out the host if you are running the examples directly on the server.

You may also want to create a *~/.pgpass (http://bit.ly/12scPrZ)* file to store all passwords. *pg_dump* and *pg_dumpall* don't have password options. Alternatively, you can set a password in the PGPASSWORD environment variable.

Selective Backup Using pg_dump

For day-to-day backup, *pg_dump* is more expeditious than *pg_dumpall* because *pg_dump* can selectively back up tables, schemas, and databases. *pg_dump* can back up to plain SQL, as well as compressed, TAR, and directory formats. Compressed, TAR, and directory format backups can take advantage of the parallel restore feature of *pg_restore*. Directory backups allow parallel *pg_dump* of a large database. Because we believe you'll be using *pg_dump* as part of your daily regimen, we have included a full dump of the help in "Database Backup Using pg_dump" on page 271 so you can see the myriad switches in a single glance.

The next examples demonstrate a few common backup scenarios and corresponding *pg_dump* options. They should work for any version of PostgreSQL.

To create a compressed, single database backup:

```
pg_dump -h localhost -p 5432 -U someuser -F c -b -v -f mydb.backup mydb
```

To create a plain-text single database backup, including a -C option, which stands for CREATE DATABASE:

```
pg_dump -h localhost -p 5432 -U someuser -C -F p -b -v -f mydb.backup mydb
```

To create a compressed backup of tables whose names start with *pay* in any schema:

```
pg_dump -h localhost -p 5432 -U someuser -F c -b -v -t *.pay* -f pay.backup mydb
```

To create a compressed backup of all objects in the hr and payroll schemas:

```
pg_dump -h localhost -p 5432 -U someuser -F c -b -v \
-n hr -n payroll -f hr.backup mydb
```

To create a compressed backup of all objects in all schemas, excluding the public schema:

```
pg_dump -h localhost -p 5432 -U someuser -F c -b -v -N public \
-f all_sch_except_pub.backup mydb
```

To create a plain-text SQL backup of select tables, useful for porting structure and data to lower versions of PostgreSQL or non-PostgreSQL databases (plain text generates an SQL script that you can run on any system that speaks SQL):

```
pg_dump -h localhost -p 5432 -U someuser -F p --column-inserts \
-f select_tables.backup mydb
```

 If your file paths contain spaces or other characters that could throw off the command-line interpreter, wrap the file path in double quotes: `"/path with spaces/mydb.backup"`. As a general rule, you can always use double quotes if you aren't sure.

The directory format option was introduced in version PostgreSQL 9.1. This option backs up each table as a separate file in a folder and gets around file size limitations. This option is the only *pg_dump* backup format option that results in multiple files, as shown in Example 2-10. It creates a new directory and populates it with a gzipped file for each table; also included is a file listing the hierarchy. This backup command exits with an error if the directory already exists.

Example 2-10. Directory format backup

```
pg_dump -h localhost -p 5432 -U someuser -F d -f /somepath/a_directory mydb
```

A parallel backup option was introduced in version 9.3 using the `--jobs` or `-j` option and specifying the number of jobs. For example: `--jobs=3` (`-j 3`) runs three backups in parallel. Parallel backup makes sense only with the directory format option, because it's the only backup where multiple files are created. Example 2-11 demonstrates its use.

Example 2-11. Directory format parallel backup

```
pg_dump -h localhost -p 5432 -U someuser -j 3 -Fd -f /somepath/a_directory mydb
```

Systemwide Backup Using pg_dumpall

Use the *pg_dumpall* utility to back up all databases on a server into a single plain-text file. This comprehensive backup automatically includes server globals such as tablespace definitions and roles. See "Server Backup: pg_dumpall" on page 273 for a listing of available *pg_dumpall* command options.

It's a good idea to back up globals on a daily basis. Although you can use *pg_dumpall* to back up databases as well, we prefer backing up databases individually using *pg_dump* or using *pg_basebackup* to do a PostgreSQL service-level backup. Restoring from a huge plain-text backup tries our patience. Using *pg_basebackup* in conjunction with streaming replication is the fastest way to recover from major server failure.

To back up all globals and tablespace definitions only, use the following:

```
pg_dumpall -h localhost -U postgres --port=5432 -f myglobals.sql --globals-only
```

To back up specific global settings, use the following:

```
pg_dumpall -h localhost -U postgres --port=5432 -f myroles.sql --roles-only
```

Restoring Data

There are two ways to restore data in PostgreSQL from backups created with *pg_dump* or *pg_dumpall*:

- Use psql to restore plain-text backups generated with *pg_dumpall* or *pg_dump*.
- Use *pg_restore* to restore compressed, TAR, and directory backups created with *pg_dump*.

Using psql to restore plain-text SQL backups

A plain SQL backup is nothing more than a text file containing a hefty SQL script. It's the least convenient backup to have, but it's the most versatile. With SQL backup, you must execute the entire script. You can't cherry-pick objects unless you're willing to manually edit the file. Run all of the following examples from the OS console or *psql*.

To restore a backup and ignore errors:

```
psql -U postgres -f myglobals.sql
```

To restore, stopping if any error is found:

```
psql -U postgres --set ON_ERROR_STOP=on -f myglobals.sql
```

To restore to a specific database:

```
psql -U postgres -d mydb -f select_objects.sql
```

Using pg_restore

If you backed up using *pg_dump* and chose a format such as TAR, custom, or directory, you have to use the *pg_restore* utility to restore. *pg_restore* provides a dizzying array of options, far surpassing the restore utility found in other database products we've used. Some of its outstanding features include:

- You can perform parallel restores using the -j (equivalent to --jobs=) option to indicate the number of threads to use. This allows each thread to restore a separate table simultaneously, significantly picking up the pace of what could otherwise be a lengthy process.

- You can use *pg_restore* to generate a table of contents file from your backup file to check what has been backed up. You can also edit this table of contents and use the revised file to control what gets restored.

- *pg_restore* allows you to selectively restore, even from within a backup of a full database. If you just need one table restored, you can do that.

- *pg_restore* is backward-compatible, for the most part. You can back up a database on an older version of PostgreSQL and restore to a newer version.

See "Database Restore: pg_restore" on page 274 for a listing of *pg_restore* options.

To perform a restore using *pg_restore*, first create the database anew using SQL:

```
CREATE DATABASE mydb;
```

Then restore:

```
pg_restore --dbname=mydb --jobs=4 --verbose mydb.backup
```

If the name of the database is the same as the one you backed up, you can create and restore the database in one step:

```
pg_restore --dbname=postgres --create --jobs=4 --verbose mydb.backup
```

When you use the --create option, the database name is always the name of the one
you backed up. You can't rename it. If you're also using the --dbname option, that
database name must be different from the name of the database being restored. We
usually just specify the postgres database.

Normally, a restore will not re-create objects already present in a database. If you have
data in the database, and you want to replace it with what's in the backup, you need to
add the --clean switch to the pg_restore command. This will cause objects to be
dropped from the current database so that restore can re-create them.

 If you restore over an existing database, the content of the backup
may replace things in your current database. Be careful during a
restore: don't accidentally pick the wrong backup file or the wrong
database to restore to!

With PostgreSQL 9.2 or later, you can take advantage of the --section option to
restore just the structure without the data. This is useful if you want to use an existing
database as a template for a new one. To do so, first create the target database:

```
CREATE DATABASE mydb2;
```

Then use pg_restore:

```
pg_restore --dbname=mydb2 --section=pre-data --jobs=4 mydb.backup
```

Managing Disk Storage with Tablespaces

PostgreSQL uses tablespaces to ascribe logical names to physical locations on disk.
Initializing a PostgreSQL cluster automatically begets two tablespaces: pg_default,
which stores all user data, and pg_global, which stores all system data. These are located in the same folder as your default data cluster. You're free to create tablespaces at
will and house them on any serverdisks. You can explicitly assign default tablespaces
for new objects by database. You can also move existing database objects to new ones.

Creating Tablespaces

To create a new tablespace, specify a logical name and a physical folder and make sure
that the postgres service account has full access to the physical folder. If you are on a
Windows server, use the following command (note the use of Unix-style forward-
slashes):

```
CREATE TABLESPACE secondary LOCATION 'C:/pgdata94_secondary';
```

For Unix-based systems, you first must create the folder or define an fstab location,
then use this command:

```
CREATE TABLESPACE secondary LOCATION '/usr/data/pgdata94_secondary';
```

Moving Objects Among Tablespaces

You can shuffle database objects among different tablespaces. To move all objects in the database to your secondary tablespace, issue the following SQL command:

```
ALTER DATABASE mydb SET TABLESPACE secondary;
```

To move just one table:

```
ALTER TABLE mytable SET TABLESPACE secondary;
```

New in PostgreSQL 9.4 is the ability move a group of objects from one tablespace to another. If the role running the command is a superuser, all objects will be moved. If not, only the owned objects will be moved.

To move all objects from default tablespace to secondary use:

```
ALTER TABLESPACE pg_default MOVE ALL TO secondary;
```

During the move, your database or table will be locked.

Verboten Practices

We have acted as first responders to many PostgreSQL accidents, so we thought it best to end this chapter by itemizing the most common mistakes.

For starters, if you don't know what you did wrong, the logfile could provide clues. Look for the *pg_log* folder in your PostgreSQL data folder or the root of the PostgreSQL data folder. It's also possible that your server shut down before a log entry could be written, in which case the log won't help you. If your server fails to restart, try the following from the OS command line:

```
path/to/your/bin/pg_ctl -D your_postgresql_data_folder
```

Don't Delete PostgreSQL Core System Files and Binaries

Perhaps this is stating the obvious, but when people run out of disk space, the first thing they do is start deleting files from the PostgreSQL data cluster folder because it's so darn big. Part of the reason this mistake happens so frequently is that some folders sport innocuous names such as *pg_log*, *pg_xlog*, and *pg_clog*. Yes, there are some files you can safely delete, but unless you know precisely which ones, you could end up destroying your data.

The *pg_log* folder, often found in your data folder, is a folder that builds up quickly, especially if you have logging enabled. You can always purge files from this folder without harm. In fact, many people schedule jobs to remove logfiles on a regular basis.

Files in the other folders, except for *pg_xlog*, should never be deleted, even if they have log-sounding names. Don't even think of touching `pg_clog`, the active commit log, unless you want to invite disaster.

pg_xlog stores transaction logs. Some systems we've seen are configured to move processed transaction logs into a subfolder called *archive*. You'll often have an archive folder somewhere (not necessarily as a subfolder of *pg_xlog*) if you are running synchronous replication, doing continuous archiving, or just keeping logs around in case you need to revert to a different point in time. Deleting files in the root of *pg_xlog* will mess up the process. Deleting files in the archived folder will just prevent you from performing point-in-time recovery, or if a slave server hasn't played back the logs, will prevent the slave from fetching them. If these scenarios don't apply to you, it's safe to remove files in the *archive* folder.

Be leery of overzealous antivirus programs, especially on Windows. We've seen cases in which antivirus software removed important binaries in the PostgreSQL *bin* folder. If PostgreSQL fails to start on a Windows system, the event viewer is the first place to look for clues as to why.

 In version 10, the *pg_xlog* folder was renamed to *pg_wal* and *pg_clog* was renamed to *pg_xact* to prevent people from thinking these are log folders where contents can be deleted without destructive consequences.

Don't Grant Full OS Administrative Privileges to the Postgres System Account (postgres)

Many people are under the misconception that the postgres account needs to have full administrative privileges to the server. In fact, depending on your PostgreSQL version, if you give the postgres account full administrative privileges to the server, your database server might not even start.

The postgres account should always be created as a regular system user in the OS with privileges just to the data cluster and additional tablespace folders. Most installers will set up the correct permissions without you needing to worry. Don't try to do postgres any favors by giving it more access than it needs. Granting unnecessary access leaves your system vulnerable if you fall victim to an SQL injection attack.

There are cases where you'll need to give the postgres account write/delete/read rights to folders or executables outside of the data cluster. With scheduled jobs that execute batch files and FDWs that have foreign tables in files, this need often arises. Practice restraint and bestow only the minimum access necessary to get the job done.

Don't Set shared_buffers Too High

Loading up your server with RAM doesn't mean you can set the shared_buffers as high as your physical RAM. Try it and your server may crash or refuse to start. If you are running PostgreSQL on 32-bit Windows, setting it higher than 512 MB often results in instability. With 64-bit Windows, you can push the envelope higher, and can even exceed 8 GB without any issues. On some Linux systems, shared_buffers can't be higher than the SHMMAX variable, which is usually quite low.

PostgreSQL 9.3 changed how kernel memory is used, so that many of the issues people ran into with limitations in prior versions are no longer issues. You can find more details in Kernel Resources (*http://bit.ly/12scSDW*).

Don't Try to Start PostgreSQL on a Port Already in Use

If you try to start PostgreSQL on a port that's already in use, you'll see errors in your *pg_log* files of the form: `make sure PostgreSQL is not already running`. Here are the common reasons why this happens:

- You've already started the postgres service.
- You are trying to run PostgreSQL on a port already in use by another service.
- Your postgres service had a sudden shutdown and you have an orphan *postgresql.pid* file in the data folder. Delete the file and try again.
- You have an orphaned PostgreSQL process. When all else fails, kill all running PostgreSQL processes and then try starting again.

psql

psql is the *de rigueur* command-line utility packaged with PostgreSQL. Aside from its common use of running queries, you can use psql to execute scripts, import and export data, restore tables, do other database administration, and even generate reports. If you have access only to a server's command line with no GUI, psql is your only choice to interact with PostgreSQL. If you fall into this group, you have to be intimate with myriad commands and options. We suggest that you print out the dump of psql help as discussed in "psql Interactive Commands" on page 276 and enshrine it above your workstation.

Environment Variables

As with other command-line tools packaged with PostgreSQL, you can forgo specifying your connection settings—host, port, user—by initializing the PGHOST, PGPORT, and PGUSER environment variables. To avoid having to retype the password, you can initialize the variable PGPASSWORD. For more secure access, create a password file as described in PostgreSQL Password File (*http://bit.ly/12scPrZ*). Since version 9.2 psql accepts two new environment variables:

PSQL_HISTORY
   Sets the name of the psql history file that lists all commands executed in the recent past. The default is *~/.psql_history*.

PSQLRC
   Specifies the location and name of a custom configuration file. Should you decide to create this file, you can place most of your settings in here. At startup, psql will read settings from your configuration file before loading default values, and your file's settings will override the defaults.

If you omit the parameters when starting psql and failed to initialize environment variables, psql will use the standard defaults.

 If you use pgAdmin3, once connected to a database, you can click an icon to open up psql with the same parameters you have in pgAdmin.

Interactive versus Noninteractive psql

Run psql interactively by typing **psql** from your OS command line. Your prompt will transfigure to the psql prompt, signaling that you are now in the interactive psql console. Begin typing in commands. For SQL statements, terminate with a semicolon. If you press Enter without a semicolon, psql will assume that your statement continues to the next line.

Typing \? while in the psql console brings up a list of available commands. For convenience, we've reprinted this list in Appendix B, highlighting new additions in the latest versions; see "psql Interactive Commands" on page 276. Typing \h followed by the command will bring up the relevant sections of the PostgreSQL documentation pertaining to the command.

To run commands repeatedly or in a sequence, you're better off creating a script first and then running it using psql noninteractively. At your OS prompt, type **psql** followed by the name of the script file. Within this script you can mix an unlimited number of SQL and psql commands. Alternatively, you can pass in one or more SQL statements surrounded by double quotes. Noninteractive psql is well-suited for automated tasks. Batch your commands into a file; then schedule it to run at regular intervals using a scheduling daemon like pgAgent, crontab in Linux/Unix, or Windows Scheduler.

Noninteractive psql offers few command-line options because the script file does most of the work. For a listing of all options, see "psql Noninteractive Commands" on page 278. To execute a file, use the -f option, as in the following:

```
psql -f some_script_file
```

To execute SQL on the fly, use the -c option. Separate multiple statements with a semicolon as in the following:

```
psql -d postgresql_book -c "DROP TABLE IF EXISTS dross; CREATE SCHEMA staging;"
```

You can embed interactive commands inside script files. Example 3-1 is the contents of a script named *build_stage.psql*, which we will use to create a staging table called *staging.factfinder_import* that is loaded in Example 3-10. The script first generates a

CREATE TABLE statement, which it writes to a new file called *create_script.sql*. It then executes the generated *create_script.sql*.

Example 3-1. Script that includes psql interactive commands

```
\a ❶
\t
\g create_script.sql
SELECT
    'CREATE TABLE staging.factfinder_import (
        geo_id varchar(255), geo_id2 varchar(255), geo_display varchar(255),' ||
        array_to_string(array_agg('s' ||
        lpad(i::text,2,'0') || ' varchar(255),s' ||
        lpad(i::text,2,'0') || '_perc varchar(255)'),',') ||
    ');'
FROM generate_series(1,51) As i;
\o ❷
\i create_script.sql ❸
```

❶ Since we want the output of our query to be saved as an executable statement, we need to remove the headers by using the \t option (shorthand for --tuples-only) and use the \a option to get rid of the extra breaking elements that psql normally puts in. We then use the \g option to force our query output to be redirected to a file.

❷ We call the \o without file arguments to stop redirection of query results to file.

❸ To execute our generated script, we use the \i followed by the generated script name *create_script.sql*. The \i is the interactive version of the noninteractive -f option.

To run Example 3-1, we enter the following at an OS prompt:

```
psql -f build_stage.psql -d postgresql_book
```

Example 3-1 is an adaptation of an approach we describe in How to Create an N-column Table (*http://bit.ly/12scVQi*). As noted in the article, you can perform this without an intermediary file by using the DO command introduced in PostgreSQL 9.0.

psql Customizations

If you spend most of your day in psql, consider tailoring the psql environment to make you more productive. psql reads settings from a configuration file called *psqlrc*, if present. When psql launches, it searches for this file and runs all commands therein.

On Linux/Unix, the file is customarily named *.psqlrc* and should be placed in your home directory. On Windows, the file is called *psqlrc.conf* and should be placed in the *%APPDATA%\postgresql* folder, which usually resolves to *C:\Users\username\App-Data\Roaming\postgresql*. Don't worry if you can't find the file right after installation; you usually need to create it. Any settings in the file will override psql defaults.

Example 3-2 is a glimpse into the contents of a *psqlrc* file. You can include any psql command.

Example 3-2. Example psqlrc file

```
\pset null 'NULL'
\encoding latin1
\set PROMPT1 '%n@%M:%>%x %/# '
\pset pager always
\timing on
\set qstats92 '
    SELECT usename, datname, left(query,100) || ''...'' As query
    FROM pg_stat_activity WHERE state != ''idle'' ;
'
```

 Each command must be on a single line without breaks. Our examples may add line breaks to accommodate printing.

When you launch psql now, the result of executing the configuration file echoes to the screen:

```
Null display is "NULL".
Timing is on.
Pager is always used.
psql (9.6beta3)
Type "help" for help.
postgres@localhost:5442 postgresql_book#
```

Some commands work only on Linux/Unix systems, while others work only on Windows. In either OS, you should use the Linux/Unix–style slash (forward slash) for path. If you want to bypass the configuration file and start psql with all its defaults, start it with the -X option.

You can change settings on the fly while in psql, though the change will only be in effect during your psql session. To remove a configuration variable or set it back to the default, issue the \unset command followed by the setting, as in: \unset qstat92.

When using set, keep in mind that the variable you set is case sensitive. Use all caps to set system options, and lowercase for your own variables. In Example 3-2, PROMPT1 is a system setting for how the psql prompt should appear, whereas qstats92 is a variable initialized as shorthand to display current activities on the PostgreSQL server.

Custom Prompts

If you spend your waking hours playing with psql connecting to multiple servers and databases, customizing your prompt to display the connected server and database will enhance your situational awareness and possibly avoid disaster. Here's a simple way to set a highly informational prompt:

```
\set PROMPT1 '%n@%M:%>%x %/# '
```

This includes whom we are logged in as (%n), the host server (%M), the port (%>), the transaction status (%x), and the database (%/). This is probably overkill, so economize as you see fit. The complete listing of prompt symbols is documented in the psql Reference Guide (*http://www.postgresql.org/docs/current/interactive/app-psql.html*).

When we connect with psql to our database, our enhanced prompt looks like:

```
postgres@localhost:5442 postgresql_book#
```

Should we switch to another database using \connect postgis_book, our prompt changes to:

```
postgres@localhost:5442 postgis_book#
```

Timing Executions

You may find it instructive to have psql output the time it took for each query to execute. Use the \timing command to toggle it on and off.

When enabled, each query you run will report the duration at the end. For example, with \timing on, executing SELECT COUNT(*) FROM pg_tables; outputs:

```
count
--------
73
(1 row)
Time: 18.650 ms
```

Autocommit Commands

By default, autocommit is on, meaning any SQL command you issue that changes data will immediately commit. Each command is its own transaction and is irreversible. If you are running a large batch of precarious updates, you may want a safety net.

Start by turning off autocommit: `\set AUTOCOMMIT off`. Now, you have the option to roll back your statements:

```
UPDATE census.facts SET short_name = 'This is a mistake.';
```

To undo the update, run:

```
ROLLBACK;
```

To make the update permanent, run:

```
COMMIT;
```

 Don't forget to commit your changes if autocommit is off; otherwise, they roll back when you exit psql.

Shortcuts

You can use the `\set` command to create useful keyboard shortcuts. Store universally applicable shortcuts in your *psqlrc* file. For example, if you use EXPLAIN ANALYZE VERBOSE once every 10 minutes, create a shortcut as follows:

```
\set eav 'EXPLAIN ANALYZE VERBOSE'
```

Now, all you have to type is `:eav` (the colon resolves the variable):

```
:eav SELECT COUNT(*) FROM pg_tables;
```

You can even save entire queries as shortcuts as we did in Example 3-2. Use lowercase to name your shortcuts to distinguish them from system settings.

Retrieving Prior Commands

As with many command-line tools, you can use the up arrows in psql to recall commands. The HISTSIZE variable determines the number of previous commands that you can recall. For example, `\set HISTSIZE 10` lets you recover the past 10 commands.

If you spent time building and testing a difficult query or performing a series of important updates, you may want to have the history of commands piped into separate files for perusal later:

```
\set HISTFILE ~/.psql_history - :DBNAME
```

Windows does not store the command history unless you're running a Linux/Unix virtual environment such as Cygwyn, MingW, or MSYS.

psql Gems

In this section, we cover helpful featurettes buried inside the psql documentation.

Executing Shell Commands

In psql, you can call out to the OS shell with the \! command. Let's say you're on Windows and need a directory listing. Instead of exiting psql or opening another window, you can just type **\! dir** at the psql prompt.

Watching Statements

The \watch command has been in psql since PostgreSQL 9.3. Use it to repeatedly run an SQL statement at fixed intervals so you can monitor the output. For example, suppose you want to keep tabs on queries that have yet to complete. Tag the watch command to the end of the query as shown in Example 3-3.

Example 3-3. Watching connection traffic every 10 seconds

```
SELECT datname, query
FROM pg_stat_activity
WHERE state = 'active' AND pid != pg_backend_pid();
\watch 10
```

Although \watch is primarily for monitoring query output, you can use it to execute statements at fixed intervals. In Example 3-4, we first create a table using bulk insert syntax ❶ and then log activity every five seconds after. Only the ❷ last statement that does the insert is repeated every five seconds.

Example 3-4. Log traffic every five seconds

```
SELECT * INTO log_activity
FROM pg_stat_activity; ❶
INSERT INTO log_activity
SELECT * FROM pg_stat_activity; \watch 5 ❷
```

❶ Create table and do first insert.

❷ Insert every five seconds.

To kill a watch, use CTRL-X CTRL-C.

Retrieving Details of Database Objects

Various psql *describe* commands list database objects along with details. Example 3-5 demonstrates how to list all tables and their sizes on disk in the pg_catalog schema that begins with the letters pg_t.

Example 3-5. List tables with \dt+

```
\dt+ pg_catalog.pg_t*

 Schema     | Name            | Type  | Owner    | Size   | Description
------------+-----------------+-------+----------+--------+------------
 pg_catalog | pg_tablespace   | table | postgres | 40 kB  |
 pg_catalog | pg_trigger      | table | postgres | 16 kB  |
 pg_catalog | pg_ts_config    | table | postgres | 40 kB  |
 pg_catalog | pg_ts_config_map| table | postgres | 48 kB  |
 pg_catalog | pg_ts_dict      | table | postgres | 40 kB  |
 pg_catalog | pg_ts_parser    | table | postgres | 40 kB  |
 pg_catalog | pg_ts_template  | table | postgres | 40 kB  |
 pg_catalog | pg_type         | table | postgres | 112 kB |
```

If you need further detail on a particular object, use the \d+ command as shown in Example 3-6.

Example 3-6. Describe object with \d+

```
\d+ pg_ts_dict

Table "pg_catalog.pg_ts_dict"
 Column         | Type | Modifiers | Storage  | Stats target | Description
----------------+------+-----------+----------+--------------+------------
 dictname       | name | not null  | plain    |              |
 dictnamespace  | oid  | not null  | plain    |              |
 dictowner      | oid  | not null  | plain    |              |
 dicttemplate   | oid  | not null  | plain    |              |
 dictinitoption | text |           | extended |              |
Indexes:
"pg_ts_dict_dictname_index" UNIQUE, btree (dictname, dictnamespace)
"pg_ts_dict_oid_index" UNIQUE, btree (oid)
Has OIDs: yes
```

Crosstabs

New in PostgreSQL 9.6 psql is the \crosstabview command, which greatly simplifies crosstab queries. This labor-saving command is available only in the psql enviroment. We'll illustrate with an example in Example 3-7, following it with an explanation.

Example 3-7. Crosstab view

```
SELECT student, subject, AVG(score)::numeric(5,2) As avg_score
FROM test_scores
GROUP BY student, subject
ORDER BY student, subject
\crosstabview student subject avg_score

 student | algebra | calculus | chemistry | physics | scheme
---------+---------+----------+-----------+---------+--------
 alex    |   74.00 |    73.50 |     82.00 |   81.00 |
 leo     |   82.00 |    65.50 |     75.50 |   72.00 |
 regina  |   72.50 |    64.50 |     73.50 |   84.00 |  90.00
 sonia   |   76.50 |    67.50 |     84.00 |   72.00 |
(4 rows)
```

The \crosstabview immediately follows the query you want to cross tabulate. The \crosstabview should list three columns selected by the query, with an optional fourth column to control sorting. The cross tabulation outputs a table where the first column serves as a row header, the second column as a column header, and the last as the value that goes in each cell. You can also omit the column names from the \cross tabview command, in which case the SELECT statement must request exactly three columns used in order for the cross tabulation.

In Example 3-7, student is the row header and subject is the column header. The average score column provides the entry for each pivoted cell. Should our data contain a missing student-subject pair, the corresponding cell would be null. We specified all the columns in the \crosstabview command, but we could have omitted them because they are in our SELECT in the right order.

Dynamic SQL Execution

Suppose you wanted to construct SQL statements to run based on the output of a query. In prior versions of PostgreSQL, you would build the SQL, output it to a file, then execute the file. Alternatively you could use the DO construct, which could be unwieldy in psql for long SQL statements. Starting with PostgreSQL 9.6, you can execute generated SQL in a single step with the new *\gexec* command, which iterates through each cell of your query and executes the SQL therein. Iteration is first by row then by column. It's not yet smart enough to discern whether each cell contains a legitimate SQL. gexec is also oblivious to the result of the SQL execution. Should the SQL within a particular cell throw an error, gexec merrily treads along. However, it skips over nulls. Example 3-8 creates two tables and inserts one row in each table using the *\gexec* command.

Example 3-8. Using gexec to create tables and insert data

```
SELECT
    'CREATE TABLE ' || person.name || '( a integer, b integer)' As create,
    'INSERT INTO ' || person.name || ' VALUES(1,2) ' AS insert
  FROM (VALUES ('leo'),('regina')) AS person (name) \gexec

CREATE TABLE
INSERT 0 1
CREATE TABLE
INSERT 0 1
```

In the next example we use `gexec` to obtain metadata by querying `information_schema`.

Example 3-9. Using gexec to retrieve counts of records in each table

```
SELECT
'SELECT ' || quote_literal(table_name) || ' AS table_name,
COUNT(*) As count FROM ' || quote_ident(table_name) AS cnt_q
FROM information_schema.tables
WHERE table_name IN ('leo','regina') \gexec

table_name | count
-----------+------
leo        | 1
(1 row)

table_name | count
-----------+------
 regina    | 1
(1 row)
```

Importing and Exporting Data

psql has a \copy command that lets you import data from and export data to a text file. The tab is the default delimiter, but you can specify others. Newline breaks must separate the rows. For our first example, we downloaded data from US Census Fact Finder (*http://factfinder2.census.gov*) covering racial demographics of housing in Massachusetts. You can download the file we use in this example, *DEC_10_SF1_QTH1_with_ann.csv*, from the PostgreSQL Book Data (*http://bit.ly/1tZXANx*).

psql Import

Our usual sequence in loading denormalized or unfamiliar data is to create a staging schema to accept the incoming data. We then write explorative queries to get a sense of what we have on our hands. Finally, we distribute the data into various normalized production tables and delete the staging schema.

Before bringing the data into PostgreSQL, you must first create a table to store the incoming data. The data must match the file both in the number of columns and in data types. This could be an annoying extra step for a well-formed file, but it does obviate the need for psql to guess at data types.

psql processes the entire import as a single transaction; if it encounters any errors in the data, the entire import fails. If you're unsure about the data contained in the file, we recommend setting up the table with the most accommodating data types and then recasting them later if necessary. For example, if you can't be sure that a column will have just numeric values, make it character varying to get the data in for inspection and then recast it later.

Example 3-10 loads data into the table we created in Example 3-1. Launch psql from the command line and run the commands in Example 3-10.

Example 3-10. Importing data with psql

```
\connect postgresql_book
\cd /postgresql_book/ch03
\copy staging.factfinder_import FROM DEC_10_SF1_QTH1_with_ann.csv CSV
```

In Example 3-10, we launch interactive psql, connect to our database, use \cd to change the current directory to the folder containing our file, and import our data using the \copy command. Because the default delimiter is a tab, we augment our statement with CSV to tell psql that our data is comma-separated instead.

If your file has nonstandard delimiters such as pipes, indicate the delimiter as follows:

```
\copy sometable FROM somefile.txt DELIMITER '|';
```

During import, you can replace null values with something of your own choosing by adding a NULL AS, as in the following:

```
\copy sometable FROM somefile.txt NULL As '';
```

 Don't confuse the \copy command in psql with the COPY statement provided by the SQL language. Because psql is a client utility, all paths are interpreted relative to the connected client. The SQL copy is server-based and runs under the context of the postgres service OS account. The input file for an SQL copy must reside in a path accessible by the postgres service account.

psql Export

Exporting data is even easier than importing. You can even export selected rows from a table. Use the psql \copy command to export. Example 3-11 demonstrates how to export the data we just loaded back to a tab-delimited file.

Example 3-11. Exporting data with psql

```
\connect postgresql_book
\copy (SELECT * FROM staging.factfinder_import  WHERE s01 ~ E'^[0-9]+' )
TO '/test.tab'
WITH DELIMITER E'\t' CSV HEADER
```

The default behavior of exporting data without qualifications is to export to a tab-delimited file. However, the tab-delimited format does not export header columns. You can use the HEADER option only with the comma-delimited format (see Example 3-12).

Example 3-12. Exporting data with psql

```
\connect postgresql_book
\copy staging.factfinder_import TO '/test.csv'
WITH CSV HEADER QUOTE '"' FORCE QUOTE *
```

FORCE QUOTE * double quotes all columns. For clarity, we specified the quoting character even though psql defaults to double quotes.

Copying from or to Program

Since PostgreSQL 9.3, psql can fetch data from the output of command-line programs such as *curl*, *ls*, and *wget*, and dump the data into a table. Example 3-13 imports a directory listing using a *dir* command.

Example 3-13. Import directory listing with psql

```
\connect postgresql_book
CREATE TABLE dir_list (filename text);
\copy dir_list FROM PROGRAM 'dir C:\projects /b'
```

Hubert Lubaczewski has more examples of using \copy. Visit Depesz: Piping copy to from an external program (*http://bit.ly/1BlpKLt*).

Basic Reporting

Believe it or not, psql is capable of producing basic HTML reports. Try the following and check out the generated output, shown in Figure 3-1.

```
psql -d postgresql_book -H -c "
SELECT category, COUNT(*) As num_per_cat
FROM pg_settings
WHERE category LIKE '%Query%'
GROUP BY category
ORDER BY category;
" -o test.html
```

category	num_per_cat
Query Tuning / Genetic Query Optimizer	7
Query Tuning / Other Planner Options	5
Query Tuning / Planner Cost Constants	6
Query Tuning / Planner Method Configuration	11
Statistics / Query and Index Statistics Collector	6

(5 rows)

Figure 3-1. Minimalist HTML report

Not too shabby. But the command outputs only an HTML table, not a fully qualified HTML document. To create a meatier report, compose a script, as shown in Example 3-14.

Example 3-14. Script to generate report

```
\o settings_report.html ❶
\T 'cellspacing=0 cellpadding=0' ❷
\qecho '<html><head><style>H2{color:maroon}</style>' ❸
\qecho '<title>PostgreSQL Settings</title></head><body>'
\qecho '<table><tr valign=''top''><td><h2>Planner Settings</h2>'
\x on ❹
\t on ❺
\pset format html ❻
SELECT category,
string_agg(name || '=' || setting, E'\n' ORDER BY name) As settings ❼
FROM pg_settings
WHERE category LIKE '%Planner%'
GROUP BY category
ORDER BY category;
\H
\qecho '</td><td><h2>File Locations</h2>'
\x off ❽
\t on
```

```
\pset format html
SELECT name, setting FROM pg_settings WHERE category = 'File Locations'
ORDER BY name;
\qecho '<h2>Memory Settings</h2>'
SELECT name, setting, unit FROM pg_settings WHERE category ILIKE '%memory%'
ORDER BY name;
\qecho '</td></tr></table>'
\qecho '</body></html>'
\o
```

❶ Redirects query output to a file.

❷ CSS table settings for query output.

❸ Appends additional HTML.

❹ Expand mode. Repeats the column headers for each row and outputs each column of each row as a separate row.

❺ Forces the queries to output as an HTML table.

❻ string_agg(), introduced in PostgreSQL 9.0, concatenates all properties in the same category into a single column.

❼ Turns off expand mode. The second and third queries should output one row per table row.

❽ Toggles tuples mode. When on, column headers and row counts are omitted.

Example 3-14 demonstrates that by interspersing SQL and psql commands, you can create a comprehensive tabular report replete with subreports. Run Example 3-14 by connecting interactively with psql and executing \i settings_report.psql. Alternatively, run psql noninteractively by executing psql -f settings_report.psql from your OS command line. The output generated by *settings_report.html* is shown in Figure 3-2.

Planner Settings

category	Query Tuning / Other Planner Options
settings	constraint_exclusion=partition cursor_tuple_fraction=0.1 default_statistics_target=100 from_collapse_limit=8 join_collapse_limit=8
category	Query Tuning / Planner Cost Constants
settings	cpu_index_tuple_cost=0.005 cpu_operator_cost=0.0025 cpu_tuple_cost=0.01 effective_cache_size=16384 random_page_cost=4 seq_page_cost=1
category	Query Tuning / Planner Method Configuration
settings	enable_bitmapscan=on enable_hashagg=on enable_hashjoin=on enable_indexonlyscan=on enable_indexscan=on enable_material=on

File Locations

config_file	C:/projects/pg/pg92edb/data/postgresql.conf
data_directory	C:/projects/pg/pg92edb/data
external_pid_file	
hba_file	C:/projects/pg/pg92edb/data/pg_hba.conf
ident_file	C:/projects/pg/pg92edb/data/pg_ident.conf

Memory Settings

maintenance_work_mem	16384	kB
max_prepared_transactions	0	
max_stack_depth	2048	kB
shared_buffers	4096	8kB
temp_buffers	1024	8kB
track_activity_query_size	1024	
work_mem	1024	kB

Figure 3-2. Advanced HTML report

As demonstrated, composing psql scripts lets you show output from many queries within a single report. Further, after you write a script, you can schedule its execution in the future, and at fixed intervals. Use a daemon like pgAgent, crontab, or Windows Scheduler.

## CHAPTER 4

Using pgAdmin

pgAdmin4 version 1.6 is the current rendition of the tried-and-true graphical administration tool for PostgreSQL. It is a complete rewrite of the predecessor pgAdmin3. Some features of pgAdmin3 have not been ported to pgAdmin4, though they may be in the future. In this chapter we'll focus on what's available in pgAdmin4. Much of the functionality you will find in pgAdmin4 was present in pgAdmin3, so this discussion will be valuable even if you are still using pgAdmin3. We will also cover some popular features of pgAdmin3 not yet ported to pgAdmin4. For the rest of this chapter, we'll simply refer to both as pgAdmin, and only make distinguishing version notes where the functionality is different.

Most of the key changes thus far with pgAdmin4 compared to pgAdmin3 is that pgAdmin4 better supports the new 9.6 and 10 constructs including the ability to run in a server or desktop mode; an improved query results pane with ability to edit records and also select noncontiguous rows; and improved performance. If you are using Windows, make sure to use pgAdmin4 1.6 or above. Prior pgAdmin4 versions had performance issues on Windows when running in desktop mode.

Although pgAdmin has shortcomings, we are always encouraged by not only how quickly bugs are fixed, but also how quickly new features are added. Because the PostgreSQL developers position pgAdmin as the most commonly used graphical-administration tool for PostgreSQL and it is packaged with many binary distributions of PostgreSQL, the developers have taken on the responsibility of keeping pgAdmin always in sync with the latest PostgreSQL releases. If a new release of PostgreSQL introduces new features, you can count on the latest pgAdmin to let you manage it. If you're new to PostgreSQL, you should definitely start with pgAdmin before exploring other tools.

Getting Started

pgAdmin4 comes packaged with many distributions. The BigSQL and EDB distributions from PostgreSQL 9.6 on include pgAdmin4 as an option. Note if you have a need for pgAdmin3 for PostgreSQL 9.6+, you'll want to use the BigSQL pgAdmin3 LTS (*https://www.bigsql.org/pgadmin3/*), which has been patched to handle versions 9.6 and 10. pgAdmin3 LTS is installable via the BigSQL package manager. After version 9.5, the EDB package only includes pgAdmin4. The pgAdmin group will no longer be making updates or enhancements to pgAdmin3.

If you are installing pgAdmin without PostgreSQL, you can download pgAdmin from pgadmin.org. While on the site, you can opt to peruse one of the guides introducing pgAdmin. The tool is well-organized and, for the most part, guides itself quite well. Adventurous users can always try beta and alpha releases of pgAdmin. Your help in testing would be greatly appreciated by the PostgreSQL community.

Overview of Features

To whet your appetite, here's a list of our favorite goodies in pgAdmin. More are listed in pgAdmin Features (*http://pgadmin.org/features.php*):

Server and Desktop mode
> pgAdmin4 can be installed in desktop mode or as a web server WSGI application. pgAdmin3 was a desktop-only application.

Graphical explain for your queries
> This awesome feature offers pictorial insight into what the query planner is thinking. While verbose text-based planner output still has its place, a graphical explain provides a more digestible bird's-eye view.

SQL pane
> pgAdmin ultimately interacts with PostgreSQL via SQL, and it's not shy about letting you see the generated SQL. When you use the graphical interface to make changes to your database, pgAdmin automatically displays, in an SQL pane, the underlying SQL that will perform the tasks. For novices, studying the generated SQL is a superb learning opportunity. For pros, taking advantage of the generated SQL is a great timesaver.

GUI editor for configuration files such as postgresql.conf and pg_hba.conf
> You no longer need to dig around for the files and use another editor. This is currently only present in pgAdmin3, and to use it, you also need to install the `pgad min` extension in the database called `postgres`.

Data export and import

pgAdmin can easily export query results as a CSV file or other delimited format and import such files as well. pgAdmin3 can even export results as HTML, providing you with a turnkey reporting engine, albeit a bit crude.

Backup and restore wizard

Can't remember the myriad commands and switches to perform a backup or restore using *pg_restore* and *pg_dump*? pgAdmin has a nice interface that lets you selectively back up and restore databases, schemas, single tables, and globals. You can view and copy the underlying *pg_dump* or *pg_restore* command that pgAdmin used in the Message tab.

Grant wizard

This timesaver allows you to change privileges on many database objects in one fell swoop.

pgScript engine

This is a quick-and-dirty way to run scripts that don't have to complete as transactions. With this you can execute loops that commit on each iteration, unlike functions that require all steps to be completed before the work is committed. Unfortunately, you cannot use this engine outside of pgAdmin and it is currently only available in pgAdmin3 (not 4).

SQL Editor Autocomplete feature

To trigger the autocomplete popup use CTRL-Space. The autocomplete feature is improved in pgAdmin4.

pgAgent

We'll devote an entire section to this cross-platform job scheduling agent. pgAdmin provides a cool interface to it.

Connecting to a PostgreSQL Server

Connecting to a PostgreSQL server with pgAdmin is straightforward. The General and Connection tabs are shown in Figure 4-1.

Figure 4-1. pgAdmin4 register server connection dialog

Navigating pgAdmin

The tree layout of pgAdmin is intuitive to follow but does engender some possible anxiety, because it starts off by showing you every esoteric object found in the database. You can pare down the tree display by going into the Browser section of Preferences and deselecting objects that you would rather not have to stare at every time you use pgAdmin. To declutter the browse tree sections, go to Files→Preferences→Browser→Nodes. You will see the screen shown in Figure 4-2.

Figure 4-2. Hide or unhide database objects in the pgAdmin4 browse tree

If you select Show System Objects in the Display section, you'll see the guts of your server: internal functions, system tables, hidden columns in tables, and so forth. You will also see the metadata stored in the PostgreSQL system catalogs: `informa tion_schema` catalog and the `pg_catalog`. `information_schema` is an ANSI SQL standard catalog found in other databases such as MySQL and SQL Server. You may recognize some of the tables and columns from working with other database products.

pgAdmin Features

pgAdmin is chock full of goodies. We don't have the space to bring them all to light, so we'll just highlight the features that many use on a regular basis.

Autogenerating Queries from Table Definitions

pgAdmin has this menu option that will autogenerate a template for SELECT, INSERT, and UPDATE statements from a table definition. You access this feature by right-clicking the table and accessing the SCRIPTS context menu option as shown in Figure 4-3.

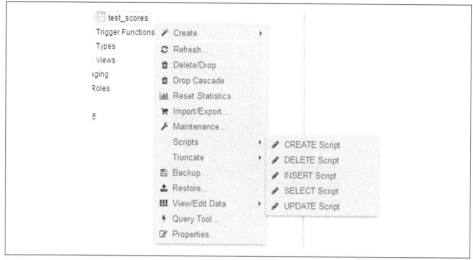

Figure 4-3. Table Scripts menu

The "SELECT Script" option is particularly handy because it will create a query that lists all the columns in the table. If you have a lot of columns in a table and want to select a large subset but not all columns, this is a great timesaver. You can remove columns you don't need in your query from the autogenerated statement.

Accessing psql from pgAdmin3

Although pgAdmin is a great tool, psql does a better job in a few cases. One of them is the execution of very large SQL files, such as those created by *pg_dump* and other dump tools. You can easily jump to psql from pgAdmin3, but this feature is not available in pgAdmin4. Click the plugin menu, as shown in Figure 4-4, and then click PSQL Console. This opens a psql session connected to the database you are currently connected to in pgAdmin. You can then use the \cd and \i commands to change directory and run the SQL file.

PSQL Console

Figure 4-4. psql plugin

Because this feature relies on a database connection, you'll see it disabled until you're connected to a database.

Editing postgresql.conf and pg_hba.conf from pgAdmin3

You can edit configuration files directly from pgAdmin, provided that you installed the adminpack extension on your server. PostgreSQL one-click installers generally create the adminpack extension. If it's present, you should see the Server Configuration menu enabled, as shown in Figure 4-5.

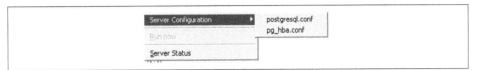

Figure 4-5. PgAdmin3 configuration file editor

If the menu is grayed out and you are connected to a PostgreSQL server, either you don't have the adminpack installed on that server or you are not logged in as a superuser. To install the adminpack run the SQL statement `CREATE EXTENSION adminpack;` or use the graphical interface for installing extensions, as shown in Figure 4-6. Disconnect from the server and reconnect; you should see the menu enabled.

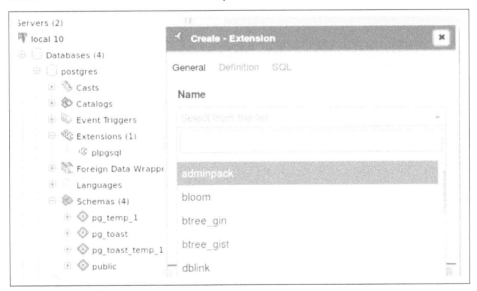

Figure 4-6. Installing extensions using pgAdmin4

Creating Database Assets and Setting Privileges

pgAdmin lets you create all kinds of database assets and assign privileges.

Creating databases and other database assets

Creating a new database in pgAdmin is easy. Just right-click the database section of the tree and choose New Database, as shown in Figure 4-7. The Definition tab provides a drop-down menu for you to select a template database, similar to what we did in "Template Databases" on page 38.

Figure 4-7. Creating a new database in pgAdmin4

Follow the same steps to create roles, schemas, and other objects. Each will have its own relevant set of tabs for you to specify additional attributes.

Privilege management

To manage the privileges of database assets, nothing beats the pgAdmin Grant Wizard, which you access from the Tools→Grant Wizard menu of pgAdmin. If you are interested in granting permissions only for objects in a specific schema, right-click the schema and choose "Grant Wizard." The list will be filtered to just objects in the schema. As with many other features, this option is grayed out unless you are connected to a database. It's also sensitive to the location in the tree you are on. For example, to set privileges for items in the census schema, select the schema and then choose Grant Wizard. The Grant Wizard screen is shown in Figure 4-8. You can then select all or some of the items and switch to the Privileges tab to set the roles and privileges you want to grant.

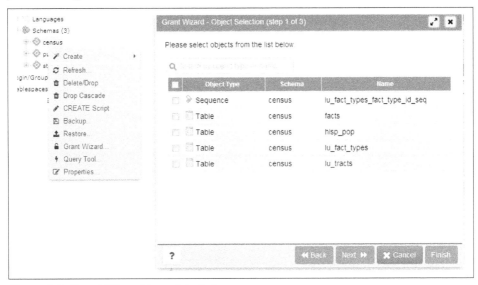

Figure 4-8. Grant Wizard in pgAdmin4

More often than setting privileges on existing objects, you may want to set default privileges for new objects in a schema or database. To do so, right-click the schema or database, select Properties, and then go to the Default Privileges tab, as shown in Figure 4-9.

Figure 4-9. Granting default privileges in pgAdmin4

When setting privileges for a schema, make sure to also set the usage privilege on the schema to the groups you will be giving access to.

Import and Export

Like psql, pgAdmin allows you to import and export text files.

Importing files

The import/export feature is really a wrapper around the psql \copy command and requires the table that will receive the data to exist already. In order to import data, right-click the table you want to import/export data to. Figure 4-10 shows the menu that comes up after we right-click the lu_fact_types table on the left.

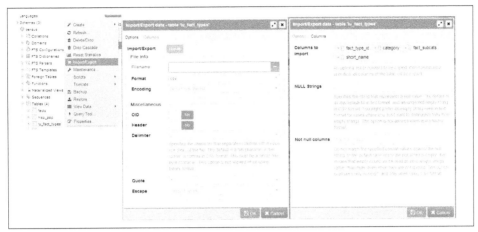

Figure 4-10. Import menu in pgAdmin4

Exporting queries as a structured file or report in pgAdmin

In addition to importing data, you can export your queries as well. pgAdmin3 allows exporting to delimited CSV, HTML, or XML formats. The pgAdmin4 export feature is much simpler and basic than pgAdmin3.

In pgAdmin to export with delimiters, perform the following:

1. Open the query window (Query Tool).
2. Write the query.
3. Run the query.
4. In pgAdmin3, you'd choose File→Export. In pgAdmin4, you click the download icon ( ) and browse to where you want to save.
5. For pgAdmin3, you get additional prompts before being given a save option. Fill out the settings as shown in Figure 4-11.

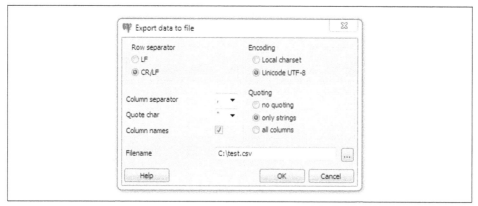

Figure 4-11. Export menu

Exporting as HTML or XML is much the same, except you use the File→Quick Report option (see Figure 4-12).

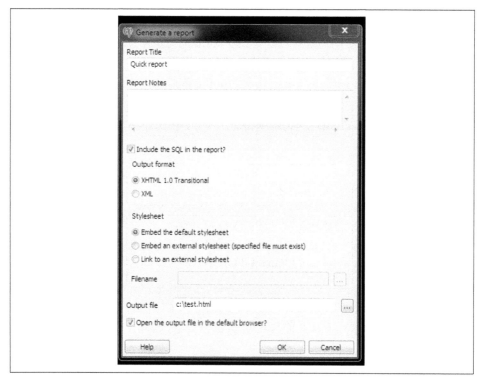

Figure 4-12. Export report options

Backup and Restore

pgAdmin offers a graphical interface to `pg_dump` and `pg_restore`, covered in "Backup and Restore" on page 50. In this section, we'll repeat some of the same examples using pgAdmin instead of the command line.

If several versions of PostgreSQL or pgAdmin are installed on your computer, it's a good idea to make sure that the pgAdmin version is using the versions of the utilities that you expect. Check what the *bin* setting in pgAdmin is pointing to in order to ensure it's the latest available, as shown in Figure 4-13.

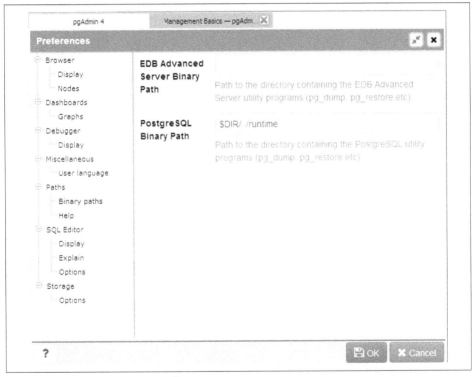

Figure 4-13. pgAdmin File→Preferences

 If your server is remote or your databases are huge, we recommend using the command-line tools for backup and restore instead of pgAdmin to avoid adding another layer of complexity to what could already be a pretty lengthy process. Also keep in mind that if you do a compressed/TAR/directory backup with a newer version of `pg_dump`, you need to use the same or later version of `pg_restore`.

Backing up an entire database

In "Selective Backup Using pg_dump" on page 51, we demonstrated how to back up a database. To repeat the same steps using the pgAdmin interface, right-click the database you want to back up and choose Custom for Format, as shown in Figure 4-14.

Figure 4-14. Backup database

Backing up systemwide objects

pgAdmin provides a graphical interface to `pg_dumpall` for backing up system objects. To use the interface, first connect to the server you want to back up. Then, from the top menu, choose Tools→Backup Globals.

pgAdmin doesn't give you control over which global objects to back up, as the command-line interface does. pgAdmin backs up all tablespaces and roles.

If you ever want to back up the entire server, invoke `pg_dumpall` by going to the top menu and choosing Tools→Backup Server.

Selective backup of database assets

pgAdmin provides a graphical interface to `pg_dump` for selective backup. Right-click the asset you want to back up and select Backup (see Figure 4-15). You can back up an entire database, a particular schema, a table, or anything else.

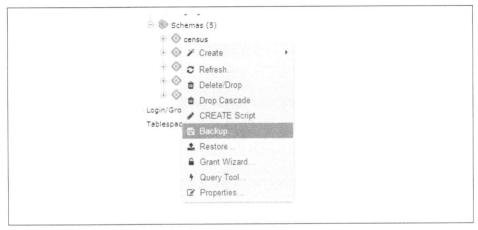

Figure 4-15. pgAdmin schema backup

To back up the selected asset, you can forgo the other tabs (see Figure 4-14). In pgAdmin3, you can selectively drill down to more items by clicking the Objects tab, as shown in Figure 4-16. This feature is not yet present in pgAdmin4.

Figure 4-16. pgAdmin3 selective backup Objects tab

Behind the scenes, pgAdmin simply runs pg_dump to perform backups. If you ever want to know the actual commands pgAdmin is using, say for scripting, look at the Messages tab after you click the Backup button. You'll see the exact call with arguments to pg_dump.

pgScript

pgScript is a built-in scripting tool in pgAdmin3 but is not present in pgAdmin4. It's most useful for running repetitive SQL tasks. pgScript can make better use of memory, and thus be more efficient, than equivalent PostgreSQL functions. This is because stored functions maintain all their work in memory and commit all the results of a function in a single batch. In contrast, pgScript commits each SQL insert or update statement as it runs through the script. This makes pgScript particularly handy for memory-hungry processes that you don't need completed as single transactions. After each transaction commits, memory becomes available for the next one. You can see an example where we use pgScript for batch geocoding at Using pgScript for Geocoding (*http://bit.ly/126mRPB*).

The pgScript language is lazily typed and supports conditionals, loops, data generators, basic print statements, and record variables. The general syntax is similar to that of Transact SQL, the stored procedure language of Microsoft SQL Server. Variables, prepended with @, can hold scalars or arrays, including the results of SQL commands. Commands such as DECLARE and SET, and control constructs such as IF-ELSE and WHILE loops, are part of the pgScript language.

Launch pgScript by opening a regular SQL query window. After typing in your script, execute it by clicking the pgScript icon (🐢).

We'll now show you some examples of pgScripts. Example 4-1 demonstrates how to use pgScript record variables and loops to build a crosstab table, using the lu_fact_types table we create in Example 7-22. The pgScript creates an empty table called census.hisp_pop with numeric columns: hispanic_or_latino, white_alone, black_or_african_american_alone, and so on.

Example 4-1. Create a table using record variables in pgScript

```
DECLARE @I, @labels, @tdef;
SET @I = 0;

Labels will hold records.
SET @labels =
    SELECT
        quote_ident(
            replace(
                replace(lower(COALESCE(fact_subcats[4], fact_subcats[3])), ' ', '_')
```

```
,':',''
            )
        ) As col_name,
    fact_type_id
    FROM census.lu_fact_types
    WHERE category = 'Population' AND fact_subcats[3] ILIKE 'Hispanic or Latino%'
    ORDER BY short_name;

SET @tdef = 'census.hisp_pop(tract_id varchar(11) PRIMARY KEY ';

Loop through records using LINES function.
WHILE @I < LINES(@labels)
BEGIN
    SET @tdef = @tdef + ', ' + @labels[@I][0] + ' numeric(12,3) ';
    SET @I = @I + 1;
END

SET @tdef = @tdef + ')';

Print out table def.
PRINT @tdef;

create the table.
CREATE TABLE @tdef;
```

Although pgScript does not have an execute command that allows you to run dynamically generated SQL, we accomplished the same thing in Example 4-1 by assigning an SQL string to a variable. Example 4-2 pushes the envelope a bit further by populating the census.hisp_pop table we just created.

Example 4-2. Populating tables with pgScript loop

```
DECLARE @I, @labels, @tload, @tcols, @fact_types;
SET @I = 0;
SET @labels =
    SELECT
        quote_ident(
            replace(
                replace(
                    lower(COALESCE(fact_subcats[4], fact_subcats[3])), ' ', '_'),':'
,''
            )
        ) As col_name,
    fact_type_id
    FROM census.lu_fact_types
    WHERE category = 'Population' AND fact_subcats[3] ILIKE 'Hispanic or Latino%'
    ORDER BY short_name;

SET @tload = 'tract_id';
SET @tcols = 'tract_id';
SET @fact_types = '-1';
```

```
WHILE @I < LINES(@labels)
BEGIN
    SET @tcols = @tcols + ', ' + @labels[@I][0] ;
    SET @tload = @tload +
        ', MAX(CASE WHEN fact_type_id = ' +
        CAST(@labels[@I][1] AS STRING) +
        ' THEN val ELSE NULL END)';
    SET @fact_types = @fact_types + ', ' + CAST(@labels[@I][1] As STRING);
    SET @I = @I + 1;
END

INSERT INTO census.hisp_pop(@tcols)
SELECT @tload FROM census.facts
WHERE fact_type_id IN(@fact_types) AND yr=2010
GROUP BY tract_id;
```

The lesson to take away from Example 4-2 is that you can dynamically append SQL fragments into a variable.

Graphical Explain

One of the great gems in pgAdmin is its at-a-glance graphical explain of the query plan. You can access the graphical explain plan by opening up an SQL query window, writing a query, and clicking the explain icon (▨).

Suppose we run the query:

```
SELECT left(tract_id, 5) As county_code, SUM(hispanic_or_latino) As tot,
    SUM(white_alone) As tot_white,
    SUM(COALESCE(hispanic_or_latino,0) - COALESCE(white_alone,0)) AS non_white
FROM census.hisp_pop
GROUP BY county_code
ORDER BY county_code;
```

We will get the graphical explain shown in Figure 4-17. Here's a quick tip for interpreting the graphical explain: trim the fat! The fatter the arrow, the longer a step takes to complete.

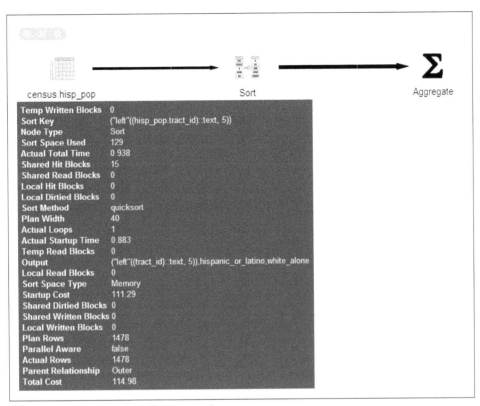

Temp Written Blocks	0
Sort Key	("left"((hisp_pop.tract_id)::text, 5))
Node Type	Sort
Sort Space Used	129
Actual Total Time	0.938
Shared Hit Blocks	15
Shared Read Blocks	0
Local Hit Blocks	0
Local Dirtied Blocks	0
Sort Method	quicksort
Plan Width	40
Actual Loops	1
Actual Startup Time	0.883
Temp Read Blocks	0
Output	("left"((tract_id)::text, 5)),hispanic_or_latino,white_alone
Local Read Blocks	0
Sort Space Type	Memory
Startup Cost	111.29
Shared Dirtied Blocks	0
Shared Written Blocks	0
Local Written Blocks	0
Plan Rows	1478
Parallel Aware	false
Actual Rows	1478
Parent Relationship	Outer
Total Cost	114.98

Figure 4-17. Graphical explain example

Graphical explain is disabled if Query→Explain→Buffers is enabled. So make sure to uncheck buffers before trying a graphical explain. In addition to the graphical explain, the Data Output tab shows the textual explain plan, which for this example looks like:

```
GroupAggregate  (cost=111.29..151.93 rows=1478 width=20)
  Output: ("left"((tract_id)::text, 5)), sum(hispanic_or_latino),
sum(white_alone), ...
    -> Sort  (cost=111.29..114.98 rows=1478 width=20)
      Output: tract_id, hispanic_or_latino, white_alone,
      ("left"((tract_id)::text, 5))
        Sort Key: ("left"((tract_id)::text, 5))
          -> Seq Scan on census.hisp_pop  (cost=0.00..33.48 rows=1478 width=20)
                Output: tract_id, hispanic_or_latino
                  , white_alone, "left"((tract_id)::text, 5)
```

Job Scheduling with pgAgent

pgAgent is a handy utility for scheduling PostgreSQL jobs. But it can also execute batch scripts on the OS, replacing `crontab` on Linux/Unix and the Task Scheduler on Windows. pgAgent goes even further: you can schedule jobs to run on any other host regardless of OS. All you have to do is install the pgAgent service on the host and point it to use a specific PostgreSQL database with pgAgent tables and functions installed. The PostgreSQL server itself is not required, but the client connection libraries are. Because pgAgent is built atop PostgreSQL, you are blessed with the added advantage of having access to all the tables controlling the agent. If you ever need to replicate a complicated job multiple times, you can go straight into the database tables directly and insert the records for new jobs, skipping the pgAdmin interface.

We'll get you started with pgAgent in this section. Visit Setting Up pgAgent and Doing Scheduled Backups (*http://bit.ly/1AvqVVs*) to see more working examples and details on how to set it up.

Installing pgAgent

You can download pgAgent from pgAgent Download (*http://www.pgadmin.org/down load/pgagent.php*). It is also available via the EDB Application Stackbuilder and BigSQL package. The packaged extension script creates a new schema named pgAgent in the `postgres` database. When you connect to your server via pgAdmin, you will see a new section called Jobs, as shown in Figure 4-18.

Figure 4-18. pgAdmin4 with pgAgent installed

Although pgAgent is installed by default in postgres db, you can install in a different database using `CREATE EXTENSION pgagent;`. If you decide to install in a different database, make sure to set your pgagent service to use that database and in pgAdmin set the maintenance db in the server connection tab to be this database.

If you want pgAgent to run batch jobs on additional servers, follow the same steps, except that you don't have to reinstall the SQL script packaged with pgAgent. Pay particular attention to the OS permission settings of the pgAgent service/daemon account. Make sure each agent has sufficient privileges to execute the batch jobs that you will be scheduling.

 Batch jobs often fail in pgAgent even when they might run fine from the command line. This is often due to permission issues. pgAgent always runs under the same account as the pgAgent service/daemon. If this account doesn't have sufficient privileges or the necessary network path mappings, jobs fail.

Scheduling Jobs

Each scheduled job has two parts: the execution steps and the schedule. When creating a new job, start by adding one or more job steps. Figure 4-19 shows what the step add/edit screen looks like.

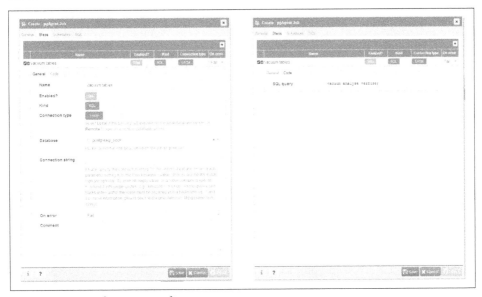

Figure 4-19. pgAdmin4 step edit screen

For each step, you can enter an SQL statement to run, point to a shell script on the OS, or even cut and paste in a full shell script as we commonly do.

If you choose SQL, the connection type option becomes enabled and defaults to local. With a local connection, the job step runs on the same server as the pgAgent and uses the same authentication username and password. You need to additionally specify the database that pgAgent should connect to in order to run the jobs. The screen offers you a drop-down list of databases to choose from. If you choose a remote connection type, the text box for entering a connection string becomes enabled. Type in the full connection string, including credentials and the database. When you connect to a remote PostgreSQL server with an earlier version of PostgreSQL, make sure that all the SQL constructs you use are supported on that version.

If you choose to run batch jobs, the syntax must be specific to the OS running the job. For example, if your pgAgent is running on Windows, your batch jobs should have valid DOS commands. If you are on Linux, your batch jobs should have valid shell or Bash commands.

Steps run in alphabetical order, and you can decide what kinds of actions you want to take upon success or failure of each step. You have the option of disabling steps that should remain dormant but that you don't want to delete because you might reactivate them later.

Once you have the steps ready, go ahead and set up a schedule to run them. You can set up intricate schedules with the scheduling screen. You can even set up multiple schedules.

If you installed pgAgent on multiple servers and have them all pointing to the same pgAgent database, all these agents by default will execute all jobs.

If you want to run the job on just one specific machine, fill in the host agent field when creating the job. Agents running on other servers will skip the job if it doesn't match their hostname.

 pgAgent consists of two parts: the data defining the jobs and the logging of the job. Log information resides in the pgAgent schema, usually in the postgres database; the job agents query the jobs for the next job to run and then insert relevant logging information in the database. Generally, both the PostgreSQL server holding the data and the job agent executing the jobs reside on the same server, but they are not required to. Additionally, a single PostgreSQL server can service many job agents residing on different servers.

A fully formed job is shown in Figure 4-20.

Figure 4-20. pgAgent jobs in pgAdmin

Helpful pgAgent Queries

With your finely honed SQL skills, you can easily replicate jobs, delete jobs, and edit jobs directly by messing with pgAgent metatables. Just be careful! For example, to get a glimpse inside the tables controlling all of your agents and jobs, connect to the `post gres` database and execute the query in Example 4-3.

Example 4-3. Description of pgAgent tables

```
SELECT c.relname As table_name, d.description
FROM
    pg_class As c INNER JOIN
    pg_namespace n ON n.oid = c.relnamespace INNER JOIN
    pg_description As d ON d.objoid = c.oid AND d.objsubid = 0
WHERE n.nspname = 'pgagent'
ORDER BY c.relname;

table_name     |       description
---------------+-------------------------
pga_job        | Job main entry
pga_jobagent   | Active job agents
pga_jobclass   | Job classification
pga_joblog     | Job run logs.
pga_jobstep    | Job step to be executed
pga_jobsteplog | Job step run logs.
pga_schedule   | Job schedule exceptions
```

Although pgAdmin already provides an intuitive interface to pgAgent scheduling and logging, you may find the need to generate your own job reports. This is especially true if you have many jobs or you want to compile stats from your job results. Example 4-4 demonstrates the one query we use often.

Example 4-4. List log step results from today

```
SELECT j.jobname, s.jstname, l.jslstart,l.jslduration, l.jsloutput
FROM
    pgagent.pga_jobsteplog As l INNER JOIN
    pgagent.pga_jobstep As s ON s.jstid = l.jsljstid INNER JOIN
    pgagent.pga_job As j ON j.jobid = s.jstjobid
WHERE jslstart > CURRENT_DATE
ORDER BY j.jobname, s.jstname, l.jslstart DESC;
```

We find this query essential for monitoring batch jobs because sometimes a job will report success even though it failed. pgAgent can't always discern the success or failure of a shell script on the OS. The `jsloutput` field in the logs provides the shell output, which usually details what went wrong.

In some versions of pgAgent running on Windows, shell scripts often default to failed even when they succeeded. If this happens, you should set the step status to `ignore`. This is a known bug that we hope will be fixed in a future release.

## CHAPTER 5

Data Types

PostgreSQL supports the workhorse data types of any database: numerics, strings, dates, times, and booleans. But PostgreSQL sprints ahead by adding support for arrays, time zone–aware datetimes, time intervals, ranges, JSON, XML, and many more. If that's not enough, you can invent custom types. In this chapter, we don't intend to cover every data type. For that, there's always the manual. We showcase data types that are unique to PostgreSQL and nuances in how PostgreSQL handles common data types.

No data type would be useful without a cast of supporting functions and operators. And PostgreSQL has plenty of them. We'll cover the more popular ones in this chapter.

 When we use the term *function*, we're talking about something that's of the form f(x). When we use the term operator, we're talking about something that's symbolic and either unary (having one argument) or binary (having two arguments) such as +, -, *, or /. When using operators, keep in mind that the same symbol can take on a different meaning when applied to different data types. For example, the plus sign means adding for numerics but unioning for ranges.

Numerics

You will find your everyday integers, decimals, and floating-point numbers in PostgreSQL. Of the numeric types, we want to discuss serial data types and a nifty function to quickly generate arithmetic series of integers.

Serials

Serial and its bigger sibling, bigserial, are auto-incrementing integers often used as primary keys of tables in which a natural key is not apparent. This data type goes by different names in different database products, with *autonumber* being the most common alternative moniker. When you create a table and specify a column as serial, PostgreSQL first creates an integer column and then creates a sequence object named `table_name_column_name_seq` located in the same schema as the table. It then sets the default of the new integer column to read its value from the sequence. If you drop the column, PostgreSQL also drops the companion sequence object.

In PostgreSQL, the sequence type is a database asset in its own right. You can inspect and edit the sequences using SQL with the `ALTER SEQUENCE` command or using PGAdmin. You can set the current value, boundary values (both the upper and lower bounds), and even how many numbers to increment each time. Though decrementing is rare, you can do it by setting the increment value to a negative number. Because sequences are independent database assets, you can create them separately from a table using the `CREATE SEQUENCE` (*http://bit.ly/1w5Hvgn*) command, and you can use the same sequence across multiple tables. The cross-table sharing of the same sequence comes in handy when you're assigning a universal key in your database.

To use an extant sequence for subsequent tables, create a new column in the table as integer or bigint—not as serial—then set the default value of the column using the `nextval(sequence_name)` (*http://bit.ly/1yx5TXd*) function as shown in Example 5-1.

Example 5-1. Using existing sequence for new tables

```
CREATE SEQUENCE s START 1;
CREATE TABLE stuff(id bigint DEFAULT nextval('s') PRIMARY KEY, name text);
```

 If you rename a table that has a serial based on a sequence, PostgreSQL will not automatically rename the sequence object. To avoid confusion, you should rename the sequence object.

Generate Series Function

PostgreSQL has a nifty function called `generate_series` (*http://bit.ly/1yUbohy*) not found in other database products. The function comes in two forms. One is a numeric version that creates a sequence of integers incremented by some value and one that creates a sequence of dates or timestamps incremented by some time interval. What makes `generate_series` so convenient is that it allows you to effectively mimic a for loop in SQL. Example 5-2 demonstrates the numeric version. Example 5-13 demonstrates the temporal version.

Example 5-2 uses integers with an optional step parameter.

Example 5-2. generate_series() with stepping of 13

```
SELECT x FROM generate_series(1,51,13) As x;
x
----
1
14
27
40
```

The default step is 1. As demonstrated in Example 5-2, you can pass in an optional step argument to specify how many steps to skip for each successive element. The end value will never exceed our prescribed range, so although our range ends at 51, our last number is 40 because adding another 13 to our 40 busts the upper bound.

Textuals

There are three primitive textual types in PostgreSQL: character (abbreviable as char), character varying (abbreviable as varchar), and text.

Use char only when the values stored are fixed length, such as postal codes, phone numbers, and Social Security numbers in the US. If your value is under the length specified, PostgreSQL automatically adds spaces to the end. When compared with varchar or text, the right-padding takes up more superfluous storage, but you get the assurance of an invariable length. There is absolutely no speed performance benefit of using char over varchar or text and char will always take up more disk space. Use character varying to store strings with varying length. When defining varchar columns, you should specify the maximum length of a varchar. Text is the most generic of the textual data types. With text, you cannot specify a maximum length.

The max length modifier for varchar is optional. Without it, varchar behaves almost identically to text. Subtle differences do surface when connecting to PostgreSQL via drivers. For instance, the ODBC driver cannot sort text columns. Both varchar and text have a maximum storage of 1G for each value—that's a lot! Behind the scenes, any value larger than what can fit in a record page gets pushed to TOAST (*http://bit.ly/12sdEAM*).

Some folks advocate abandoning varchar and always using text. Rather than waste space arguing about it here, read the debate at In Defense of Varchar(X) (*http://bit.ly/1vwE68w*).

Often, for cross-system compatibility, you want to remove case sensitivity from your character types. To do this, you need to override comparison operators that take case into consideration. Overriding operators is easier for varchar than it is for text. We demonstrate an example in Using MS Access with PostgreSQL (*http://bit.ly/ 1w5HIQF*), where we show how to make varchar behave without case sensitivity and still be able to use an index.

String Functions

Common string manipulations are padding (`lpad`, `rpad`), trimming whitespace (`rtrim`, `ltrim`, `trim`, `btrim`), extracting substrings (`substring`), and concatenating (`||`). Example 5-3 demonstrates padding, and Example 5-4 demonstrates trimming.

Example 5-3. Using lpad and rpad

```
SELECT
    lpad('ab', 4, '0') As ab_lpad,
    rpad('ab', 4, '0') As ab_rpad,
    lpad('abcde', 4, '0') As ab_lpad_trunc; ❶

ab_lpad | ab_rpad | ab_lpad_trunc
--------+---------+--------------
00ab    | ab00    | abcd
```

❶ lpad truncates instead of padding if the string is too long.

By default, trim functions remove spaces, but you can pass in an optional argument indicating other characters to trim.

Example 5-4. Trimming spaces and characters

```
SELECT
    a As a_before, trim(a) As a_trim, rtrim(a) As a_rt,
    i As i_before, ltrim(i, '0') As i_lt_0,
    rtrim(i, '0') As i_rt_0, trim(i, '0') As i_t_0
FROM (
        SELECT repeat(' ', 4) || i || repeat(' ', 4) As a, '0' || i As i
        FROM generate_series(0, 200, 50) As i
) As x;

a_before | a_trim | a_rt | i_before | i_lt_0 | i_rt_0 | i_t_0
---------+--------+------+----------+--------+--------+------
0        | 0      | 0    | 00       |        |        |
50       | 50     | 50   | 050      | 50     | 05     | 5
100      | 100    | 100  | 0100     | 100    | 01     | 1
150      | 150    | 150  | 0150     | 150    | 015    | 15
200      | 200    | 200  | 0200     | 200    | 02     | 2
```

A helpful function for aggregating strings is the string_agg function, which we demonstrate in Examples 3-14 and 5-26.

Splitting Strings into Arrays, Tables, or Substrings

There are a couple of useful functions in PostgreSQL for tearing strings apart.

The `split_part` function is useful for extracting an element from a delimited string, as shown in Example 5-5. Here, we select the second item in a string of items delimited by periods.

Example 5-5. Getting the nth element of a delimited string

```
SELECT split_part('abc.123.z45','.',2) As x;

x
---
123
```

The `string_to_array` function is useful for creating an array of elements from a delimited string. By combining `string_to_array` with the `unnest` function, you can expand the returned array into a set of rows, as shown in Example 5-6.

Example 5-6. Converting a delimited string to an array to rows

```
SELECT unnest(string_to_array('abc.123.z45', '.')) As x;

x
---
abc
123
z45
```

Regular Expressions and Pattern Matching

PostgreSQL's regular expression support is downright fantastic. You can return matches as tables or arrays and choreograph replaces and updates. Back-referencing and other fairly advanced search patterns are also supported. In this section, we'll provide a small sampling. For more information, see Pattern Matching (*http://bit.ly/1s2nQXB*) and String Functions (*http://bit.ly/1Iaix2K*).

Example 5-7 shows you how to format phone numbers stored simply as contiguous digits.

Example 5-7. Reformat a phone number using back-referencing

```
SELECT regexp_replace(
'6197306254',
'([0-9]{3})([0-9]{3})([0-9]{4})',
 E'\(\\1\) \\2-\\3'
 ) As x;
```

```
x
--------------
(619) 730-6254
```

The \\1, \\2, etc., refer to elements in our pattern expression. We use a backslash (\) to escape the parentheses. The E' construct is PostgreSQL syntax for denoting that the string to follow should be taken literally.

Suppose some field contains text with embedded phone numbers; Example 5-8 shows how to extract the phone numbers and turn them into rows all in one step.

Example 5-8. Return phone numbers in piece of text as separate rows

```
SELECT unnest(regexp_matches(
'Cell (619) 852-5083. Work (619)123-4567 , Casa 619-730-6254. Bésame mucho.',
E'[(]{0,1}[0-9]{3}[)-.]{0,1}[\\s]{0,1}[0-9]{3}[-.]{0,1}[0-9]{4}', 'g')
) As x;

x
--------------
(619) 852-5083
(619)123-4567
619-730-6254
(3 rows)
```

The matching rules for Example 5-8 are:

- [(]{0,1}: starts with zero or one open parenthesis.
- [0-9]{3}: followed by three digits.
-)-.]{0,1}: followed by zero or one closed parenthesis, hyphen, or period.
- [\\s]+: followed by zero or more spaces.
- [0-9]{4}: followed by four digits.
- regexp_matches returns a string array consisting of matches of a regular expression. The last input to our function is the flags parameter. We set this to g, which stands for *global* and returns all matches of a regular expression as separate elements. If you leave out this flags parameter, then your array will only contain the first match. The flags parameter can consist of more than one flag. For example, if you have letters in your regular expression and text and you want to make the check case insensitive and global, you would use two flags, gi. In addition to the global flag, other allowed flags are listed in POSIX EMBEDDED OPTIONS (*http://bit.ly/2kDHYao*).
- unnest explodes an array into a row set.

There are many ways to compose the same regular expression. For instance, \\d is shorthand for [0-9]. But given the few characters you'd save, we prefer the more descriptive longhand.

If you only care about the first match, you can utilize the substring function, which will return the first matching value as shown in Example 5-9.

Example 5-9. Return first phone number in piece of text

```
SELECT substring(
'Cell (619) 852-5083. Work (619)123-4567 , Casa 619-730-6254. Bésame mucho.'
from E'[(]{0,1}[0-9]{3}[)-.]{0,1}[\\s]{0,1}[0-9]{3}[-.]{0,1}[0-9]{4}')
 As x;

       x
----------------
 (619) 852-5083
(1 row)
```

In addition to the wealth of regular expression functions, you can use regular expressions with the SIMILAR TO (~) operators. The following example returns all description fields with embedded phone numbers:

```
SELECT description
FROM mytable
WHERE description ~
E'[(]{0,1}[0-9]{3}[)-.]{0,1}[\\s]{0,1}[0-9]{3}[-.]{0,1}[0-9]{4}';
```

Temporals

PostgreSQL support for temporal data is second to none. In addition to the usual dates and times types, PostgreSQL supports time zones, enabling the automatic handling of daylight saving time (DST) conversions by region. Specialized data types such as interval offer datetime arithmetic. PostgreSQL also understands infinity and negative infinity, relieving us from having to create conventions that we'll surely forget. Range types (*http://bit.ly/126nQPP*) provide support for temporal ranges with a slew of companion operators, functions, and indexes. We cover range types in "Range Types" on page 116.

At last count, PostgreSQL has nine temporal data types. Understanding their distinctions is important in ensuring that you choose the right data type for the job. All the types except range abide by ANSI SQL standards. Other leading database products support some, but not all, of these data types. Oracle has the most varieties of temporal types; SQL Server ranks second; and MySQL comes in last.

PostgreSQL temporal types vary in a number of ways to handle different situations. If a type is time zone–aware, the time changes if you change your server's time zone. The types are:

date

> Stores the month, day, and year, with no time zone awareness and no concept of hours, minutes, or seconds.

time *(aka* time without time zone*)*

> Stores hours, minutes, and seconds with no awareness of time zone or calendar dates.

timestamp *(aka* timestamp without time zone*)*

> Stores both calendar dates and time (hours, minutes, seconds) but does not care about the time zone.

timestamptz *(aka* timestamp with time zone*)*

> A time zone–aware date and time data type. Internally, timestamptz is stored in Coordinated Universal Time (UTC), but its display defaults to the time zone of the server, the service config, the database, the user, or the session. Yes, you can observe different time zones at different levels. If you input a timestamp with no time zone and cast it to one with the time zone, PostgreSQL assumes the default time zone in effect. If you don't set your time zone in *postgresql.conf*, the server's default takes effect. This means that if you change your server's time zone, you'll see all the displayed times change after the PostgreSQL server restarts.

timetz *(aka* time with time zone*)*

> The lesser-used sister of timestamptz. It is time zone–aware but does not store the date. It always assumes DST of the current date and time. Some program‐ ming languages with no concept of time without date might map timetz to a timestamp with some arbitrary date such as Unix Epoch 1970, resulting in year 1970 being assumed.

interval

> A duration of time in hours, days, months, minutes, and others. It comes in handy for datetime arithmetic. For example, if the world is supposed to end in exactly 666 days from now, all you have to do is add an interval of 666 days to the current time to get the exact moment (and plan accordingly).

tsrange

> Allows you to define opened and closed ranges of timestamp with no time zone. The type consists of two timestamps and opened/closed range qualifiers. For example, '[2012-01-01 14:00, 2012-01-01 15:00)'::tsrange defines a period starting at 14:00 but ending before 15:00. Refer to Range Types (*http:// bit.ly/1vXxIXI*) for details.

`tstzrange`

　Allows you to define opened and closed ranges of `timestamp with timezone`.

`daterange`

　Allows you to define opened and closed ranges of dates.

Time Zones: What They Are and Are Not

A common misconception with PostgreSQL time zone–aware data types is that Post-greSQL records an extra time marker with the datetime value itself. This is incorrect. If you save `2012-2-14 18:08:00-8` (-8 being the Pacific offset from UTC), Post-greSQL internally thinks like this:

1. Calculate the UTC time for 2012-02-14 18:08:00-8. This is 2012-02-15 04:08:00-0.

2. Store the value `2012-02-15 04:08:00`.

When you call the data back for display, PostgreSQL internally works like this:

1. Start with the requested time zone, defaulting to the server time zone if none is requested.

2. Compute the offset for time zone for this UTC time (-5 for `America/New_York`).

3. Determine the datetime with the offset (2012-02-15 16:08:00 with a -5 offset becomes 2012-02-15 21:08:00).

4. Display the result (`2012-02-15 21:08:00-5`).

So PostgreSQL doesn't store the time zone, but uses it only to convert the datetime to UTC before storage. After that, the time zone information is discarded. When Post-greSQL displays datetime, it does so in the default time zone dictated by the session, user, database, or server, in that order. If you use time zone–aware data types, you should consider the consequence of a server move from one time zone to another. Suppose you based a server in New York City and subsequently restored the database in Los Angeles. All timestamps with time zone fields could suddenly display in Pacific time. This is fine as long as you anticipate this behavior.

Here's an example of how something can go wrong. Suppose that McDonald's had its server on the East Coast and the opening time for stores is stored as `timetz`. A new McDonald's opens up in San Francisco. The new franchisee phones McDonald's headquarters to add its store to the master directory with an opening time of 7 a.m. The data entry dude entered the information as he is told: 7 a.m. The East Coast Post-greSQL server interprets this to mean 7 a.m. Eastern, and now early risers in San Francisco are lining up at the door wondering why they can't get their McBreakfasts at 4 a.m. Being hungry is one thing, but we can imagine many situations in which confusion over a difference of three hours could mean life or death.

Given the pitfalls, why would anyone want to use time zone–aware data types? First, it does spare you from having to do time zone conversions manually. For example, if a flight leaves Boston at 8 a.m. and arrives in Los Angeles at 11 a.m., and your server is in Europe, you don't want to have to figure out the offset for each time manually. You could just enter the data with the Boston and Los Angeles local times. There's another convincing reason to use time zone–aware data types: the automatic handling of DST. With countries deviating more and more from one another in DST schedules, manually keeping track of DST changes for a globally used database would require a dedicated programmer who does nothing but keep up-to-date with the latest DST schedules and map them to geographic enclaves.

Here's an interesting example: a traveling salesperson catches a flight home from San Francisco to nearby Oakland. When she boards the plane, the clock at the terminal reads 2012-03-11 1:50 a.m. When she lands, the clock in the terminal reads 2012-03-11 3:10 a.m. How long was the flight? The key to the solution is that the change to DST occurred during the flight—the clocks sprang forward. With time zone–aware timestamps, you get 20 minutes, to which is a plausible answer for a short flight across the Bay. We get the wrong answer if we don't use time zone–aware timestamps:

```
SELECT '2012-03-11 3:10 AM America/Los_Angeles'::timestamptz
 - '2012-03-11 1:50 AM America/Los_Angeles'::timestamptz;
```

gives you 20 minutes, whereas:

```
SELECT '2012-03-11 3:10 AM'::timestamp - '2012-03-11 1:50 AM'::timestamp;
```

gives you 1 hour and 20 minutes.

Let's drive the point home with more examples, using a Boston server. For Example 5-10, I input my time in Los Angeles local time, but because my server is in Boston, I get a time returned in Boston local time. Note that it does give me the offset but that is merely display information. The timestamp is internally stored in UTC.

Example 5-10. Inputting time in one time zone and output in another

```
SELECT '2012-02-28 10:00 PM America/Los_Angeles'::timestamptz;
```

```
2012-02-29 01:00:00-05
```

In Example 5-11, we are getting back a timestamp without time zone. So the answer you get when you run this same query will be the same as mine, regardless of where in the world you are.

Example 5-11. Timestamp with time zone to timestamp at location

```
SELECT '2012-02-28 10:00 PM America/Los_Angeles'::timestamptz
AT TIME ZONE 'Europe/Paris';

2012-02-29 07:00:00
```

The query is asking: what time is it in Paris if it's 2012-02-28 10:00 p.m. in Los Angeles? Note the absence of the UTC offset in the result. Also, notice how you can specify a time zone with its official name rather than just an offset. Visit Wikipedia for a list of official time zone names (*http://en.wikipedia.org/wiki/Zoneinfo*).

Datetime Operators and Functions

The inclusion of a temporal interval data type greatly eases date and time arithmetic in PostgreSQL. Without it, we'd have to create another family of functions or use a nesting of functions as many other databases do. With intervals, we can add and subtract timestamp data simply by using the arithmetic operators we're intimately familiar with. The following examples demonstrate operators and functions used with date and time data types.

The addition operator (+) adds an interval to a timestamp:

```
SELECT '2012-02-10 11:00 PM'::timestamp + interval '1 hour';

2012-02-11 00:00:00
```

You can also add intervals:

```
SELECT '23 hours 20 minutes'::interval + '1 hour'::interval;

24:20:00
```

The subtraction operator (-) subtracts an interval from a temporal type:

```
SELECT '2012-02-10 11:00 PM'::timestamptz - interval '1 hour';

2012-02-10 22:00:00-05
```

OVERLAPS, demonstrated in Example 5-12, returns true if two temporal ranges overlap. This is an ANSI SQL predicate equivalent to the overlaps function. OVERLAPS takes four parameters, the first pair constituting one range and the last pair constituting the other range. An overlap considers the time periods to be half open, meaning that the start time is included but the end time is outside the range. This is slightly different behavior from the common BETWEEN predicate, which considers both start and end to be included. This quirk won't make a difference unless one of your ranges is a fixed point in time (a period for which start and end are identical). Watch out for this if you're an avid user of the OVERLAPS function.

Example 5-12. OVERLAPS for timestamp and date

```
SELECT
        ('2012-10-25 10:00 AM'::timestamp, '2012-10-25 2:00 PM'::timestamp)
        OVERLAPS
        ('2012-10-25 11:00 AM'::timestamp,'2012-10-26 2:00 PM'::timestamp) AS x,
        ('2012-10-25'::date,'2012-10-26'::date)
        OVERLAPS
        ('2012-10-26'::date,'2012-10-27'::date) As y;

x  |y
---+---
t  |f
```

In addition to operators and predicates, PostgreSQL comes with functions supporting temporal types. A full listing can be found at Datetime Functions and Operators (*http://bit.ly/1A0Wju9*). We'll demonstrate a sampling here.

Once again, we start with the versatile `generate_series` function. You can use this function with temporal types and interval steps.

As you can see in Example 5-13, we can express dates in our local datetime format or the more global ISO yyyy-mm-dd format. PostgreSQL automatically interprets differing input formats. To be safe, we tend to stick with entering dates in ISO, because date formats vary from culture to culture, server to server, or even database to database.

Example 5-13. Generate time series using generate_series()

```
SELECT (dt - interval '1 day')::date As eom
FROM generate_series('2/1/2012', '6/30/2012', interval '1 month') As dt;

eom
-----------
2012-01-31
2012-02-29
2012-03-31
2012-04-30
2012-05-31
```

Another popular activity is to extract or format parts of a datetime value. Here, the functions `date_part` and `to_char` (*http://bit.ly/15SXGCd*) fit the bill. Example 5-14 also drives home the behavior of DST for a time zone–aware data type. We intentionally chose a period that crosses a daylight saving switchover in US/East. Because the clock springs forward at 2 a.m., the final row of the table reflects the new time.

Example 5-14. Extracting elements of a datetime value

```
SELECT dt, date_part('hour',dt) As hr, to_char(dt,'HH12:MI AM') As mn
FROM
```

```
generate_series(
        '2012-03-11 12:30 AM',
        '2012-03-11 3:00 AM',
        interval '15 minutes'
) As dt;

dt                      | hr | mn
------------------------+----+----------
2012-03-11 00:30:00-05  |  0 | 12:30 AM
2012-03-11 00:45:00-05  |  0 | 12:45 AM
2012-03-11 01:00:00-05  |  1 | 01:00 AM
2012-03-11 01:15:00-05  |  1 | 01:15 AM
2012-03-11 01:30:00-05  |  1 | 01:30 AM
2012-03-11 01:45:00-05  |  1 | 01:45 AM
2012-03-11 03:00:00-04  |  3 | 03:00 AM
```

By default, `generate_series` assumes `timestamptz` if you don't explicitly cast values to `timestamp`.

Arrays

Arrays play an important role in PostgreSQL. They are particularly useful in building aggregate functions, forming `IN` and `ANY` clauses, and holding intermediary values for morphing to other data types. In PostgreSQL, every data type has a companion array type. If you define your own data type, PostgreSQL creates a corresponding array type in the background for you. For example, `integer` has an integer array type `integer[]`, `character` has a character array type `character[]`, and so forth. We'll show you some useful functions to construct arrays short of typing them in manually. We will then point out some handy functions for array manipulations. You can get the complete listing of array functions and operators in the Official Manual: Array Functions and Operators (*http://www.postgresql.org/docs/current/interactive/functions-array.html*).

Array Constructors

The most rudimentary way to create an array is to type the elements:

```
SELECT ARRAY[2001, 2002, 2003] As yrs;
```

If the elements of your array can be extracted from a query, you can use the more sophisticated constructor function, `array()`:

```
SELECT array(
SELECT DISTINCT date_part('year', log_ts)
FROM logs
ORDER BY date_part('year', log_ts)
);
```

Although the `array` function has to be used with a query returning a single column, you can specify a composite type as the output, thereby achieving multicolumn results. We demonstrate this in "Custom and Composite Data Types" on page 142.

You can cast a string representation of an array to an array with syntax of the form:

```
SELECT '{Alex,Sonia}'::text[] As name, '{46,43}'::smallint[] As age;

name         | age
-------------+--------
{Alex,Sonia} | {46,43}
```

You can convert delimited strings to an array with the `string_to_array` function, as demonstrated in Example 5-15.

Example 5-15. Converting a delimited string to an array

```
SELECT string_to_array('CA.MA.TX', '.') As estados;

estados
----------
{CA,MA,TX}
(1 row)
```

`array_agg` is an aggregate function that can take a set of any data type and convert it to an array, as demonstrated in Example 5-16.

Example 5-16. Using array_agg

```
SELECT array_agg(log_ts ORDER BY log_ts) As x
FROM logs
WHERE log_ts BETWEEN '2011-01-01'::timestamptz AND '2011-01-15'::timestamptz;

x
------------------------------------------
{'2011-01-01', '2011-01-13', '2011-01-14'}
```

PostgreSQL 9.5 introduced `array_agg` function support for arrays. In prior versions if you wanted to aggregate rows of arrays with array_agg, you'd get an error. array_agg support for arrays makes it much easier to build multidimensional arrays from one-dimensional arrays, as shown in Example 5-17.

Example 5-17. Creating multidimensional arrays from one-dimensional arrays

```
SELECT array_agg(f.t)
 FROM ( VALUES ('{Alex,Sonia}'::text[]),
    ('{46,43}'::text[] ) ) As f(t);

array_agg
---------------------
```

```
{{Alex,Sonia},{46,43}}
(1 row)
```

In order to aggregate arrays, they must be of the same data type and the same dimension. To force that in Example 5-17, we cast the ages to text. We also have the same number of items in the arrays being aggregated: two people and two ages. Arrays with the same number of elements are called *balanced* arrays.

Unnesting Arrays to Rows

A common function used with arrays is unnest, which allows you to expand the elements of an array into a set of rows, as demonstrated in Example 5-18.

Example 5-18. Expanding arrays with unnest

```
SELECT unnest('{XOX,OXO,XOX}'::char(3)[]) As tic_tac_toe;

tic_tac_toe
---
XOX
OXO
XOX
```

Although you can add multiple unnests to a single SELECT, if the number of resultant rows from each array is not balanced, you may get some head-scratching results.

A balanced unnest, as shown in Example 5-19, yields three rows.

Example 5-19. Unnesting balanced arrays

```
SELECT
unnest('{three,blind,mice}'::text[]) As t,
unnest('{1,2,3}'::smallint[]) As i;

t     |i
------+-
three |1
blind |2
mice  |3
```

If you remove an element of one array so that you don't have an equal number of elements in both, you get the result shown in Example 5-20.

Example 5-20. Unnesting unbalanced arrays

```
SELECT
unnest( '{blind,mouse}'::varchar[]) AS v,
unnest('{1,2,3}'::smallint[]) AS i;
```

```
v     |i
------+-
blind |1
mouse |2
blind |3
mouse |1
blind |2
mouse |3
```

Version 9.4 introduced a multiargument unnest function that puts in null placeholders where the arrays are not balanced. The main drawback with the new unnest is that it can appear only in the FROM clause. Example 5-21 revisits our unbalanced arrays using the version 9.4 construct.

Example 5-21. Unnesting unbalanced arrays with multiargument unnest

```
SELECT * FROM unnest('{blind,mouse}'::text[], '{1,2,3}'::int[]) AS f(t,i);

t      | i
-------+---
blind  | 1
mouse  | 2
<NULL> | 3
```

Array Slicing and Splicing

PostgreSQL also supports array slicing using the *start:end* syntax. It returns another array that is a subarray of the original. For example, to return new arrays that just contain elements 2 through 4 of each original array, type:

```
SELECT fact_subcats[2:4] FROM census.lu_fact_types;
```

To glue two arrays together end to end, use the concatenation operator ||:

```
SELECT fact_subcats[1:2] || fact_subcats[3:4] FROM census.lu_fact_types;
```

You can also add additional elements to an existing array as follows:

```
SELECT '{1,2,3}'::integer[] || 4 || 5;
```

The result is {1,2,3,4,5}.

Referencing Elements in an Array

Elements in arrays are most commonly referenced using the index of the element. PostgreSQL array indexes start at 1. If you try to access an element above the upper bound, you won't get an error—only NULL will be returned. The next example grabs the first and last element of our array column:

```
SELECT
    fact_subcats[1] AS primero,
```

```
        fact_subcats[array_upper(fact_subcats, 1)] As segundo
    FROM census.lu_fact_types;
```

We used the `array_upper` function to get the upper bound of the array. The second required parameter of the function indicates the dimension. In our case, our array is one-dimensional, but PostgreSQL does support multidimensional arrays.

Array Containment Checks

PostgreSQL has several operators for working with array data. We already saw the concatenation operator (||) for combining multiple arrays into one or adding an element to an array in "Array Slicing and Splicing" on page 114. Arrays also support the following comparison operators: =, <>, <, >, @>, <@, and &&. These operators require both sides of the operator to be arrays of the same array data type. If you have a GiST or GIN index on your array column, the comparison operators can utilize them.

The overlap operator (&&) returns `true` if two arrays have any elements in common. Example 5-22 will list all records in our table where the *fact_subcats* contains elements OCCUPANCY STATUS or For rent.

Example 5-22. Array overlaps operator

```
SELECT fact_subcats
FROM census.lu_fact_types
WHERE fact_subcats && '{OCCUPANCY STATUS,For rent}'::varchar[];

fact_subcats
-----------------------------------------------------------
{S01,"OCCUPANCY STATUS","Total housing units"...}
{S02,"OCCUPANCY STATUS","Total housing units"...}
{S03,"OCCUPANCY STATUS","Total housing units"...}
{S10,"VACANCY STATUS","Vacant housing units","For rent"...}
(4 rows)
```

The equality operator (=) returns `true` only if elements in all the arrays are equal and in the same order. If you don't care about order of elements, and just need to know whether all the elements in one array appear as a subset of the other array, use the containment operators (@> , <@). Example 5-23 demonstrates the difference between the contains (@>) and contained by (@<) operators.

Example 5-23. Array containment operators

```
SELECT '{1,2,3}'::int[] @> '{3,2}'::int[] AS contains;

contains
--------
t
(1 row)
```

```
SELECT '{1,2,3}'::int[] <@ '{3,2}'::int[] AS contained_by;

contained_by
------------
f
(1 row)
```

Range Types

Range data types (http://www.postgresql.org/docs/current/interactive/rangetypes.html) represent data with a beginning and an end. PostgreSQL also rolled out many operators and functions to identify overlapping ranges, check to see whether a value falls inside the range, and combine adjacent smaller ranges into larger ranges. Prior to range types, we had to kludge our own functions. These often were clumsy and slow, and didn't always produce the expected results. We've been so happy with ranges that we've converted all of our temporal tables to use them where possible. We hope you share our joy.

Range types replace the need to use two separate fields to represent ranges. Suppose we want all integers between −2 and 2, but not including 2. The range representation would be [-2,2). The square bracket indicates a range that is closed on that end, whereas a parenthesis indicates a range that is open on that end. Thus, [-2,2) includes exactly four integers: −2, −1, 0, 1. Similarly:

- The range (-2,2] includes four integers: -1, 0, 1, 2.
- The range (-2,2) includes three integers: -1, 0, 1.
- The range [-2,2] includes five integers: -2, -1, 0, 1, 2.

Discrete Versus Continuous Ranges

PostgreSQL makes a distinction between discrete and continuous ranges. A range of integers or dates is discrete because you can enumerate each value within the range. Think of dots on a number line. A range of numerics or timestamps is continuous, because an infinite number of values lies between the end points.

A discrete range has multiple representations. Our earlier example of [-2,2) can be represented in the following ways and still include the same number of values in the range: [-2,1], (-3,1], (-3,2), [-2,2). Of these four representations, the one with [) is considered the canonical form. There's nothing magical about closed-open ranges except that if everyone agrees to using that representation for discrete ranges, we can easily compare among many ranges without having to worry first about converting open to close or vice versa. PostgreSQL canonicalizes all discrete ranges, for both storage and display. So if you enter a date range as (2014-1-5,2014-2-1], PostgreSQL rewrites it as [2014-01-06,2014-02-02).

Built-in Range Types

PostgreSQL comes with six built-in range types for numbers and datetimes:

int4range, int8range
> A range of integers. Integer ranges are discrete and subject to canonicalization.

numrange
> A continuous range of decimals, floating-point numbers, or double-precision numbers.

daterange
> A discrete date range of calendar dates without time zone awareness.

tsrange, tstzrange
> A continuous date and time (timestamp) range allowing for fractional seconds. tstrange is not time zone–aware; tstzrange is time zone–aware.

For number-like ranges, if either the start point or the end point is left blank, PostgreSQL replaces it with a null. For practicality, you can interpret the null to represent either -infinity on the left or infinity on the right. In actuality, you're bound by the smallest and largest values for the particular data type. So a int4range of (,) would be [-2147483648,2147483647).

For temporal ranges, -infinity and infinity are valid upper and lower bounds.

In addition to the built-in range types, you can create your own range types. When you do, you can set the range to be either discrete or continuous.

Defining Ranges

A range, regardless of type, is always comprised of two elements of the same type with the bounding condition denoted by brackets or parentheses, as shown in Example 5-24.

Example 5-24. Defining ranges with casts

```
SELECT '[2013-01-05,2013-08-13]'::daterange; ❶
SELECT '(2013-01-05,2013-08-13]'::daterange; ❷
SELECT '(0,)'::int8range; ❸
SELECT '(2013-01-05 10:00,2013-08-13 14:00]'::tsrange; ❹

[2013-01-05,2013-08-14)
[2013-01-06,2013-08-14)
[1,)
("2013-01-05 10:00:00","2013-08-13 14:00:00"]
```

❶ A date range between 2013-01-05 and 2013-08-13 inclusive. Note the canonicalization on the upper bound.

❷ A date range greater than 2013-01-05 and less than or equal to 2013-08-13. Notice the canonicalization.

❸ All integers greater than 0. Note the canonicalization.

❹ A timestamp greater than 2013-01-05 10:00 AM and less than or equal to 2013-08-13 2 PM.

 Datetimes in PostgreSQL can take on the values of -infinity and infinity. For uniformity and in keeping with convention, we suggest that you always use [for the former and) for the latter as in [-infinity, infinity).

Ranges can also be defined using range constructor functions, which go by the same name as the range and can take two or three arguments. Here's an example:

```
SELECT daterange('2013-01-05','infinity','[]');
```

The third argument denotes the bound. If omitted, the open-close [ ) convention is used by default. We suggest that you always include the third element for clarity.

Defining Tables with Ranges

Temporal ranges are popular. Suppose you have an employment table that stores employment history. Instead of creating separate columns for start and end dates, you can design a table as shown in Example 5-25. In the example, we added an index to the period column to speed up queries using our range column.

Example 5-25. Table with date range

```
CREATE TABLE employment (id serial PRIMARY KEY, employee varchar(20),
period daterange);
CREATE INDEX ix_employment_period ON employment USING gist (period); ❶
INSERT INTO employment (employee,period)
VALUES
        ('Alex','[2012-04-24, infinity)'::daterange),
        ('Sonia','[2011-04-24, 2012-06-01)'::daterange),
        ('Leo','[2012-06-20, 2013-04-20)'::daterange),
        ('Regina','[2012-06-20, 2013-04-20)'::daterange);
```

❶ Add a GiST index on the range field.

Range Operators

Two range operators tend to be used most often: overlap (&&) and contains (@>).
Those are the ones we'll cover. To see the full catalog of range operators, go to Range
Operators (*http://bit.ly/1s2o6WE*).

Overlap operator

As the name suggests, the overlap operator && returns true if two ranges have any
values in common. Example 5-26 demonstrates this operator and puts to use the
string_agg function for aggregating the list of employees into a single text field.

Example 5-26. Who worked with whom?

```
SELECT
       e1.employee,
       string_agg(DISTINCT e2.employee, ', ' ORDER BY e2.employee) As colleagues
FROM employment As e1 INNER JOIN employment As e2
ON e1.period && e2.period
WHERE e1.employee <> e2.employee
GROUP BY e1.employee;

employee | colleagues
---------+------------------
Alex     | Leo, Regina, Sonia
Leo      | Alex, Regina
Regina   | Alex, Leo
Sonia    | Alex
```

Contains and contained in operators

In the contains operator (@>), the first argument is a range and the second is a value.
If the second is within the first, the contains operator returns true. Example 5-27
demonstrates its use.

Example 5-27. Who is currently working?

```
SELECT employee FROM employment WHERE period @> CURRENT_DATE GROUP BY employee;

employee
--------
Alex
```

The reverse of the contains operator is the contained operator (<@), whose first argument is the value and the second the range.

JSON

PostgreSQL provides JSON (*http://json.org*) (JavaScript Object Notation) and many support functions. JSON has become the most popular data interchange format for web applications. Version 9.3 significantly beefed up JSON support with new functions for extracting, editing, and casting to other data types. Version 9.4 introduced the JSONB data type, a binary form of JSON that can also take advantage of indexes. Version 9.5 introduced more functions for jsonb, including functions for setting elements in a jsonb object. Version 9.6 introduced the jsonb_insert function for inserting elements into an existing jsonb array or adding a new key value.

Inserting JSON Data

To create a table to store JSON, define a column as a `json` type:

```
CREATE TABLE persons (id serial PRIMARY KEY, person json);
```

Example 5-28 inserts JSON data. PostgreSQL automatically validates the input to make sure what you are adding is valid JSON. Remember that you can't store invalid JSON in a JSON column, nor can you cast invalid JSON to a JSON data type.

Example 5-28. Populating a JSON field

```
INSERT INTO persons (person)
VALUES (
    '{
        "name":"Sonia",
        "spouse":
        {
            "name":"Alex",
            "parents":
            {
                "father":"Rafael",
                "mother":"Ofelia"
            },
            "phones":
            [
                {
                    "type":"work",
                    "number":"619-722-6719"
                },
                {
                    "type":"cell",
                    "number":"619-852-5083"
                }
            ]
        },
        "children":
        [
```

```
        {
            "name":"Brandon",
            "gender":"M"
        },
        {
            "name":"Azaleah",
            "girl":true,
            "phones": []
        }
    ]
}'
);
```

Querying JSON

The easiest way to traverse the hierarchy of a JSON object is by using pointer symbols. Example 5-29 shows some common usage.

Example 5-29. Querying the JSON field

```
SELECT person->'name' FROM persons;
SELECT person->'spouse'->'parents'->'father' FROM persons;
```

You can also write the query using a path array as in the following example:

```
SELECT person#>array['spouse','parents','father'] FROM persons;
```

Notice that you must use the #> pointer symbol if what comes after is a path array.

To penetrate JSON arrays, specify the array index. JSON arrays is zero-indexed, unlike PostgreSQL arrays, whose indexes start at 1.

```
SELECT person->'children'->0->'name' FROM persons;
```

And the path array equivalent:

```
SELECT person#>array['children','0','name'] FROM persons;
```

All queries in the prior examples return the value as JSON primitives (numbers, strings, booleans). To return the text representation, add another greater-than sign as in the following examples:

```
SELECT person->'spouse'->'parents'->>'father' FROM persons;
SELECT person#>>array['children','0','name'] FROM persons;
```

If you are chaining the -> operator, only the very last one can be a ->> operator.

The json_array_elements function takes a JSON array and returns each element of the array as a separate row as in Example 5-30.

Example 5-30. json_array_elements to expand JSON array

```
SELECT json_array_elements(person->'children')->>'name' As name FROM persons;

name
-------
Brandon
Azaleah
(2 rows)
```

 We strongly encourage you to use pointer symbols when drilling down into a JSON object. The syntax is more succinct and you can use the same operators as for JSONB (which we'll cover shortly). PostgreSQL does offer functional equivalents if you need them: json_extract_path is a variadic function (functions with an unlimited number of arguments). The first argument is always the JSON object you are trying to navigate; subsequent parameters are the key value for each tier of the hierarchy. The equivalent to ->> and #>> is json_extract_path_text.

Outputting JSON

In addition to querying JSON data, you can convert other data to JSON. In these next examples, we'll demonstrate the use of JSON built-in functions to create JSON objects.

Example 5-31 demonstrates the use of row_to_json to convert a subset of columns in each record from the table we created and loaded in Example 5-28.

Example 5-31. Converting rows to individual JSON objects (requires version 9.3 or later)

```
SELECT row_to_json(f) As x
FROM (
    SELECT id, json_array_elements(person->'children')->>'name' As cname FROM persons
) As f;

             x
---------------------------
{"id":1,"cname":"Brandon"}
{"id":1,"cname":"Azaleah"}
(2 rows)
```

To output each row in our persons table as JSON:

```
SELECT row_to_json(f) As jsoned_row FROM persons As f;
```

The use of a row as an output field in a query is a feature unique to PostgreSQL. It's handy for creating complex JSON objects. We describe it further in "Composite Types in Queries" on page 177, and Example 7-20 demonstrates the use of array_agg and

---

`array_to_json` to output a set of rows as a single JSON object. In version 9.3 we have at our disposal the `json_agg` function. We demonstrate its use in Example 7-21.

Binary JSON: jsonb

New in PostgreSQL 9.4 is the `jsonb` data type. It is handled through the same operators as those for the `json` type, and similarly named functions, plus several additional ones. `jsonb` performance is much better than `json` performance because `jsonb` doesn't need to be reparsed during operations. There are a couple of key differences between the `jsonb` and `json` data types:

- `jsonb` is internally stored as a binary object and does not maintain the formatting of the original JSON text as the `json` data type does. Spaces aren't preserved, numbers can appear slightly different, and attributes become sorted. For example, a number input as `e-5` would be converted to its decimal representation.

- `jsonb` does not allow duplicate keys and silently picks one, whereas the `json` type preserves duplicates. This is demonstrated in Michael Paquier's article "Manipulating jsonb data by abusing of key uniqueness" (*http://bit.ly/2v1E1wV*).

- `jsonb` columns can be directly indexed using the GIN index method (covered in "Indexes" on page 157), whereas `json` requires a functional index to extract key elements.

To demonstrate these concepts, we'll create another `persons` table, replacing the `json` column with a `jsonb`:

```
CREATE TABLE persons_b (id serial PRIMARY KEY, person jsonb);
```

To insert data into our new table, we would repeat Example 5-28.

So far, working with JSON and binary JSON has been the same. Differences appear when you query. To make the binary JSON readable, PostgreSQL converts it to a canonical text representation, as shown in Example 5-32.

Example 5-32. jsonb versus json output

```
SELECT person As b FROM persons_b WHERE id = 1; ❶
SELECT person As j FROM persons WHERE id = 1;❷

b
---------------------------------------------------------------------------
{"name": "Sonia",
 "spouse": {"name": "Alex", "phones": [{"type": "work", "number": "619-722-6719"},
 {"type": "cell", "number": "619-852-5083"}],
 "parents": {"father": "Rafael", "mother": "Ofelia"}},
 "children": [{"name": "Brandon", "gender": "M"},
```

```
{"girl": true, "name": "Azaleah", "phones": []}]}
(1 row)

                                j
-------------------------------------------------
{
    "name":"Sonia",
        "spouse":
        {
            "name":"Alex",
            "parents":
            {
                "father":"Rafael",
                "mother":"Ofelia"
            },
            "phones":
            [
                {
                    "type":"work",
                    "number":"619-722-6719"+
                },
                {
                    "type":"cell",
                    "number":"619-852-5083"+
                }
            ]
        },
        "children":
        [
            {
                "name":"Brandon",
                "gender":"M"
            },
            {
                "name":"Azaleah",
                "girl":true,
                "phones": []
            }
        ]
    }
(1 row)
```

❶ jsonb reformats input and removes whitespace. Also, the order of attributes is not maintained from the insert.

❷ json maintains input whitespace and the order of attributes.

jsonb has similarly named functions as json, plus some additional ones. So, for example, the json family of functions such as json_extract_path_text and json_each are matched in jsonb by jsonb_extract_path_text, jsonb_each, etc. However, the equivalent operators are the same, so you will find that the examples in

"Querying JSON" on page 121 work largely the same without change for the `jsonb` type—just replace the table name and `json_array_elements` with `jsonb_array_elements`.

In addition to the operators supported by `json`, `jsonb` has additional comparator operators for equality (=), contains (@>), contained (<@), key exists (?), any of array of keys exists (?|), and all of array of keys exists (?&).

So, for example, to list all people that have a child named Brandon, use the contains operator as demonstrated in Example 5-33.

Example 5-33. jsonb contains operator

```
 SELECT person->>'name' As name
FROM persons_b
WHERE person @> '{"children":[{"name":"Brandon"}]}';

name
-----
Sonia
```

These additional operators provide very fast checks when you complement them with a GIN index on the `jsonb` column:

```
    CREATE INDEX ix_persons_jb_person_gin ON persons_b USING gin (person);
```

We don't have enough records in our puny table for the index to kick in, but for more rows, you'd see that Example 5-33 utilizes the index.

Editing JSONB data

PostgreSQL 9.5 introduced native jsonb concatenation (||) and subtraction operators (-, #-) as well as companion functions for setting data. These operators do not exist for the json datatype. To be able to accomplish these tasks in prior versions, you'd have to lean on "Writing PL/V8, PL/CoffeeScript, and PL/LiveScript Functions" on page 214 to do the work.

The concatenation operator can be used to add and replace attributes of a jsonb object. In Example 5-34 we add an address attribute to the Gomez family and use the RETURNING construct covered in "Returning Affected Records to the User" on page 176 to return the updated value. The new value has an address attribute.

Example 5-34. Using JSONB || to add address

```
UPDATE persons_b
SET person = person || '{"address": "Somewhere in San Diego, CA"}'::jsonb
WHERE person @> '{"name":"Sonia"}'
RETURNING person;
```

```
profile
------------------------------------------------------------------------
{"name": "Sonia", ... "address": "Somewhere in San Diego, CA", "children": ...}
(1 row)
UPDATE 1
```

Because JSONB requires that keys be unique, if you try to add a duplicate key, the original value will be replaced instead. So to update with a new address, we would repeat the exercise in Example 5-34, but replacing *Somewhere in San Diego, CA* with something else.

If we decided we no longer wanted an address, we could use the - as shown in Example 5-35.

Example 5-35. Using JSONB - to remove an element

```
UPDATE persons_b
SET person = person - 'address'
WHERE person @> '{"name":"Sonia"}';
```

The simple - operator works for first-level elements, but what if you wanted to remove an attribute from a particular member? This is when you'd use the #- operator. #- takes an array of text values that denotes the path of the element you want to remove. In Example 5-36 we remove the `girl` designator of Azaleah.

Example 5-36. Using JSONB #- to remove nested element

```
UPDATE persons_b
SET  person = person #- '{children,1,girl}'::text[]
WHERE person @> '{"name":"Sonia"}'
RETURNING person->'children'->1;

{"name": "Azaleah", "phones": []}
```

When removing elements from an array, you need to denote the index. Because Java-Script indexes start at 0, to remove an element from the second child, we use 1 instead of 2. If we wanted to remove Azaleah entirely, we would have used '{chil dren,1}'::text[].

To add a gender attribute, or replace one that was previously set, we can use the jsonb_set function as shown in Example 5-37.

Example 5-37. Using the jsonb_set function to change a nested value

```
UPDATE persons_b
SET person = jsonb_set(person,'{children,1,gender}'::text[],'"F"'::jsonb, true)
WHERE person @> '{"name":"Sonia"}';
```

jsonb_set takes three arguments of form jsonb_set(*jsonb_to_update*, *text_array_path*, *new_jsonb_value*,*allow_creation*). If you set *allow_creation* to false when the property did not already exist, the statement will return an error.

XML

The XML data type, similar to JSON, is "controversial" in a relational database because it violates the principles of normalization. Nonetheless, all of the high-end relational database products (IBM DB2, Oracle, SQL Server) support XML. PostgreSQL also jumped on the bandwagon and offers plenty of functions to boot. (We've authored many articles on working with XML in PostgreSQL (*http://bit.ly/1yx7ixc*).) PostgreSQL comes packaged with functions for generating, manipulating, and parsing XML data. These are outlined in XML Functions (*http://bit.ly/1BlrAvL*). Unlike the jsonb type, there is currently no direct index support for it. So you need to use functional indexes to index subparts, similar to what you can do with the plain json type.

Inserting XML Data

When you create a column of the xml data type, PostgreSQL automatically ensures that only valid XML values populate the rows. This is what distinguishes an XML column from just any text column. However, the XML is not validated against any Document Type Definition (DTD) or XML Schema Definition (XSD), even if it is specified in the XML document. To freshen up on what constitutes valid XML, Example 5-38 shows you how to append XML data to a table by declaring a column as xml and inserting into it as usual.

Example 5-38. Populate an XML field

```
CREATE TABLE families (id serial PRIMARY KEY, profile xml);
INSERT INTO families(profile)
VALUES (
    '<family name="Gomez">
        <member><relation>padre</relation><name>Alex</name></member>
        <member><relation>madre</relation><name>Sonia</name></member>
        <member><relation>hijo</relation><name>Brandon</name></member>
        <member><relation>hija</relation><name>Azaleah</name></member>
        </family>');
```

Each XML value could have a different XML structure. To enforce uniformity, you can add a check constraint, covered in "Check Constraints" on page 155, to the XML column. Example 5-39 ensures that all family has at least one relation element. The '/family/member/relation' is XPath syntax, a basic way to refer to elements and other parts of XML.

Example 5-39. Ensure that all records have at least one member relation

```
ALTER TABLE families ADD CONSTRAINT chk_has_relation
CHECK (xpath_exists('/family/member/relation', profile));
```

If we then try to insert something like:

```
INSERT INTO families (profile) VALUES ('<family name="HsuObe"></family>');
```

we will get this error: ERROR: new row for relation "families" violates check constraint "chk_has_relation".

For more involved checks that require checking against DTD or XSD, you'll need to resort to writing functions and using those in the check constraint, because PostgreSQL doesn't have built-in functions to handle those kinds of checks.

Querying XML Data

To query XML, the xpath function is really useful. The first argument is an XPath query, and the second is an xml object. The output is an array of XML elements that satisfies the XPath query. Example 5-40 combines xpath with unnest to return all the family members. unnest unravels the array into a row set. We then cast the XML fragment to text.

Example 5-40. Query XML field

```
SELECT ordinality AS id, family,
    (xpath('/member/relation/text()', f))[1]::text As relation,
    (xpath('/member/name/text()', f))[1]::text As mem_name ❶
FROM (
    SELECT
        (xpath('/family/@name', profile))[1]::text As family, ❷
        f.ordinality, f.f
        FROM families, unnest(xpath('/family/member', profile)) WITH ORDINALITY AS f
) x; ❸

 id | family | relation | mem_name
----+--------+----------+----------
  1 | Gomez  | padre    | Alex
  2 | Gomez  | madre    | Sonia
  3 | Gomez  | hijo     | Brandon
  4 | Gomez  | hija     | Azaleah
(4 rows)
```

❶ Get the text element in the relation and name tags of each member element. We need to use array subscripting because xpath always returns an array, even if only one element is returned.

❷   Get the name attribute from `family` root. For this we use `@attribute_name`.

❸   Break the result of the SELECT into the subelements `<member>`, `<relation>`, `</relation>`, `<name>`, `</name>`, and `</member>` tags. The slash is a way of getting at subtag elements. For example, `xpath('/family/member', 'profile')` will return an array of all members in each family that is defined in a profile. The `@` sign is used to select attributes of an element. So, for example, `family/@name` returns the name attribute of a `family`. By default, `xpath` always returns an element, including the tag part. The `text()` forces a return of just the text body of an element.

New in version 10 is the ANSI-SQL standard XMLTABLE construct. XMLTABLE converts text of XML into individual rows and columns based on some defined transformation. We'll repeat Example 5-40 using XMLTABLE.

Example 5-41. Query XML using XMLTABLE

```
SELECT xt.*
  FROM families,
       XMLTABLE ('/family/member' PASSING profile ❶
                 COLUMNS ❷
                     id FOR ORDINALITY ❸,
                     family text PATH '../@name' ❹,
                     relation text NOT NULL ❺,
                     member_name text PATH 'name' NOT NULL
                ) AS xt;
 id | family | relation | mem_name
----+--------+----------+----------
  1 | Gomez  | padre    | Alex
  2 | Gomez  | madre    | Sonia
  3 | Gomez  | hijo     | Brandon
  4 | Gomez  | hija     | Azaleah
(4 rows)
```

❶   The first part is an XML path element that defines the row. The word PASSING is followed by the table column to parse out rows. This column has to be of type `xml`. We use the `families.profile` column of our families table.

❷   The COLUMNS component should define the list of columns to be parsed out of the xml.

❸   Similar to WITH ORDINALITY in conjunction with set-returning functions, you can use FOR ORDINALITY to assign numeric order to each record.

❹ You can use ../ to move up a level above the base of the row. In this case we use ./ @name to get the family name, which is one level above family/member. The @ is used to denote this is an attribute (something of form `name='a value'`) and not an element.

❺ If a path element matches the name of your defined column, you don't need to specify the PATH. In this case, because */family/member/relation* matches our column name `relation`, we can skip the PATH clause.

Full Text Search

I'm sure you've seen websites where you can search by typing in keywords. An ecommerce site will bring up a list of matching products; a film site will bring up a list of matching movies; a knowledgebase site will bring up matching questions and answers, etc.

To search textual data by keywords, you have at your disposal the `like` or `ilike` (case insensitive) commands. You can also avail yourself of powerful regular expression and Soundex searches. But both of these methods stop short of offering natural language–based match conditions. For example, if you're looking for LGBT movies and type that abbreviation into your search, you're going to miss movies described as lesbian, gay, bisexual, or transgendered. If you type in the search term *lots of steamy sex scenes*, you may end up with nothing unless the description very closely matches what you typed in.

FTS is a suite of tools that adds a modicum of "intelligence" to your searches. Though it's far from being able to read your mind, it can find words that are close in meaning, rather than spelling. FTS is packaged into PostgreSQL, with no additional installation necessary.

At the core of FTS is an FTS configuration. The configuration codifies the rules under which match will occur by referring to one or more dictionaries. For instance, if your dictionary contains entries that equate the words *love, romance, infatuation, lust,* then any search by one of the words will find matches with any of the words. Dictionaries may also equate words with the same stem. For example, *love, loving,* and *loved* share a common stem. A dictionary could equate all principle parts of a verb; for example, *eat, eats, ate,* and *eaten* could be considered the same.

A dictionary can also list stop words. These are usually parts of speech that add little to the meaning. Articles, conjunctions, prepositions, and pronouns such as *a, the, on,* and *that* often make up the list of stop words.

Beyond matching synonyms and pruning stop words, FTS can be used to rank searches. FTS can utilize the proximity of words to each other and the frequency of terms in text to rank search results. For example, if you're interested in viewing movies where sex is depicted with smoking, you could search for the two words *sex* and *smoking*, but also specify that the two words must be two words apart and rank higher if they appear in the title. *And so they smoked after sex* would hit, whereas *sex took place in a hotel, which has a foyer for smoking guests* would miss. FTS can apply unequal weights to the places where the sought-after words appear in the text. For instance, if you have a movie where the word *sex* appears in either the title or the byline, you could make this movie rank higher than movies where *sex* is only in the description.

FTS Configurations

Most PostgreSQL distributions come packaged with over 10 FTS configurations. All these are installed in the pg_catalog schema.

To see the listing of installed FTS configurations, run the query SELECT cfgname FROM pg_ts_config;. Or use the \dF command in psql. A typical list follows:

```
cfgname
----------
simple
danish
dutch
english
finnish
french
german
hungarian
italian
norwegian
portuguese
romanian
russian
spanish
swedish
turkish
(16 rows)
```

If you need to create your own configurations or dictionaries, refer to PostgreSQL Manual: Full Text Search Configuration (*https://www.postgresql.org/docs/current/static/textsearch-configuration.html*) and PostgreSQL Manual: Full Text Search Dictionaries (*https://www.postgresql.org/docs/current/static/textsearch-dictionaries.html*).

You're not limited to built-in FTS configurations. You can create your own. But before you do, you may wish to see what other users have already created that may suit your needs. If your text is medical-related, you may be able to find a configuration with dictionaries chock full of specialized anatomy terms. If your text is in Spanish, find a configuration that tailors to your particular dialect of Spanish.

Once you locate a configuration that you'd like added to your arsenal, installation is quite simple and usually doesn't require additional compilation. We demonstrate by installing the popular hunspell configuration.

Start by downloading hunspell configurations from hunspell_dicts (*https://github.com/postgrespro/hunspell_dicts*). You'll be greeted by hunspell for many different languages. We'll go with hunspell_en_us:

1. Download everything in the folder.

2. Copy *en_us.affix* and *en_us.dict* to your PostgreSQL installation directory *share/tsearch_data*.

3. Copy the *hunspell_en_us--*.sql* and *hunspell_en_us.control* files to your PostgreSQL installation directory *share/extension* folder.

Next, run:

```
CREATE EXTENSION hunspell_en_us SCHEMA pg_catalog;
```

From psql, if you now run Example 5-42, you'll see details of the hunspell configuration and dictionary we just installed.

Example 5-42. FTS configuration hunspell

```
\dF+ english_hunspell;

Text search configuration "pg_catalog.english_hunspell"
Parser: "pg_catalog.default"
Token           | Dictionaries
----------------+-----------------------------
asciihword      | english_hunspell,english_stem
asciiword       | english_hunspell,english_stem
email           | simple
file            | simple
float           | simple
host            | simple
hword           | english_hunspell,english_stem
hword_asciipart | english_hunspell,english_stem
hword_numpart   | simple
hword_part      | english_hunspell,english_stem
int             | simple
numhword        | simple
numword         | simple
sfloat          | simple
uint            | simple
url             | simple
url_path        | simple
version         | simple
word            | english_hunspell,english_stem
```

Keep in mind that not all FTS configurations install in the same way. Read the instructions.

Contrast that output to the built-in English configuration in Example 5-43, which gives you the dictionaries used by the English configuration.

Example 5-43. FTS English configuration

```
\dF+ english;

Text search configuration "pg_catalog.english"
Parser: "pg_catalog.default"
Token           | Dictionaries
----------------+--------------
asciihword      | english_stem
asciiword       | english_stem
email           | simple
file            | simple
float           | simple
host            | simple
hword           | english_stem
hword_asciipart | english_stem
hword_numpart   | simple
hword_part      | english_stem
int             | simple
numhword        | simple
numword         | simple
sfloat          | simple
uint            | simple
url             | simple
url_path        | simple
version         | simple
word            | english_stem
```

The only difference between the two is that hunspell draws from an additional dictionary.

Not sure which configuration is the default? Run:

```
SHOW default_text_search_config;
```

To replace the default with another, run:

```
ALTER DATABASE postgresql_book
SET default_text_search_config = 'pg_catalog.english';
```

This replacement takes place at the database level, but as with most PostgreSQL configuration settings, you can make the change at the server, user, or session levels.

TSVectors

A text column must be vectorized before FTS can search against it. The resultant vector column is a tsvector data type. To create a tsvector from text, you must specify the FTS configuration to use. The vectorization reduces the original text to a set of word skeletons, referred to as lexemes, by removing stop words. For each lexeme, the TSVector records where in the original text it appears. The more frequently a lexeme appears, the higher the weight. Each lexeme therefore is imbued with at least one position, much like a vector in the physical sense.

Use the to_tsvector function to vectorize a blob of text. This function will resort to the default FTS configuration unless you specify another.

Example 5-44 shows how TSVectors differ depending on which FTS configuration was used in their construction.

Example 5-44. TSVector derived from different FTS configurations

```
SELECT
    c.name,
    CASE
        WHEN c.name ='default' THEN to_tsvector(f.t)
        ELSE to_tsvector(c.name::regconfig,f.t)
    END As vect
FROM (
    SELECT 'Just dancing in the rain. I like to dance.'::text) As f(t), (
        VALUES ('default'),('english'),('english_hunspell'),('simple')
    ) As c(name);
name             | vect
-----------------+-----------------------------------------------------------------
default          | 'danc':2,9 'like':7 'rain':5
english          | 'danc':2,9 'like':7 'rain':5
english_hunspell | 'dance':2,9 'dancing':2 'like':7 'rain':5
simple           | 'dance':9 'dancing':2 'i':6 'in':3 'just':1 'like':7
'rain':5 'the':4 'to':8
(4 rows)
```

Example 5-44 demonstrates how four different FTS configurations result in different vectors. Note how the English and Hunspell configurations remove all stop words, such as *just* and *to*. English and Hunspell also convert words to their normalized form as dictated by their dictionaries, so *dancing* becomes *danc* and *dance*, respectively. The simple configuration has no concept of stemming and stop words.

The to_tsvector function returns where each lexeme appears in the text. So, for example, 'danc':2,9 means that *dancing* and *dance* appear as the second and the ninth words.

To incorporate FTS into your database, add a tsvector column to your table. You then either schedule the tsvector column to be updated regularly, or add a trigger to the table so that whenever relevant fields update, the tsvector field recomputes.

For our examples, we gathered fictitious movie data (*https://www.postgresql.org/ftp/ projects/pgFoundry/dbsamples/pagila/pagila/*). Load the tables from psql using the *file.sql* script as follows:

```
\encoding utf8;
\i film.sql
```

Next, we add and compute a tsvector column to the film table as shown in Example 5-45.

Example 5-45. Add tsvector column and populate with weights

```
ALTER TABLE film ADD COLUMN fts tsvector;
UPDATE film
SET fts =
    setweight(to_tsvector(COALESCE(title,'')),'A') ||
    setweight(to_tsvector(COALESCE(description,'')),'B');
CREATE INDEX ix_film_fts_gin ON film USING gin (fts);
```

Example 5-45 vectorizes the title and description columns and stores the vector in a newly created tsvector column. To speed up searches, we add a GIN index on the tsvector column. GIN is a lossless index. You can also add a GiST index on a vector column. GiST is lossy and slower to search but builds quicker and takes up less disk space. We explore indexes in more detail in "Indexes" on page 157.

By populating the *fts* column, we've introduced two new constructs, the `setweight` function and the concatenation operator (||), to tsvector.

To distinguish the relative importance of different lexemes, you could assign a weight to each. The weights must be A, B, C, or D, with A ranking highest in importance. In Example 5-45, we assigned A to lexemes culled from the title and B to lexemes from the description. If our search term matches a lexeme from the title, we deem the match to be more relevant than a match from the description of the movie.

TSVectors can be formed from other tsvectors using the concatenation (||) operator. We used it here to combine the title and description into a single tsvector. This way when we search, we have to contend with only a single column.

Should data change in one of the basis columns forming the tsvector, you must re-vectorize. To avoid having to manually run to_tsvector every time data changes, create a trigger that responds to updates. In the trigger, use the handy tsvec-tor_update_trigger function as shown in Example 5-46.

Example 5-46. Trigger to automatically update tsvector

```
CREATE TRIGGER trig_tsv_film_iu
BEFORE INSERT OR UPDATE OF title, description ON film FOR EACH ROW
EXECUTE PROCEDURE tsvector_update_trigger(fts,'pg_catalog.english',
title,description);
```

Example 5-46 reacts to an insert or update in the title or description by revectoring the fts column. One shortcoming though: tsvector_update_trigger does not support weighting.

TSQueries

A FTS, or any text search for that matter, has two components: the searched text and the search terms. For FTS to work, both must be vectorized. We have already seen how to vectorize the searched text to create tsvector columns. We now show you how to vectorize the search terms.

FTS refers to vectorized search terms as tsqueries, and PostgreSQL offers several functions that will convert plain-text search terms to tsqueries: to_tsquery, plainto_tsquery, and phraseto_tsquery. The latter is a new function in 9.6 and takes the ordering of words in the search term into consideration.

tsqueries are normally created on the fly rather than being stored in a table. However, if you are building a system where people can save their queries and run them, you could define a tsquery column in a table.

Example 5-47 shows the output using the to_tsquery functions against two configurations: the default English configuration and the Hunspell configuration.

Example 5-47. TSQuery constructions: to_query

```
SELECT to_tsquery('business & analytics');

to_tsquery
----------------
'busi' & 'analyt'

SELECT to_tsquery('english_hunspell','business & analytics');

to_tsquery
--------------------------------
('business' | 'busy') & 'analyt'
```

Both examples are akin to searching for text containing the words *business* and *analytics*. The and operator (&) means that both words must appear in the searched text. The or operator (|) means one or both of the words must appear in the searched text. If the configuration in use finds multiple stems for a word, they are stitched together by the or operator.

You should use the same FTS configuration as the one you used to build the tsvector.

A slight variant of to_tsquery is plain_totsquery. This function automatically inserts the and operator between words for you, saving you a few key clicks. See Example 5-48.

Example 5-48. TSQuery constructions: plainto_query

```
SELECT plainto_tsquery('business analytics');

plainto_tsquery
-----------------
'busi' & 'analyt'
```

to_tsquery and plainto_tsquery look only at words, not their sequence. So *business analytics* and *analytics business* produce the same tsquery. This is a shortcoming because you're limited to searching by single words only. Version 9.6 addressed this with the function phraseto_tsquery. In Example 5-49, the phraseto_tsquery vectorizes the words, inserting the distance operator between the words. This means that the searched text must contain the words *business* and *analytics* in that order, upgrading a word search to a phrase search.

Example 5-49. TSQuery constructions: phraseto_query

```
SELECT phraseto_tsquery('business analytics');

phraseto_tsquery
-------------------
'busi' <-> 'analyt'

SELECT phraseto_tsquery('english_hunspell','business analytics');

phraseto_tsquery
---------------------------------------------
'business' <-> 'analyt' | 'busy' <-> 'analyt'
```

You can also cast text to tsquery without using any functions, as in `'business & ana lytics'::tsquery`. However, with casts, words are not replaced with lexemes and are taken literally.

TSQueries can be combined using the *or* operator (||) or the *and* operator (&&). The expression `tsquery1 || tsquery2` means matching text must satisfy either tsquery1 *or* tsquery2. The expression `tsquery1 && tsquery2` means matching text must satisfy both tsquery1 and tsquery2.

Examples of each are shown in Example 5-50.

Example 5-50. Combining tsqueries

```
SELECT plainto_tsquery('business analyst') || phraseto_tsquery('data scientist');
tsquery
-------------------------------------------
'busi' & 'analyst' | 'data' <-> 'scientist'
SELECT plainto_tsquery('business analyst') && phraseto_tsquery('data scientist');
tsquery
-------------------------------------------
'busi' & 'analyst' & ('data' <-> 'scientist')
```

tsqueries and tsvectors have additional operators for doing things like determining if one is a subset of another, and several other functions. All this is detailed in Post-greSQL Manual: Text Search Functions and Operators (*https://www.postgresql.org/docs/current/static/functions-textsearch.html*).

Using Full Text Search

We have created a tsvector from our text; we have created a tsquery from our search terms. Now, we can perform an FTS. We do so by using the @@ operator. Example 5-51 demonstrates it.

Example 5-51. FTS in action

```
SELECT left(title,50) As title, left(description,50) as description
FROM film
WHERE fts @@ to_tsquery('hunter & (scientist | chef)') AND title > '';
title                  | description
-----------------------+---------------------------------------------------
ALASKA PHANTOM         | A Fanciful Saga of a Hunter And a Pastry Chef who
CAUSE DATE             | A Taut Tale of a Explorer And a Pastry Chef who mu
CINCINATTI WHISPERER   | A Brilliant Saga of a Pastry Chef And a Hunter who
COMMANDMENTS EXPRESS   | A Fanciful Saga of a Student And a Mad Scientist w
DAUGHTER MADIGAN       | A Beautiful Tale of a Hunter And a Mad Scientist w
GOLDFINGER SENSIBILITY | A Insightful Drama of a Mad Scientist And a Hunter
HATE HANDICAP          | A Intrepid Reflection of a Mad Scientist And a Pio
INSIDER ARIZONA        | A Astounding Saga of a Mad Scientist And a Hunter
WORDS HUNTER           | A Action-Packed Reflection of a Composer And a Mad
(9 rows)
```

Example 5-51 finds all films with a title or description containing the word *hunter* and either the word *scientist*, or the word *chef*, or both.

If you are running PostgreSQL 9.6, you can specify the proximity and order of words. See Example 5-52.

Example 5-52. FTS with order and proximity

```
SELECT left(title,50) As title, left(description,50) as description
FROM film
WHERE fts @@ to_tsquery('hunter <4> (scientist | chef)') AND title > '';

title            | description
-----------------+-----------------------------------------------------------
ALASKA PHANTOM   | A Fanciful Saga of a Hunter And a Pastry Chef who
DAUGHTER MADIGAN | A Beautiful Tale of a Hunter And a Mad Scientist w
(2 rows)
```

Example 5-52 requires that the word *hunter* precede *scientist* or *chef* by exactly four words.

Ranking Results

FTS includes functions for ranking results. These functions are ts_rank and ts_rank_cd. ts_rank considers only the frequency of terms and weights, while ts_rank_cd (cd stands for coverage density) also considers the position of the search term within the searched text. If lexemes are found closer together, the result ranks higher. ts_rank_cd is meaningful only if you have position markers in your tsvector; otherwise, it returns zero. The frequency with which a search term appears also depends on position markers. So the ts_rank function will consider only weights if positional markers are missing. By default, ts_rank and ts_rank_cd apply the weights 0.1, 0.2, 0.4, and 1.0, respectively, for D, C, B, and A. Example 5-53 follows the default order.

Example 5-53. Ranking search results

```
SELECT title, left(description,50) As description,
    ts_rank(fts,ts)::numeric(10,3) AS r
FROM film, to_tsquery('english','love  & (wait | indian | mad)') AS ts
WHERE fts @@ ts AND title > ''
ORDER BY r DESC;

title         | description                                        | r
--------------+----------------------------------------------------+------
INDIAN LOVE   | A Insightful Saga of a Mad Scientist And a Mad Sci | 0.999
LAWRENCE LOVE | A Fanciful Yarn of a Database Administrator And a   | 0.252
(2 rows)
```

Let's suppose we wish to retrieve a field only if the search terms appear in the title. For this situation we would assign 1 to the title field and 0 to all others. Example 5-54 repeats Example 5-53, passing in an array of weights.

Example 5-54. Ranking search results using custom weights

```
SELECT
    left(title,40) As title,
    ts_rank('{0,0,0,1}'::numeric[],fts,ts)::numeric(10,3) AS r,
    ts_rank_cd('{0,0,0,1}'::numeric[],fts,ts)::numeric(10,3) As rcd
FROM film, to_tsquery('english', 'love  & (wait | indian | mad )') AS ts
WHERE fts @@ ts AND title > ''
ORDER BY r DESC;

title          | r     | rcd
---------------+-------+------
INDIAN LOVE    | 0.991 | 1.000
LAWRENCE LOVE  | 0.000 | 0.000
(2 rows)
```

Notice how in Example 5-54 the second entry has a ranking of zero because the title does not contain all the words to satisfy the tsquery.

 If performance is a concern, you should explicitly declare the FTS configuration in queries instead of allowing the default behavior. As noted in Some FTS Tricks by Oleg Bartunov (*http://obartu nov.livejournal.com/189806.html*), you can achieve twice the speed by using to_tsquery('english','social & (science | scien tist)') in lieu of to_tsquery('social & (science | scien tist)').

Full Text Stripping

By default, vectorization adds markers (location of the lexemes within the vector) and optionally weights (A, B, C, D). If your searches care only whether a particular term can be found, regardless of where it is in the text, how frequently it occurs, or its prominence, you can declutter your vectors using the strip function. This saves disk space and gains some speed. Example 5-55 compares what an unstripped versus stripped vector looks like.

Example 5-55. Unstripped versus stripped vector

```
SELECT fts
FROM film
WHERE film_id = 1;

'academi':1A 'battl':15B 'canadian':20B 'dinosaur':2A 'drama':5B 'epic':4B
'feminist':8B 'mad':11B 'must':14B 'rocki':21B 'scientist':12B 'teacher':17B

SELECT strip(fts)
FROM film
WHERE film_id = 1;
```

```
'academi' 'battl' 'canadian' 'dinosaur' 'drama' 'epic' 'feminist' 'mad'
'must' 'rocki' 'scientist' 'teacher'
```

Keep in mind that although a stripped vector is faster to search and takes up less disk space, many operators and functions cannot be used in conjunction with them. For instance, because a stripped vector has no markers, distance operators cannot be used.

Full Text Support for JSON and JSONB

New in version 10 are `ts_headline` and `to_tsvector`, which take as input json and jsonb data. The functions work just like the text ones, except they consider only the values of json/jsonb data and not the keys or json markup. Example 5-56 applies the function to the json person column of the table we created in Example 5-28.

Example 5-56. Converting json/jsonb to tsvector

```
SELECT to_tsvector(person)
    FROM persons WHERE id=1;

      to_tsvector
---------------------------------------------------------------------------
 '-5083':19 '-6719':13 '-722':12 '-852':18 '619':11,17 'alex':3 'azaleah':25
 'brandon':21 'cell':15 'm':23 'ofelia':7 'rafael':5 'sonia':1 'work':9
(1 row)
```

To apply this function to the jsonb table `persons_b`, swap out the `persons` table for `persons_b`. Similar to the to_tsvector for text, these functions also have a variant that takes the FTS configuration to use as their first argument. To make best use of these functions, create a tsvector column in your table and populate the field using either a trigger or update as needed.

Also available now for json and jsonb is the `ts_headline` function, which tags as HTML all matching text in the json document. Example 5-57 flags all references to Rafael in the document.

Example 5-57. Tag matching words

```
SELECT ts_headline(person->'spouse'->'parents', 'rafael'::tsquery)
FROM persons_b WHERE id=1;

{"father": "<b>Rafael</b>", "mother": "Ofelia"}
(1 row)
```

Note the bold HTML tags around the matching value.

Custom and Composite Data Types

This section demonstrates how to define and use a custom type. The composite (aka record, row) object type is often used to build an object that is then cast to a custom type, or as a return type for functions needing to return multiple columns.

All Tables Are Custom Data Types

PostgreSQL automatically creates custom types for all tables. For all intents and purposes, you can use custom types just as you would any other built-in type. So we could conceivably create a table that has a column type that is another table's custom type, and we can go even further and make an array of that type. We demonstrate this "turducken" in Example 5-58.

Example 5-58. Turducken

```
CREATE TABLE chickens (id integer PRIMARY KEY);
CREATE TABLE ducks (id integer PRIMARY KEY, chickens chickens[]);
CREATE TABLE turkeys (id integer PRIMARY KEY, ducks ducks[]);

INSERT INTO ducks VALUES (1, ARRAY[ROW(1)::chickens, ROW(1)::chickens]);
INSERT INTO turkeys VALUES (1, array(SELECT d FROM ducks d));
```

We create an instance of a chicken without adding it to the chicken table itself; hence we're able to repeat id with impunity. We take our array of two chickens, stuff them into one duck, and add it to the ducks table. We take the duck we added and stuff it into the turkeys table.

Finally, let's see what we have in our turkey:

```
SELECT * FROM turkeys;

output
------------------------
id | ducks
---+--------------------
 1 | {"(1,\"{(1),(1)}\")"}
```

We can also replace subelements of our turducken. This next example replaces our second chicken in our first turkey with a different chicken:

```
UPDATE turkeys SET ducks[1].chickens[2] = ROW(3)::chickens
WHERE id = 1 RETURNING *;

output
------------------------
id | ducks
---+--------------------
 1 | {"(1,\"{(1),(3)}\")"}
```

We used the RETURNING clause as discussed in "Returning Affected Records to the User" on page 176 to output the changed record.

Any complex row or column, regardless of how complex, can be converted to a json or jsonb column like so:

```
SELECT id, to_jsonb(ducks) AS ducks_jsonb
FROM turkeys;

id | ducks_jsonb
---+-----------------------------------------------
 1 | [{"id": 1, "chickens": [{"id": 1}, {"id": 3}]}]
(1 row)
```

PostgreSQL internally keeps track of object dependencies. The ducks.chickens column is dependent on the chickens table. The turkeys.ducks column is dependent on the ducks table. You won't be able to drop the chickens table without specifying CASCADE or first dropping the ducks.chickens column. If you do a CASCADE, the ducks.chickens column will be gone, and without warning, your turkeys will have no chickens in their ducks.

Building Custom Data Types

Although you can easily create composite types just by creating a table, at some point, you'll probably want to build your own from scratch. For example, let's build a complex number data type with the following statement:

```
CREATE TYPE complex_number AS (r double precision, i double precision);
```

We can then use this complex number as a column type:

```
CREATE TABLE circuits (circuit_id serial PRIMARY KEY, ac_volt complex_number);
```

We can then query our table with statements such as:

```
SELECT circuit_id, (ac_volt).* FROM circuits;
```

or an equivalent:

```
SELECT circuit_id, (ac_volt).r, (ac_volt).i FROM circuits;
```

 Puzzled by the parentheses surrounding ac_volt? If you leave them out, PostgreSQL will raise the error missing FROM-clause entry for table "ac_volt" because it assumes ac_volt without parentheses refers to a table.

Composites and NULLs

NULL is a confusing concept in the ANSI SQL Standard, primarily because NULL != NULL. When working with NULLs, instead, you need to use IS NULL, IS NOT NULL, or NOT (`somevalue IS NULL`). With noncomposite types, `something IS NULL` is generally the antithesis to `something IS NOT NULL`. This is not the case with composites, however.

PostgreSQL abides by the ANSI SQL standard specs when dealing with NULLs. The specs require that in order for a composite to be IS NULL, all elements of the composite must be NULL. Here is where confusion can enter. In order for a composite to be considered IS NOT NULL, *every* element in the composite must return true for IS NOT NULL.

Building Operators and Functions for Custom Types

After you build a custom type such as a complex number, naturally you'll want to create functions and operators for it. We'll demonstrate building a + operator for the `complex_number` we created. For more details about building functions, see Chapter 8. As stated earlier, an operator is a symbol alias for a function that takes one or two arguments. You can find more details about what symbols and sets of symbols are allowed in CREATE OPERATOR (*http://www.postgresql.org/docs/current/interactive/sql-createoperator.html*).

In addition to being an alias, an operator contains optimization information that can be used by the query optimizer to decide how indexes should be used, how best to navigate the data, and which operator expressions are equivalent. More details about these optimizations and how each can help the optimizer are in Operator Optimization (*http://bit.ly/1vXzPek*).

The first step to creating an operator is to create a function, as shown in Example 5-59.

Example 5-59. Add function for complex number

```
CREATE OR REPLACE FUNCTION add(complex_number, complex_number)
RETURNS complex_number AS
$$
    SELECT
        ((COALESCE(($1).r,0) + COALESCE(($2).r,0)),
        (COALESCE(($1).i,0) + COALESCE(($2).i,0)))::complex_number;
$$
language sql;
```

The next step is to create a symbolic operator to wrap the function, as in Example 5-60.

Example 5-60. + operator for complex number

```
CREATE OPERATOR + (
    PROCEDURE = add,
    LEFTARG = complex_number,
    RIGHTARG = complex_number,
    COMMUTATOR = +
);
```

We can then test our new + operator:

```
SELECT (1,2)::complex_number + (3,-10)::complex_number;
```

which outputs (4,-8).

Although we didn't demonstrate it here, you can overload functions and operators to take different types as inputs. For example, you can create an add function and companion + operator that takes a complex_number and an integer.

The ability to build custom types and operators pushes PostgreSQL to the boundary of a full-fledged development environment, bringing us ever closer to our utopia where everything is table-driven.

## CHAPTER 6

Tables, Constraints, and Indexes

Tables constitute the building blocks of relational database storage. Structuring tables so that they form meaningful relationships is the key to relational database design. In PostgreSQL, constraints enforce relationships between tables. To distinguish a table from just a heap of data, we establish indexes. Much like the indexes you find at the end of books or the tenant list at the entrances to grand office buildings, indexes point to locations in the table so you don't have to scour the table from top to bottom every time you're looking for something.

In this chapter, we introduce syntax for creating tables and adding rows. We then move on to constraints to ensure that your data doesn't get out of line. Finally, we show you how to add indexes to your tables to expedite searches.

Indexing a table is as much a programming task as it is an experimental endeavor. A misappropriated index is worse than useless. Not all indexes are created equal. Algorithmists have devised different kinds of indexes for different data types and different query types, all in an attempt to scrape that last morsel of speed from a query.

Tables

In addition to ordinary data tables, PostgreSQL offers several kinds of tables that are rather uncommon: temporary, unlogged, inherited, typed, and foreign (covered in Chapter 10).

Basic Table Creation

Example 6-1 shows the table creation syntax, which is similar to what you'll find in all SQL databases.

Example 6-1. Basic table creation

```
CREATE TABLE logs (
log_id serial PRIMARY KEY, ❶
user_name varchar(50), ❷
description text, ❸
log_ts timestamp with time zone NOT NULL DEFAULT current_timestamp
); ❹
CREATE INDEX idx_logs_log_ts ON logs USING btree (log_ts);
```

❶ `serial` is the data type used to represent an incrementing autonumber. Adding a serial column automatically adds an accompanying sequence object to the database schema. A serial data type is always an integer with the default value set to the next value of the sequence object. Each table usually has just one serial column, which often serves as the primary key. For very large tables, you should opt for the related `bigserial`.

❷ `varchar` is shorthand for "character varying," a variable-length string similar to what you will find in other databases. You don't need to specify a maximum length; if you don't, `varchar` will be almost identical to the text data type.

❸ `text` is a string of indeterminate length. It's never followed by a length restriction.

❹ `timestamp with time zone` (shorthand `timestamptz`) is a date and time data type, always stored in UTC. It displays date and time in the server's own time zone unless you tell it to otherwise. See "Time Zones: What They Are and Are Not" on page 107 for a more thorough discussion.

New in version 10 is the IDENTITY qualifier for a column. IDENTITY is a more standard-compliant way of generating an autonumber for a table column.

You could turn the existing log_id column to the new IDENTITY construct using a sequence object:

```
DROP SEQUENCE logs_log_id_seq CASCADE;
ALTER TABLE logs
    ALTER COLUMN log_id ADD GENERATED BY DEFAULT AS IDENTITY;
```

If we already had data in the table, we'd need to prevent the numbering from starting at 1 with a statement like this:

```
ALTER TABLE logs
    ALTER COLUMN log_id RESTART WITH 2000;
```

If we were starting with a new table, we'd create it as shown in Example 6-2 using IDENTITY instead of serial.

Example 6-2. Basic table creation using IDENTITY

```
CREATE TABLE logs (
log_id int GENERATED BY DEFAULT AS IDENTITY PRIMARY KEY,
user_name varchar(50),
description text,
log_ts timestamp with time zone NOT NULL DEFAULT current_timestamp
);
```

The structure of Example 6-2 is much the same as what we saw in Example 6-1 but more verbose.

Under what cases would you prefer to use IDENTITY over serial? The main benefit of the IDENTITY construct is that an identity is always tied to a specific table, so incrementing and resetting the value is managed with the table. A serial, on the other hand, creates a sequence object that may or may not be reused by other tables and needs to be dropped manually when it's no longer needed. If you wanted to reset the number of a serial, you'd need to modify the related SEQUENCE object, which means knowing what the name of it is.

The serial approach is still useful if you need to reuse an autonumber generator across many tables. In that case, though, you'd create the sequence object separate from the table and set the table column default to the next value of the sequence. Internally, the new IDENTITY construct behaves much the same by creating behind the scenes a sequence object, but preventing that sequence object from being edited directly.

Inherited Tables

PostgreSQL stands alone as the only database product offering inherited tables. When you specify that a table (the child table) inherits from another table (the parent table), PostgreSQL creates the child table with its own columns plus all the columns of the parent table. PostgreSQL will remember this parent-child relationship so that any subsequent structural changes to the parent automatically propagate to its children. Parent-child table design is perfect for partitioning your data. When you query the parent table, PostgreSQL automatically includes all rows in the child tables. Not every trait of the parent passes down to the child. Notably, primary key constraints, foreign key constraints, uniqueness constraints, and indexes are never inherited. Check constraints are inherited, but children can have their own check constraints in addition to the ones they inherit from their parents (see Example 6-3).

Example 6-3. Inherited table creation

```
CREATE TABLE logs_2011 (PRIMARY KEY (log_id)) INHERITS (logs);
CREATE INDEX idx_logs_2011_log_ts ON logs_2011 USING btree(log_ts);
ALTER TABLE logs_2011
    ADD CONSTRAINT chk_y2011
```

```
CHECK (
    log_ts >= '2011-1-1'::timestamptz AND log_ts < '2012-1-1'::timestamptz
); ❶
```

❶ We define a check constraint to limit data to the year 2011. Having the check
constraint in place allows the query planner to skip inherited tables that do not
satisfy the query condition.

A new feature in PostgreSQL 9.5 is inheritance between local and foreign tables: each
type can now inherit from the other. This is all in pursuit of making sharding easier.

Partitioned Tables

New in version 10 are partitioned tables. Partitioned tables are much like inherited
tables in that they allow partitioning of data across many tables and the planner can
conditionally skip tables that don't satisfy a query condition. Internally they are
implemented much the same, but use a different DDL syntax.

Although partitioned tables replace the functionality of inherited tables in many
cases, they are not complete replacements. Here are some key differences between
inherited tables and partition tables:

- A partitioned table group is created using the declarative partition syntax CREATE
  TABLE .. PARTITION BY RANGE ...

- When partitions are used, data can be inserted into the core table and is rerouted
  automatically to the matching partition. This is not the case with inherited tables,
  where you either need to insert data into the child table, or have a trigger that
  reroutes data to the child tables.

- All tables in a partition must have the same exact columns. This is unlike inherited tables, where child tables are allowed to have additional columns that are not
  in the parent tables.

- Each partitioned table belongs to a single partitioned group. Internally that
  means it can have only one parent table. Inherited tables, on other hand, can
  inherit columns from multiple tables.

- The parent of the partition can't have primary keys, unique keys, or indexes,
  although the child partitions can. This is different from the inheritance tables,
  where the parent and each child can have a primary key that needs only to be
  unique within the table, not necessarily across all the inherited children.

- Unlike inherited tables, the parent partitioned table can't have any rows of its
  own. All inserts are redirected to a matching child partition and when no matching child partition is available, an error is thrown.

We'll re-create the logs table from Example 6-1 as a partitioned table and create the child tables using partition syntax instead of the inheritance shown in Example 6-3.

First, we'll drop our existing logs table and all its child tables:

```
DROP TABLE IF EXISTS logs CASCADE;
```

For a partitioned table set, the parent table must be noted as a partitioned table through the PARTITION BY syntax, as shown in Example 6-4. Contrast that to Example 6-1 where we just start with a regular table definition. Also note that we do not define a primary key because primary keys are not supported for the parent partition table.

Example 6-4. Basic table creation for partition

```
CREATE TABLE logs (
log_id int GENERATED BY DEFAULT AS IDENTITY,
user_name varchar(50),
description text,
log_ts timestamp with time zone NOT NULL DEFAULT current_timestamp
) PARTITION BY RANGE (log_ts);
```

Similar to inheritance, we create child tables of the partition, except instead of using CHECK constraints to denote allowed data in the child table, we use the FOR VALUES FROM DDL construct. We repeat the exercise from Example 6-3 in Example 6-5 but using the FOR VALUES FROM construct instead of INHERITS.

Example 6-5. Create a child partition

```
CREATE TABLE logs_2011 PARTITION OF logs ❶
FOR VALUES FROM ('2011-1-1') TO ('2012-1-1') ❷;
CREATE INDEX idx_logs_2011_log_ts ON logs_2011 USING btree(log_ts); ❸
ALTER TABLE logs_2011 ADD CONSTRAINT pk_logs_2011  PRIMARY KEY (log_id) ❹;
```

❶ Define the new table as a partition of logs.

❷ Define the set of data to be stored in this partition. Child partitions must not have overlapping ranges, so if you try to define a range that overlaps an existing range, the CREATE TABLE command will fail with an error.

❸❹ Child partitions can have indexes and primary keys. As with inheritance, the primary key is not enforced across the whole partition set of tables.

Now if we were to insert data as follows:

```
INSERT INTO logs(user_name, description ) VALUES ('regina', 'Sleeping');
```

We'd get an error such as:

```
ERROR:  no partition of relation "logs" found for row
DETAIL:  Partition key of the failing row contains
(log_ts) = (2017-05-25 02:58:28.057101-04).
```

If we then create a partition table for the current year:

```
CREATE TABLE logs_gt_2011 PARTITION OF logs
FOR VALUES FROM ('2012-1-1') TO (unbounded);
```

Unlike Example 6-5, we opted to use the PARTITION range keyword unbounded, which allows our partition to be used for future dates.

Repeating our insert now, we can see by SELECT * FROM logs_gt_2011; that our data got rerouted to the new partition.

In the real world, you would need to create indexes and primary keys on the new child for query efficiency.

Similar to the way inheritance works, when we query the parent table, all partitions that don't satisfy the date filter are skipped, as shown in Example 6-6.

Example 6-6. Planner skipping other partitions

```
EXPLAIN ANALYZE SELECT * FROM logs WHERE log_ts > '2017-05-01';

Append  (cost=0.00..15.25 rows=140 width=162)
(actual time=0.008..0.009 rows=1 loops=1)
  -> Seq Scan on logs_gt_2011  (cost=0.00..15.25 rows=140 width=162)
(actual time=0.008..0.008 rows=1 loops=1)
        Filter: (log_ts > '2017-05-01 00:00:00-04'::timestamp with time zone)
Planning time: 0.152 ms
Execution time: 0.022 ms
```

If you are using the PSQL packaged with PostgreSQL 10, you will get more information when you use the describe table command that details the partition ranges of the parent table:

```
\d+ logs

Table "public.logs"
:
Partition key: RANGE (log_ts)
Partitions: logs_2011
    FOR VALUES FROM ('2011-01-01 00:00:00-05') TO ('2012-01-01 00:00:00-05'),
            logs_gt_2011
            FOR VALUES FROM ('2012-01-01 00:00:00-05') TO (UNBOUNDED)
```

Unlogged Tables

For ephemeral data that could be rebuilt in the event of a disk failure or doesn't need to be restored after a crash, you might prefer having more speed than redundancy.

The UNLOGGED modifier allows you to create unlogged tables, as shown in Example 6-7. These tables will not be part of any write-ahead logs. The big advantage of an unlogged table is that writing data to it is much faster than to a logged table— 10–15 times faster in our experience.

If you accidentally unplug the power cord on the server and then turn the power back on, the rollback process will wipe clean all data in unlogged tables. Another consequence of making a table unlogged is that its data won't be able to participate in PostgreSQL replication. A pg_dump option also allows you to skip the backing up of unlogged data.

Example 6-7. Unlogged table creation

```
CREATE UNLOGGED TABLE web_sessions (
        session_id text PRIMARY KEY,
        add_ts timestamptz,
        upd_ts timestamptz,
        session_state xml);
```

There are a few other sacrifices you have to make with unlogged tables. Prior to PostgreSQL 9.3, unlogged tables didn't support GiST indexes (see "PostgreSQL Stock Indexes" on page 157), which are commonly used for more advanced data types such as arrays, ranges, json, full text, and spatial. Unlogged tables in any version will accommodate the common B-Tree and GIN indexes.

Prior to PostgreSQL 9.5, you couldn't easily convert an UNLOGGED table to a logged one. To do so in version 9.5+, enter:

```
ALTER TABLE some_table SET LOGGED;
```

TYPE OF

PostgreSQL automatically creates a corresponding composite data type in the background whenever you create a new table. The reverse is not true. But you can use a composite data type as a template for creating tables. We'll demonstrate this by first creating a type with the definition:

```
CREATE TYPE basic_user AS (user_name varchar(50), pwd varchar(10));
```

We can then create a table with rows that are instances of this type as shown in Example 6-8.

Example 6-8. Using TYPE to define a new table structure

```
CREATE TABLE super_users OF basic_user (CONSTRAINT pk_su PRIMARY KEY (user_name));
```

After creating tables from data types, you can't alter the columns of the table. Instead, add or remove columns to the composite data type, and PostgreSQL will automatically propagate the changes to the table structure. Much like inheritance, the advantage of this approach is that if you have many tables sharing the same underlying structure and you need to make a universal alteration, you can do so by simply changing the underlying composite type.

Let's say we now need to add a phone number to our `super_users` table from Example 6-8. All we have to do is execute the following command:

```
ALTER TYPE basic_user ADD ATTRIBUTE phone varchar(10) CASCADE;
```

Normally, you can't change the definition of a type if tables depend on that type. The CASCADE modifier overrides this restriction, applying the same change to all dependent tables.

Constraints

PostgreSQL constraints are the most advanced (and most complex) of any database we've worked with. You can control all facets of how a constraint handles existing data, all cascade options, how to perform the matching, which indexes to incorporate, conditions under which the constraint can be violated, and more. On top of it all, you can pick your own name for each constraint. For the full treatment, we suggest you review the official documentation (*http://bit.ly/1q2fBPG*). You'll find comfort in knowing that using the default settings usually works out fine. We'll start off with something familiar to most relational folks: foreign key, unique, and check constraints. Then we'll move on to exclusion constraints.

 Names of primary key and unique key constraints must be unique within a given schema. A good practice is to include the name of the table and column as part of the name of the key. For the sake of brevity, our examples might not abide by this practice.

Foreign Key Constraints

PostgreSQL follows the same convention as most databases that support referential integrity. You can specify cascade update and delete rules to avoid pesky orphaned records. We show you how to add foreign key constraints in Example 6-9.

Example 6-9. Building foreign key constraints and covering indexes

```
SET search_path=census, public;
ALTER TABLE facts ADD CONSTRAINT fk_facts_1 FOREIGN KEY (fact_type_id)
REFERENCES lu_fact_types (fact_type_id) ❶ON UPDATE CASCADE ON DELETE RESTRICT;
```

```
CREATE INDEX fki_facts_1 ON facts (fact_type_id); ❸
```

❶ We define a foreign key relationship between our facts and fact_types tables. This prevents us from introducing fact types into facts tables unless they are already present in the fact_types lookup table.

❷ We add a cascade rule that automatically updates the fact_type_id in our facts table should we renumber our fact types. We restrict deletes from our lookup table so fact types in use cannot be removed. RESTRICT is the default behavior, but we suggest stating it for clarity.

❸ Unlike for primary key and unique constraints, PostgreSQL doesn't automatically create an index for foreign key constraints; you should add this yourself to speed up queries.

Foreign key constraints are important for data integrity. Newer versions of PostgreSQL can also use them to improve the planner's thinking. In version 9.6, the planner was revised to use foreign key relationships to infer selectivity for join predicates, thus improving many types of queries.

Unique Constraints

Each table can have no more than a single primary key. If you need to enforce uniqueness on other columns, you must resort to unique constraints or unique indexes. Adding a unique constraint automatically creates an associated unique index. Similar to primary keys, unique key constraints can participate as the foreign key in foreign key constraints, but can have null values. A unique index without a unique key constraint can also have null values and in addition can use functions in its definition. The following example shows how to add a unique key:

```
ALTER TABLE logs_2011 ADD CONSTRAINT uq UNIQUE (user_name,log_ts);
```

Often you'll find yourself needing to ensure uniqueness for only a subset of your rows. PostgreSQL does not offer conditional unique constraints, but you can achieve the same effect by using a partial uniqueness index. See "Partial Indexes" on page 162.

Check Constraints

Check constraints are conditions that must be met for a field or a set of fields for each row. The query planner takes advantage of check constraints by skipping tables that don't meet the check constraints outright. We saw an example of a check constraint in Example 6-3. That particular example prevents the planner from having to scan rows failing to satisfy the date range specified in a query. You can exercise some creativity in your check constraints, because you can use functions and Boolean expressions to build complicated matching conditions. For example, the following constraint requires all usernames in the logs tables to be lowercase:

```
ALTER TABLE logs ADD CONSTRAINT chk CHECK (user_name = lower(user_name));
```

The other noteworthy aspect of check constraints is that unlike primary key, foreign key, and unique key constraints, they inherit from parent tables.

Exclusion Constraints

Exclusion constraints allow you to incorporate additional operators to enforce uniqueness that can't be satisfied by the equality operator. Exclusion constraints are especially useful in problems involving scheduling.

PostgreSQL 9.2 introduced the range data types that are perfect candidates for exclusion constraints. You'll find a fine example of using exclusion constraints for range data types at Waiting for 9.2 Range Data Types (*http://bit.ly/1z3emS1*).

Exclusion constraints are generally enforced using GiST indexes, but you can create compound indexes that incorporate B-Tree as well. Before you do this, you need to install the btree_gist extension. A classic use of a compound exclusion constraint is for scheduling resources.

Here's an example using exclusion constraints. Suppose you have a fixed number of conference rooms in your office, and groups must book them in advance. See how we'd prevent double-booking in Example 6-10, and how we are able to use the overlap operator (&&) for our temporal comparison and the usual equality operator for the room number.

Example 6-10. Prevent overlapping bookings for the same room

```
CREATE TABLE schedules(id serial primary key, room int, time_slot tstzrange);
ALTER TABLE schedules ADD CONSTRAINT ex_schedules
EXCLUDE USING gist (room WITH =, time_slot WITH &&);
```

Just as with uniqueness constraints, PostgreSQL automatically creates a corresponding index of the type specified in the constraint declaration.

Arrays are another popular type where EXCLUSION constraints come in handy. Let's suppose you have a set of rooms that you need to assign to a group of people. We'll call these room "blocks." For expediency, you decide to store one record per party, but you want to ensure that two parties are never given the same room. So you set up a table as follows:

```
CREATE TABLE room_blocks(block_id integer primary key, rooms int[]);
```

To ensure that no two blocks have a room in common, you can set up an exclusion constraint preventing blocks from overlapping (two blocks having the same room).

Exclusion constraints unfortunately work only with GiST indexes, and because GIST indexes don't exist for arrays out of the box, you need to install an additional extension before you can do this, as shown in Example 6-11.

Example 6-11. Prevent overlapping array blocks

```
CREATE EXTENSION IF NOT EXISTS intarray;
ALTER TABLE room_blocks
 ADD CONSTRAINT ex_room_blocks_rooms
 EXCLUDE USING gist(rooms WITH &&);
```

The intarray extension provides GiST index support for integer arrays (int4, int8). After intarray is installed, you can then use GiST with arrays and create exclusion constraints on integer arrays.

Indexes

PostgreSQL comes with a lavish framework for creating and fine-tuning indexes. The art of PostgreSQL indexing could fill a tome all by itself. PostgreSQL is packaged with several types of indexes. If you find these inadequate, you can define new index operators and modifiers to supplement. If still unsatisfied, you're free to invent your own index type.

PostgreSQL also allows you to mix and match different index types in the same table with the expectation that the planner will consider them all. For instance, one column could use a B-Tree index while an adjacent column uses a GiST index, with both indexes contributing to speed up the queries. To delve more into the mechanics of how the planner takes advantage of indexes, visit Bitmap Index Scan Strategy (*http://bit.ly/1vUs2fU*).

You can create indexes on tables (with the exception of foreign tables) as well as materialized views.

Index names must be unique within a given schema.

PostgreSQL Stock Indexes

To take full advantage of all that PostgreSQL has to offer, you'll want to understand the various types of indexes and situations where they will aid or harm. Following is a list of stock indexes:

B-Tree

B-Tree is a general-purpose index common in relational databases. You can usually get by with B-Tree alone if you don't want to experiment with additional index types. If PostgreSQL automatically creates an index for you or you don't bother specifying the index method, B-Tree will be chosen. It is currently the only indexing method for primary keys and unique keys.

BRIN

Block range index (BRIN) is an index type introduced in PostgreSQL 9.4. It's designed specifically for very large tables where using an index such as B-Tree would take up too much space and not fit in memory. The approach of BRIN is to treat a range of pages as one unit. BRIN indexes are much smaller than B-Tree and other indexes and faster to build. But they are slower to use and can't be used for primary keys or certain other situations.

GiST

Generalized Search Tree (GiST) is an index optimized for FTS, spatial data, scientific data, unstructured data, and hierarchical data. Although you can't use it to enforce uniqueness, you can create the same effect by using it in an exclusion constraint.

GiST is a lossy index, in the sense that the index itself will not store the value of what it's indexing, but merely a bounding value such as a box for a polygon. This creates the need for an extra lookup step if you need to retrieve the value or do a more fine-tuned check.

GIN

Generalized Inverted Index (GIN) is geared toward the built-in full text search (*http://bit.ly/1vwG2ht*) and binary json data type of PostgreSQL. Many other extensions, such as hstore and pg_trgm, also utilize it. GIN is a descendent of GiST but without the lossiness. GIN will clone the values in the columns that are part of the index. If you ever need a query limited to covered columns, GIN is faster than GiST. However, the extra replication required by GIN means the index is larger and updating the index is slower than a comparable GiST index. Also, because each index row is limited to a certain size, you can't use GIN to index large objects such as large hstore documents or text. If there is a possibility you'll be inserting a 600-page manual into a field of a table, don't use GIN to index that column.

You can find a wonderful example of GIN in Waiting for Faster LIKE/ILIKE (*http://bit.ly/1FUiaW9*). As of version 9.3, you can index regular expressions that leverage the GIN-based pg_trgm extension (*http://bit.ly/1vnL7DJ*).

SP-GiST

Space-Partitioned Generalized Search Tree (*http://bit.ly/1vXAtIK*) (SP-GiST) can be used in the same situations as GiST but can be faster for certain kinds of data distribution. PostgreSQL's native geometric data types, such as point and box, and the text data type, were the first to support SP-GiST. In version 9.3, support extended to range types.

hash

Hash indexes were popular prior to the advent of GiST and GIN. General consensus rates GiST and GIN above hash in terms of both performance and transaction safety. The write-ahead log prior to PostgreSQL 10 did not track hash indexes; therefore, you couldn't use them in streaming replication setups. Although hash indexes were relegated to legacy status for some time, they got some love in PostgreSQL 10. In that version, they gained transactional safety and some performance improvements that made them more efficient than B-Tree in some cases.

B-Tree-GiST/B-Tree-GIN

If you want to explore indexes beyond what PostgreSQL installs by default, either out of need or curiosity, start with the composite B-Tree-GiST or B-Tree-GIN indexes, both available as extensions and included with most PostgreSQL distributions.

These hybrids support the specialized operators of GiST or GIN, but also offer indexability of the equality operator like B-Tree indexes. You'll find them indispensable when you want to create a compound index comprised of multiple columns containing both simple and complex types. For example, you can have a compound index that consists of a column of plain text and a column of full text. Normally complex types such as full-text, ltree, geometric, and spatial types can use only GIN or GiST indexes, and thus can never be combined with simpler types that can only use B-Tree. These combo methods allow you to combine columns indexed with GIST with columns indexed with B-Tree in a single index.

Although not packaged with PostgreSQL, other indexes can be found in extensions for PostgreSQL. Most popular others are the VODKA (*https://www.pgcon.org/2014/schedule/attachments/318_pgcon-2014-vodka.pdf*) and RUM (*https://github.com/postgrespro/rum*) (a variant based on GIN) index method types, which will work with PostgreSQL 9.6 and up. RUM is most suited for work with complex types such as fulltext and is required if you need index support for full-text phrase searches. It also offers additional distance operators.

Another recent addition is pgroonga (*http://pgroonga.github.io*), a PostgreSQL extension currently supported for PostgreSQL 9.5 and 9.6. It brings the power of the groonga (*http://groonga.org/*) full-text engine and column store to PostgreSQL. PGRoonga includes with it an index called *pgroonga* and companion operators.

PGRoonga supports indexing of regular text to produce full-text like functionality without needing to have a full-text vector, as the built-in PostgreSQL FTS requires. PGRoonga also makes ILIKE and LIKE '%something%' indexable similar to the pg_trgm (*http://www.postgresonline.com/journal/archives/212-PostgreSQL-9.1-Trigrams-teaching-LIKE-and-ILIKE-new-tricks.html*) extension. In addition, it supports indexing of text arrays and JSONB. There are binaries available for Linux/Mac and Windows.

Operator Classes

Most of you will skate through your index-capades without ever needing to know what operator classes (*opclasses* for short) are and why they matter for indexes. But if you falter, you'll need to understand opclasses to troubleshoot the perennial question, "Why is the planner not taking advantage of my index?"

Index architects intend for their indexes to work only against certain data types and with specific comparison operators. An expert in indexing ranges could obsess over the overlap operator (&&), whereas an expert in indexing text searches may find little meaning in an overlap. A linguist trying to index logographic languages, such as Chinese, probably has little use for inequalities, whereas a linguist trying to index alphabetic languages would find A-to-Z sorting indispensable.

PostgreSQL groups operators into operator classes. For example, the int4_ops operator class includes the operators = < > > < to be applied against the data type of int4 (commonly known as an integer). The pg_opclass system table provides a complete listing of available operator classes, both from your original install and from extensions. A particular index will work only against a given set of opclasses. To see this complete list, you can either open up pgAdmin and look under operator classes, or execute the query in Example 6-12 to get a comprehensive view.

Example 6-12. Which data types and operator classes does B-Tree support?

```
SELECT am.amname AS index_method, opc.opcname AS opclass_name,
opc.opcintype::regtype AS indexed_type, opc.opcdefault AS is_default
FROM pg_am am INNER JOIN pg_opclass opc ON opc.opcmethod = am.oid
WHERE am.amname = 'btree'
ORDER BY index_method, indexed_type, opclass_name;

index_method | opclass_name        | indexed_type | is_default
-------------+---------------------+--------------+-----------
btree        | bool_ops            | boolean      | t
:
btree        | text_ops            | text         | t
btree        | text_pattern_ops    | text         | f
btree        | varchar_ops         | text         | f
btree        | varchar_pattern_ops | text         | f
  :
```

In Example 6-12, we limit our result to B-Tree. Notice that one opclass per indexed data type is marked as the default. When you create an index without specifying the opclass, PostgreSQL chooses the default opclass for the index. Generally, this is good enough, but not always.

For instance, B-Tree against `text_ops` (aka `varchar_ops`) doesn't include the `~~` operator (the `LIKE` operator), so none of your `LIKE` searches can use an index in the `text_ops` opclass. If you plan on doing many wildcard searches on `varchar` or `text` columns, you'd be better off explicitly choosing the `text_pattern_ops`/`varchar_pat tern_ops` opclass for your index. To specify the opclass, just append the opclass after the column name, as in:

```
CREATE INDEX idx1 ON census.lu_tracts USING btree (tract_name text_pattern_ops);
```

 You will notice that the list contains both `varchar_ops` and `text_ops`, but they map only to `text`. `character varying` doesn't have B-Tree operators of its own, because it is essentially text with a length constraint. `varchar_ops` and `varchar_pattern_ops` are just aliases for `text_ops` and `text_pattern_ops` to satisfy the desire of some to maintain this symmetry of opclasses starting with the name of the type they support.

Finally, remember that each index you create works against only a single opclass. If you would like an index on a column to cover multiple opclasses, you must create separate indexes. To add the default index `text_ops` to a table, run:

```
CREATE INDEX idx2 ON census.lu_tracts USING btree (tract_name);
```

Now you have two indexes against the same column. (There's no limit to the number of indexes you can build against a single column.) The planner will choose `idx2` for basic equality queries and `idx1` for comparisons using LIKE.

You'll find operator classes detailed in the Operator Classes (*http://bit.ly/1yx8sZs*) section of the official documentation. We also strongly recommend that you read our article for tips on troubleshooting index issues, Why is My Index Not Used? (*http://bit.ly/1FZVSnP*)

Functional Indexes

PostgreSQL lets you add indexes to functions of columns. Functional indexes prove their usefulness in mixed-case textual data. PostgreSQL is a case-sensitive database. To perform a case-insensitive search you could create a functional index:

```
CREATE INDEX idx ON featnames_short
USING btree (upper(fullname) varchar_pattern_ops);
```

This next example uses the same function to uppercase the fullname column before comparing. Since we created the index with the same upper(fullname) expression, the planner will be able to use the index for this query:

```
SELECT fullname FROM featnames_short WHERE upper(fullname) LIKE 'S%';
```

 Always use the same functional expression when querying to ensure use of the index.

Partial Indexes

Partial indexes (sometimes called filtered indexes) are indexes that cover only rows fitting a predefined WHERE condition. For instance, if you have a table of 1,000,000 rows, but you care about a fixed set of 10,000, you're better off creating partial indexes. The resulting indexes can be faster because more can fit into RAM, plus you'll save a bit of disk space on the index itself.

Partial indexes let you place uniqueness constraints only on some rows of the data. Pretend that you manage newspaper subscribers who signed up in the past 10 years and want to ensure that nobody is getting more than one paper delivered per day. With dwindling interest in print media, only about 5% of your subscribers have a current subscription. You don't care about subscribers being duplicated who have stopped getting newspapers, because they're not on the carriers' list anyway. Your table looks like this:

```
CREATE TABLE subscribers (
    id serial PRIMARY KEY,
    name varchar(50) NOT NULL, type varchar(50),
    is_active boolean);
```

We add a partial index to guarantee uniqueness only for current subscribers:

```
CREATE UNIQUE INDEX uq ON subscribers USING btree(lower(name)) WHERE is_active;
```

 Functions used in the index's WHERE condition must be immutable. This means you can't use time functions like CURRENT_DATE or data from other tables (or other rows of the indexed table) to determine whether a record should be indexed.

One warning we stress is that when you query the data, in order for the index to be considered by the planner, the conditions used when creating the index must be a part of your WHERE condition and any functions used in the index must also be used in the query filter. This index is both PARTIAL and functional because what it indexes is upper(name) (not name). An easy way to not have to worry about this is to use a view. Back to our subscribers example, create a view as follows:

```
CREATE OR REPLACE VIEW vw_subscribers_current AS
SELECT id, lower(name) As name FROM subscribers WHERE is_active = true;
```

Then always query the view instead of the table (many purists advocate never querying tables directly anyway). A view is a saved query that is transparent to the planner. Any query done on a view will include the view's WHERE conditions and functional additions as well as what other additions the query adds. The view we created does two things to make indexes available to queries. The view replaces the name column with lower(name), so that when we do a query against name with the view, it's shorthand for lower(name) against the underlying table. The view also enables is_active = true, which means any query against the view will automatically have that condition in it and be able to use the PARTIAL index:

```
SELECT * FROM vw_subscribers_current WHERE name = 'sandy';
```

You can open up the planner and confirm that the planner indeed used your index.

Multicolumn Indexes

You've already seen many examples of multicolumn (aka compound) indexes in this chapter, but you can also create functional indexes using more than one underlying column. Here is an example of a multicolumn index:

```
CREATE INDEX idx ON subscribers
USING btree (type, upper(name) varchar_pattern_ops);
```

The PostgreSQL planner uses a strategy called *bitmap index scan* that automatically tries to combine indexes on the fly, often from single-column indexes, to achieve the same goal as a multicolumn index. If you're unable to predict how you'll be querying compound fields in the future, you may be better off creating single-column indexes and let the planner decide how to combine them during search.

If you have a multicolumn B-Tree index on type and upper(name), there is no need for an index on just type, because the planner can still use the compound index for cases in which you just need to filter by type. Although the planner can use the index even if the columns you are querying are not the first in the index, querying by the first column in an index is much more efficient than querying by just secondary columns.

The planner can also employ a strategy called an *index-only* scan, which enables the planner to use just the index and not the table if the index contains all the columns needed to satisfy a query. So if you commonly filter by the same set of fields and output those, a compound index can improve speed since it can skip the table. Keep in mind that the more columns you have in an index, the fatter your index and the less of it that can easily fit in RAM. Don't go overboard with compound indexes.

## CHAPTER 7

SQL: The PostgreSQL Way

PostgreSQL surpasses other database products in ANSI SQL compliance. It cements its lead by adding constructs that range from convenient syntax shorthands to avant-garde features that break the bounds of traditional SQL. In this chapter, we'll cover some SQL tidbits not often found in other databases. For this chapter, you should have a working knowledge of SQL; otherwise, you may not appreciate the labor-saving *amuse-bouche* that PostgreSQL brings to the table.

Views

Well-designed relational databases store data in normalized form. To access this data across scattered tables, you write queries to join underlying tables. When you find yourself writing the same query over and over again, create a view. Simply put, a view is nothing more than a query permanently stored in the database.

Some purists have argued that one should always query a view, never tables. This means you must create a view for every table that you intend to query directly. The added layer of indirection eases management of permissions and facilitates abstraction of table data. We find this to be sound advice, but laziness gets the better of us.

Views in PostgreSQL have evolved over the years. Version 9.3 unveiled automatically updatable views. If your view draws from a single table and you include the primary key as an output column, you can issue an update command directly against your view. Data in the underlying table will follow suit.

Version 9.3 also introduced materialized views. When you mark a view as materialized, it will requery the data only when you issue the REFRESH command. The upside is that you're not wasting resources running complex queries repeatedly; the downside is that you might not have the most up-to-date data when you use the view.

Furthermore, under some circumstances you are barred from access to the view during a refresh.

Version 9.4 allows users to access materialized views during refreshes. It also introduced the WITH CHECK OPTION modifier, which prevents inserts and updates outside the scope of the view.

Single Table Views

The simplest view draws from a single table. Always include the primary key if you intend to write data back to the table, as shown in Example 7-1.

Example 7-1. Single table view

```
CREATE OR REPLACE VIEW census.vw_facts_2011 AS
SELECT fact_type_id, val, yr, tract_id FROM census.facts WHERE yr = 2011;
```

As of version 9.3, you can alter the data in this view by using INSERT, UPDATE, or DELETE commands. Updates and deletes will abide by any WHERE condition you have as part of your view. For example, the following query will delete only records whose value is 0:

```
DELETE FROM census.vw_facts_2011 WHERE val = 0;
```

And the following will not update any records, because the view explicitly includes only records for 2011:

```
UPDATE census.vw_facts_2011 SET val = 1 WHERE yr = 2012;
```

Be aware that you can insert data that places it outside of the view's WHERE or update data so it is no longer visible from the view as shown in Example 7-2.

Example 7-2. View update that results in data no longer visible in view

```
UPDATE census.vw_facts_2011 SET yr = 2012 WHERE yr = 2011;
```

The update of Example 7-2 does not violate the WHERE condition. But, once executed, you would have emptied your view. For the sake of sanity, you may find it desirable to prevent updates or inserts that leave data invisible to further queries. Version 9.4 introduced the WITH CHECK OPTION to accomplish this. Include this modifier when creating the view and PostgreSQL will forever balk at any attempts to add records outside the view and to update records that will put them outside the view. In our example view, our goal is to limit vw_facts_2011 to allow inserts only of 2011 data and disallow updates of the yr to something other than 2011. To add this restriction, we revise our view definition as shown in Example 7-3.

Example 7-3. Single table view WITH CHECK OPTION

```
CREATE OR REPLACE VIEW census.vw_facts_2011 AS
SELECT fact_type_id, val, yr, tract_id FROM census.facts
WHERE yr = 2011 WITH CHECK OPTION;
```

Now try to run an update such as:

```
UPDATE census.vw_facts_2011 SET yr = 2012 WHERE val > 2942;
```

You'll get an error:

```
ERROR: New row violates WITH CHECK OPTION for view "vw_facts_2011"
DETAIL: Failing row contains (1, 25001010500, 2012, 2985.000, 100.00).
```

Using Triggers to Update Views

Views can encapsulate joins among tables. When a view draws from more than one table, updating the underlying data with a simple command is no longer possible. Drawing data from more than one table introduces inherent ambiguity when you're trying to update the underlying data, and PostgreSQL is not about to make an arbitrary decision for you. For instance, if you have a view that joins a table of countries with a table of provinces, and then decide to delete one of the rows, PostgreSQL won't know whether you intend to delete only a country, a province, or a particular country-province pairing. Nonetheless, you can still modify the underlying data through the view using triggers.

Let's start by creating a view that pulls rows from the facts table and a lookup table, as shown in Example 7-4.

Example 7-4. Creating view vw_facts

```
CREATE OR REPLACE VIEW census.vw_facts AS
SELECT
        y.fact_type_id, y.category, y.fact_subcats, y.short_name,
        x.tract_id, x.yr, x.val, x.perc
FROM census.facts As x INNER JOIN census.lu_fact_types As y
ON x.fact_type_id = y.fact_type_id;
```

To make this view updatable with a trigger, you can define one or more INSTEAD OF triggers. We first define the trigger function to handle the trifecta: INSERT, UPDATE, DELETE. In addition, PostgreSQL supports triggers on the TRUNCATE event. You can use any language to write the function except SQL, and you're free to name it whatever you like. We chose PL/pgSQL (*http://bit.ly/1w5ISeU*) in Example 7-5.

Example 7-5. Trigger function for vw_facts to insert, update, delete

```
CREATE OR REPLACE FUNCTION census.trig_vw_facts_ins_upd_del() RETURNS trigger AS
$$
BEGIN
    IF (TG_OP = 'DELETE') THEN ❶
        DELETE FROM census.facts AS f
        WHERE
            f.tract_id = OLD.tract_id AND f.yr = OLD.yr AND
            f.fact_type_id = OLD.fact_type_id;
        RETURN OLD;
    END IF;
    IF (TG_OP = 'INSERT') THEN ❷
        INSERT INTO census.facts(tract_id, yr, fact_type_id, val, perc)
        SELECT NEW.tract_id, NEW.yr, NEW.fact_type_id, NEW.val, NEW.perc;
        RETURN NEW;
    END IF;
    IF (TG_OP = 'UPDATE') THEN ❸
        IF
            ROW(OLD.fact_type_id, OLD.tract_id, OLD.yr, OLD.val, OLD.perc) !=
            ROW(NEW.fact_type_id, NEW.tract_id, NEW.yr, NEW.val, NEW.perc)
        THEN ❹
            UPDATE census.facts AS f
            SET
                tract_id = NEW.tract_id,
                yr = NEW.yr,
                fact_type_id = NEW.fact_type_id,
                val = NEW.val,
                perc = NEW.perc
            WHERE
                f.tract_id = OLD.tract_id AND
                f.yr = OLD.yr AND
                f.fact_type_id = OLD.fact_type_id;
            RETURN NEW;
        ELSE
            RETURN NULL;
        END IF;
    END IF;
END;
$$
LANGUAGE plpgsql VOLATILE;
```

❶ Handles deletes. Delete only records with matching keys in the OLD record.

❷ Handles inserts.

❸ Handles updates. Use the OLD record to determine which records to update. NEW record has the new data.

❹ Update rows only if at least one of the columns from the facts table has changed.

Next, we bind the trigger function to the view, as shown in Example 7-6.

Example 7-6. Bind trigger function to view

```
CREATE TRIGGER trig_01_vw_facts_ins_upd_del
INSTEAD OF INSERT OR UPDATE OR DELETE ON census.vw_facts
FOR EACH ROW EXECUTE PROCEDURE census.trig_vw_facts_ins_upd_del();
```

The binding syntax is uncharacteristically English-like.

Now when we update, delete, or insert into our view, we update the underlying `facts` table instead:

```
UPDATE census.vw_facts SET yr = 2012
WHERE yr = 2011 AND tract_id = '25027761200';
```

Upon a successful update, PostgreSQL returns the following message:

```
Query returned successfully: 56 rows affected, 40 ms execution time.
```

If we try to update a field not in our update row comparison, the update will not take place:

```
UPDATE census.vw_facts SET short_name = 'test';
```

With a message:

```
Query returned successfully: 0 rows affected, 931 ms execution time.
```

Although this example created a single trigger function to handle multiple events, we could have just as easily created a separate trigger and trigger function for each event.

PostgreSQL has another approach for updating views called *rules*, which predates the introduction of `INSTEAD OF` triggers view support. You can see an example using rules in Database Abstraction with Updatable Views (*http://bit.ly/1A0YJc4*).

You can still use rules to update view data, but `INSTEAD OF` triggers are preferred now. Internally PostgreSQL still uses rules to define the view (a view is nothing but an `INSTEAD OF SELECT` rule on a virtual table) and to implement single table updatable views. The difference between using a trigger and a rule is that a rule rewrites the underlying query and a trigger gets called for each virtual row. As such, rules become overwhelmingly difficult to write (and understand) when many tables are involved. Rules are also limited because they can be written only in SQL, not in other procedural languages.

Materialized Views

Materialized views cache the fetched data. This happens when you first create the view as well as when you run the `REFRESH MATERIALIZED VIEW` command. To use materialized views, you need at least version 9.3.

The most convincing cases for using materialized views are when the underlying query takes a long time and when having timely data is not critical. You often encounter these scenarios when building online analytical processing (OLAP) applications.

Unlike nonmaterialized views, you can add indexes to materialized views to speed up the read.

Example 7-7 demonstrates how to make a materialized version of the view in Example 7-1.

Example 7-7. Materialized view

```
CREATE MATERIALIZED VIEW census.vw_facts_2011_materialized AS
SELECT fact_type_id, val, yr, tract_id FROM census.facts WHERE yr = 2011;
```

Create an index on a materialized view as you would do on a regular table, as shown in Example 7-8.

Example 7-8. Add index to materialized view

```
CREATE UNIQUE INDEX ix
ON census.vw_facts_2011_materialized (tract_id, fact_type_id, yr);
```

For speedier access to a materialized view with a large number of records, you may want to control the physical sort of the data. The easiest way is to include an ORDER BY when you create the view. Alternatively, you can add a cluster index to the view. First, create an index in the physical sort order you want to have. Then run the CLUS TER command (*http://bit.ly/1FZWaeg*), passing it the index, as shown in Example 7-9.

Example 7-9. Clustering and reclustering a view on an index

```
CLUSTER census.vw_facts_2011_materialized USING ix; ❶
CLUSTER census.vw_facts_2011_materialized; ❷
```

❶ Name the index to cluster on. Needed only during view creation.

❷ Each time you refresh, you must recluster the data.

The advantage of using ORDER BY in the materialized view over using the CLUSTER approach is that the sort is maintained with each REFRESH MATERIALIZED VIEW call, alleviating the need to recluster. The downside is that ORDER BY generally adds more processing time to the REFRESH step of the view. You should test the effect of ORDER BY on performance of REFRESH before using it. One way to test is just to run the underlying query of the view with an ORDER BY clause.

To refresh the view in PostgreSQL 9.3, use:

```
REFRESH MATERIALIZED VIEW census.vw_facts_2011_materialized;
```

The view cannot be queried while the REFRESH MATERIALIZED VIEW step is running.

In PostgreSQL 9.4, to allow the view to be queried while it's refreshing, you can use:

```
REFRESH MATERIALIZED VIEW CONCURRENTLY census.vw_facts_2011_materialized;
```

Current limitations of materialized views include:

- You can't use CREATE OR REPLACE to edit an existing materialized view. You must drop and re-create the view even for the most trivial of changes. Use DROP MATERIALIZED VIEW *name_of_view*. Annoyingly, you'll lose all your indexes.

- You need to run REFRESH MATERIALIZED VIEW to rebuild the cache. PostgreSQL doesn't perform automatic recaching of any kind. You need to resort to mechanisms such as crontab, pgAgent jobs, or triggers to automate any kind of refresh. We have an example using triggers in Caching Data with Materialized Views and Statement-Level Triggers (*http://bit.ly/1yn1ySK*).

- Refreshing materialized views in version 9.3 is a blocking operation, meaning that the view will not be accessible during the refresh process. In version 9.4 you can lift this quarantine by adding the CONCURRENTLY keyword to your REFRESH command, provided that you have established a unique index on your view. The trade-off is concurrent refreshes could take longer to complete.

Handy Constructions

In our many years of writing SQL, we have come to appreciate the little things that make better use of our typing. Only PostgreSQL offers some of the gems we present in this section. Often this means that the construction is not ANSI-compliant. If thy God demands strict observance to the ANSI SQL standards, abstain from the shortcuts that we'll be showing.

DISTINCT ON

One of our favorites is DISTINCT ON. It behaves like DISTINCT, but with two enhancements: you can specify which columns to consider as distinct and to sort the remaining columns. One little word—ON—replaces numerous lines of additional code to achieve the same result.

In Example 7-10, we demonstrate how to get the details of the first tract for each county.

Example 7-10. DISTINCT ON

```
SELECT DISTINCT ON (left(tract_id, 5))
    left(tract_id, 5) As county, tract_id, tract_name
FROM census.lu_tracts
ORDER BY county, tract_id;

county |  tract_id   | tract_name
-------+-------------+------------------------------------------------------------
25001  | 25001010100 | Census Tract 101, Barnstable County, Massachusetts
25003  | 25003900100 | Census Tract 9001, Berkshire County, Massachusetts
25005  | 25005600100 | Census Tract 6001, Bristol County, Massachusetts
25007  | 25007200100 | Census Tract 2001, Dukes County, Massachusetts
25009  | 25009201100 | Census Tract 2011, Essex County, Massachusetts
:
(14 rows)
```

The ON modifier accepts multiple columns, considering all of them to determine distinctness. The ORDER BY clause has to start with the set of columns in the DISTINCT ON; then you can follow with your preferred ordering.

LIMIT and OFFSET

LIMIT returns only the number of rows indicated; OFFSET indicates the number of rows to skip. You can use them in tandem or separately. You almost always use them in conjunction with an ORDER BY. In Example 7-11, we demonstrate use of a positive offset. Leaving out the offset yields the same result as setting the offset to zero.

Limits and offsets are not unique to PostgreSQL and are in fact copied from MySQL, although implementation differs widely among database products.

Example 7-11. First tract for counties 2 through 5

```
SELECT DISTINCT ON (left(tract_id, 5))
    left(tract_id, 5) As county, tract_id, tract_name
FROM census.lu_tracts
ORDER BY county, tract_id LIMIT 3 OFFSET 2;

county | tract_id    | tract_name
-------+-------------+------------------------------------------------------------
25005  | 25005600100 | Census Tract 6001, Bristol County, Massachusetts
25007  | 25007200100 | Census Tract 2001, Dukes County, Massachusetts
25009  | 25009201100 | Census Tract 2011, Essex County, Massachusetts
(3 rows)
```

Shorthand Casting

ANSI SQL defines a construct called CAST that allows you to morph one data type to another. For example, CAST('2011-1-11' AS date) casts the text 2011-1-1 to a date.

PostgreSQL has shorthand for doing this, using a pair of colons, as in `'2011-1-1'::date`. This syntax is shorter and easier to apply for cases in which you can't directly cast from one type to another and have to intercede with one or more intermediary types, such as `someXML::text::integer`.

Multirow Insert

PostgreSQL supports the multirow constructor to insert more than one record at a time. Example 7-12 demonstrates how to use a multirow construction to insert data into the table we created in Example 6-3.

Example 7-12. Using a multirow constructor to insert data

```
INSERT INTO logs_2011 (user_name, description, log_ts)
VALUES
    ('robe', 'logged in', '2011-01-10 10:15 AM EST'),
    ('lhsu', 'logged out', '2011-01-11 10:20 AM EST');
```

The latter portion of the multirow constructor, starting with the VALUES keyword, is often referred to as a values list. A values list can stand alone and effectively creates a table on the fly, as in Example 7-13.

Example 7-13. Using a multirow constructor as a virtual table

```
SELECT *
FROM (
    VALUES
        ('robe', 'logged in', '2011-01-10 10:15 AM EST'::timestamptz),
        ('lhsu', 'logged out', '2011-01-11 10:20 AM EST'::timestamptz)
) AS l (user_name, description, log_ts);
```

When you use VALUES as a stand-in for a virtual table, you need to specify the names for the columns. You also need to explicitly cast the values to the data types in the table if the parser can't infer the data type from the data. The multirow VALUES construct also exists in MySQL and SQL Server.

ILIKE for Case-Insensitive Search

PostgreSQL is case-sensitive. However, it does have mechanisms in place to ignore casing. You can apply the upper function to both sides of the ANSI LIKE operator, or you can simply use the ILIKE (~~*) operator:

```
SELECT tract_name FROM census.lu_tracts WHERE tract_name ILIKE '%duke%';

tract_name
---------------------------------------------
Census Tract 2001, Dukes County, Massachusetts
```

```
Census Tract 2002, Dukes County, Massachusetts
Census Tract 2003, Dukes County, Massachusetts
Census Tract 2004, Dukes County, Massachusetts
Census Tract 9900, Dukes County, Massachusetts
```

ANY Array Search

PostgreSQL has a construct called ANY that can be used in conjunction with arrays, combined with a comparator operator or comparator keyword. If any element of the array matches a row, that row is returned.

Here is an example:

```
SELECT tract_name
FROM census.lu_tracts
WHERE tract_name ILIKE ANY(ARRAY['%99%duke%','%06%Barnstable%']::text[]);

tract_name
--------------------------------------------------
Census Tract 102.06, Barnstable County, Massachusetts
Census Tract 103.06, Barnstable County, Massachusetts
Census Tract 106, Barnstable County, Massachusetts
Census Tract 9900, Dukes County, Massachusetts
(4 rows)
```

The example just shown is a shorthand way of using multiple ILIKE OR clauses. You can use ANY with other comparators such as LIKE, =, and ~ (the regex like operator).

ANY can be used with any data types and comparison operators (operators that return a Boolean), including ones you built yourself or installed via extensions.

Set-Returning Functions in SELECT

A set-returning function is a function that could return more than one row.

PostgreSQL allows set-returning functions to appear in the SELECT clause of an SQL statement. This is not true of most other databases, in which only scalar functions can appear in the SELECT.

Interweaving some set-returning functions into an already complicated query could produce results beyond what you expect, because these functions usually result in the creation of new rows. You must anticipate this if you'll be using the results as a sub-query. In Example 7-14, we demonstrate row creation resulting from using a temporal version of generate_series. The example uses a table that we construct with:

```
CREATE TABLE interval_periods (i_type interval);
INSERT INTO interval_periods (i_type)
VALUES ('5 months'), ('132 days'), ('4862 hours');
```

Example 7-14. Set-returning function in SELECT

```
SELECT i_type,
    generate_series('2012-01-01'::date,'2012-12-31'::date,i_type) As dt
FROM interval_periods;

i_type      | dt
------------+-----------------------
5 months    | 2012-01-01 00:00:00-05
5 months    | 2012-06-01 00:00:00-04
5 months    | 2012-11-01 00:00:00-04
132 days    | 2012-01-01 00:00:00-05
132 days    | 2012-05-12 00:00:00-04
132 days    | 2012-09-21 00:00:00-04
4862 hours  | 2012-01-01 00:00:00-05
4862 hours  | 2012-07-21 15:00:00-04
```

Restricting DELETE, UPDATE, and SELECT from Inherited Tables

When you query from a table that has child tables, the query automatically drills down into the children, creating a union of all the child records satisfying the query condition. DELETE and UPDATE work the same way, drilling down the hierarchy for victims. Sometimes this is not desirable because you want data to come only from the table you specified, without the kids tagging along.

This is where the ONLY keyword comes in handy. We show an example of its use in Example 7-37, where we want to delete only those records from the production table that haven't migrated to the log table. Without the ONLY modifier, we'd end up deleting records from the child table that might have already been moved previously.

DELETE USING

Often, when you delete data from a table, you'll want to delete the data based on its presence in another set of data. Specify this additional set with the USING predicate. Then, in the WHERE clause, you can use both datasets in the USING and in the FROM to define conditions for deletion. Multiple tables can be included in USING, separated by commas. Example 7-15 deletes all records from census.facts that correspond to a fact type of short_name = 's01'.

Example 7-15. DELETE USING

```
DELETE FROM census.facts
USING census.lu_fact_types As ft
WHERE facts.fact_type_id = ft.fact_type_id AND ft.short_name = 's01';
```

The standards-compliant way would be to use a clunkier IN expression in the WHERE.

Returning Affected Records to the User

The RETURNING predicate is supported by ANSI SQL standards but not commonly found in other relational databases. We show an example in Example 7-37, where we return the records deleted. RETURNING can also be used for inserts and updates. For inserts into tables with a serial key, RETURNING is invaluable because it returns the key value of the new rows—something you wouldn't know prior to the query execution. Although RETURNING is often accompanied by * for all fields, you can limit the fields as we do in Example 7-16.

Example 7-16. Returning changed records of an UPDATE with RETURNING

```
UPDATE census.lu_fact_types AS f
SET short_name = replace(replace(lower(f.fact_subcats[4]),' ','_'),':','')
WHERE f.fact_subcats[3] = 'Hispanic or Latino:' AND f.fact_subcats[4] > ''
RETURNING fact_type_id, short_name;

 fact_type_id | short_name
--------------+--------------------------------------------------------
 96           | white_alone
 97           | black_or_african_american_alone
 98           | american_indian_and_alaska_native_alone
 99           | asian_alone
 100          | native_hawaiian_and_other_pacific_islander_alone
 101          | some_other_race_alone
 102          | two_or_more_races
```

UPSERTs: INSERT ON CONFLICT UPDATE

New in version 9.5 is the INSERT ON CONFLICT (*https://www.postgresql.org/docs/current/static/sql-insert.html*) construct, which is often referred to as an UPSERT. This feature is useful if you don't know a record already exists in a table and rather than having the insert fail, you want it to either update the existing record or do nothing.

This feature requires a unique key, primary key, unique index, or exclusion constraint in place, that when violated, you'd want different behavior like updating the existing record or not doing anything. To demonstrate, imagine we have a table of colors to create:

```
CREATE TABLE colors(color varchar(50) PRIMARY KEY, hex varchar(6));
    INSERT INTO colors(color, hex)
    VALUES('blue', '0000FF'), ('red', 'FF0000');
```

We then get a new batch of colors to add to our table, but some may be present already. If we do a regular insert, we'd get a primary key violation when we tried to add colors already in the table. When we run Example 7-17, we get only one record inserted, the green that is not already in our table, and each subsequent run would result in no records being inserted.

Example 7-17. ON CONFLICT DO NOTHING

```
INSERT INTO colors(color, hex)
   VALUES('blue', '0000FF'), ('red', 'FF0000'), ('green', '00FF00')
ON CONFLICT DO NOTHING ;
```

Someone could come and put in a different case 'Blue' in our system, and we'd then have two different cased blues. To remedy this, we can put a unique index on our table:

```
CREATE UNIQUE INDEX uidx_colors_lcolor ON colors USING btree(lower(color));
```

As before, if we tried to insert a 'Blue', we'd be prevented from doing so and the ON CONFLICT DO NOTHING would result in nothing happening. If we really wanted to spell the colors as given to us, we could use code like that given in Example 7-18.

Example 7-18. ON CONFLICT DO UPDATE

```
INSERT INTO colors(color, hex)
  VALUES('Blue', '0000FF'), ('Red', 'FF0000'), ('Green', '00FF00')
ON CONFLICT(lower(color))
    DO UPDATE SET color = EXCLUDED.color, hex = EXCLUDED.hex;
```

In Example 7-18 we specified the conflict, which matches the expression of a constraint or unique index, so using something like upper(color) would not work since the colors table has no matching index for that expression.

In the case of INSERT ON CONFLICT DO UPDATE, you need to specify the conflicting condition or CONSTRAINT name. If using a constraint, you'd use ON CON FLICT ON CONSTRAINT constraint_name_here as shown in Example 7-19.

Example 7-19. ON CONFLICT DO UPDATE

```
INSERT INTO colors(color, hex)
      VALUES('Blue', '0000FF'), ('Red', 'FF0000'), ('Green', '00FF00')
ON CONFLICT ON CONSTRAINT colors_pkey
DO UPDATE SET color = EXCLUDED.color, hex = EXCLUDED.hex;;
```

The DO part of the INSERT construct will only happen if there is a primary key, unique index, or unique key constraint error triggered. However, errors such as data type ones or check constraints will fail and never be processed by DO UPDATE.

Composite Types in Queries

PostgreSQL automatically creates data types of all tables. Because data types derived from tables contain other data types, they are often called composite data types, or just composites. The first time you see a query with composites, you might be surprised. In fact, you might come across their versatility by accident when making a typo in an SQL statement. Try the following query:

```
SELECT x FROM census.lu_fact_types As x LIMIT 2;
```

At first glance, you might think that we left out a .* by accident, but check out the result:

```
x
---------------------------------------------------------------
(86,Population,"{D001,Total:}",d001)
(87,Population,"{D002,Total:,""Not Hispanic or Latino:""}",d002)
```

Instead of erroring out, the preceding example returns the canonical representation of a lu_fact_type data type. Composites can serve as input to several useful functions, among which are array_agg and hstore (a function packaged with the hstore extension that converts a row into a key-value pair object).

If you are building web applications, you can take advantage of the built-in JSON and JSONB support we covered in "JSON" on page 120 and use a combination of array_agg and array_to_json to output a query as a single JSON object as shown in Example 7-20. In PostgreSQL 9.4, you can use json_agg. See Example 7-21.

Example 7-20. Query to JSON output

```
SELECT array_to_json(array_agg(f)) As cat ❶
FROM (
    SELECT MAX(fact_type_id) As max_type, category ❷
    FROM census.lu_fact_types
    GROUP BY category
) As f;
```

This will give you an output of:

```
cats
---------------------------------------------------------
[{"max_type":102,"category":"Population"},
{"max_type":153,"category":"Housing"}]
```

❶ Defines a subquery with name f. f can then be used to reference each row in the subquery.

❷ Aggregate each row of subquerying using array_agg and then convert the array to json with array_to_json.

In version 9.3, the json_agg function replaces the chain of array_to_json and array_agg, offering both convenience and speed. In Example 7-21, we repeat Example 7-20 using json_agg, and both examples will have the same output.

Example 7-21. Query to JSON using json_agg

```
SELECT json_agg(f) As cats
FROM (
    SELECT MAX(fact_type_id) As max_type, category
    FROM census.lu_fact_types
    GROUP BY category
) As f;
```

Dollar Quoting

In standard ANSI SQL, single quotes (') surround string literals. Should you have a single quote in the string itself, such as last names like *O'Nan*, possesives like *mon's place*, or contractions like *can't*, you need to escape it with another. The escape character is another single quote placed in front of the single quote you're trying to escape. Say you're writing an insert statement where you copied a large passage from a novel. Affixing yet another single quote to all existing single quotes is both tedious to add and challenging to read. After all, two single quotes look awfully like one double quote, which is another character entirely.

PostgreSQL lets you escape single quotes in strings of any length by surrounding them with two sequential dollar signs ($$), hence the name *dollar quoting*.

Dollar quoting is also useful in situations where you're trying to execute a piece of SQL dynamically, such as exec(*some sql*). In Example 7-5, we enclosed the body of a trigger using dollar quoting.

If you are writing an SQL statement that glues two sentences with many single quotes, the ANSI standard way would be to escape as in the following:

```
SELECT 'It''s O''Neil''s play. ' || 'It''ll start at two o''clock.'
```

With dollar quoting:

```
SELECT $$It's O'Neil's play. $$ || $$It'll start at two o'clock.$$
```

The pair of dollar signs replaces the single quote and escapes all single quotes within.

A variant of dollar quoting is *named dollar quoting*. We cover this in the following section.

DO

The DO command allows you to inject a piece of procedural code into your SQL on the fly. You can think of it as a one-time anonymous function. As an example, we'll load the data collected in Example 3-10 into production tables from our staging table. We'll use PL/pgSQL for our procedural snippet, but you're free to use other languages.

First, we'll create the table:

```
set search_path=census;
DROP TABLE IF EXISTS lu_fact_types CASCADE;
CREATE TABLE lu_fact_types (
    fact_type_id serial,
    category varchar(100),
    fact_subcats varchar(255)[],
    short_name varchar(50),
    CONSTRAINT pk_lu_fact_types PRIMARY KEY (fact_type_id)
);
```

Then we'll use DO to populate it as shown in Example 7-22. CASCADE will force the drop of any related objects such as foreign key constraints and views, so be cautious when using CASCADE.

Example 7-22 generates a series of INSERT INTO SELECT statements. The SQL also performs an unpivot operation to convert columnar data into rows.

 Example 7-22 is only a partial listing of the code needed to build lu_fact_types. For the full code, refer to the *building_census_tables.sql* file that is part of the book code and data download.

Example 7-22. Using DO to generate dynamic SQL

```
DO language plpgsql
$$
DECLARE var_sql text;
BEGIN
    var_sql := string_agg(
        $sql$ ❶
        INSERT INTO lu_fact_types(category, fact_subcats, short_name)
        SELECT
            'Housing',
            array_agg(s$sql$ || lpad(i::text,2,'0')
            || ') As fact_subcats,'
            || quote_literal('s' || lpad(i::text,2,'0')) || ' As short_name
        FROM staging.factfinder_import
        WHERE s' || lpad(I::text,2,'0') || $sql$ ~ '^[a-zA-Z]+' $sql$, ';'
    )
    FROM generate_series(1,51) As I; ❷
    EXECUTE var_sql; ❸
END
$$;
```

❶ Use of dollar quoting, so we don't need to escape ' in Housing. Since the DO command is also wrapped in dollars, we need to use a named $ delimiter inside. We chose sql.

❷ Use `string_agg` to form a set of SQL statements as a single string of the form `INSERT INTO lu_fact_type(...) SELECT ... WHERE s01 ~ '[a-zA-Z]+';`

❸ Execute the SQL.

In Example 7-22, we are using the dollar-quoting syntax covered in "Dollar Quoting" on page 179 for the body of the DO function and some fragments of the SQL statements inside the function. Since we use dollar quoting to define the whole body of the DO as well as internally, we need to use named dollar quoting for at least one part. The same dollar-quoting nested approach can be used for functon definitions as well.

FILTER Clause for Aggregates

New in version 9.4 is the `FILTER` clause for aggregates, recently standardized in ANSI SQL. This replaces the standard `CASE WHEN` clause for reducing the number of rows included in an aggregation. For example, suppose you used `CASE WHEN` to break out average test scores by student, as shown in Example 7-23.

Example 7-23. CASE WHEN used in AVG

```
SELECT student,
    AVG(CASE WHEN subject ='algebra' THEN score ELSE NULL END) As algebra,
    AVG(CASE WHEN subject ='physics' THEN score ELSE NULL END) As physics
FROM test_scores
GROUP BY student;
```

The `FILTER` clause equivalent for Example 7-23 is shown in Example 7-24.

Example 7-24. FILTER used with AVG aggregate

```
SELECT student,
    AVG(score) FILTER (WHERE subject ='algebra') As algebra,
    AVG(score) FILTER (WHERE subject ='physics') As physics
FROM test_scores
GROUP BY student;
```

In the case of averages and sums and many other aggregates, the `CASE` and `FILTER` are equivalent. The benefit is that `FILTER` is a little clearer in purpose and for large datasets is faster. However, there are some aggregates—such as `array_agg`, which considers `NULL` fields—where the `CASE` statement gives you extra `NULL` values you don't want. In Example 7-25 we try to get the list of scores for each subject of interest for each student using the `CASE .. WHEN..` approach.

Example 7-25. CASE WHEN used in array_agg

```
SELECT student,
    array_agg(CASE WHEN subject ='algebra' THEN score ELSE NULL END) As algebra,
    array_agg(CASE WHEN subject ='physics' THEN score ELSE NULL END) As physics
FROM test_scores
GROUP BY student;

student | algebra                   | physics
--------+---------------------------+---------------------------------------
jojo    | {74,NULL,NULL,NULL,74,..} | {NULL,83,NULL,NULL,NULL,79,..}
jdoe    | {75,NULL,NULL,NULL,78,..} | {NULL,72,NULL,NULL,NULL,72..}
robe    | {68,NULL,NULL,NULL,77,..} | {NULL,83,NULL,NULL,NULL,85,..}
lhsu    | {84,NULL,NULL,NULL,80,..} | {NULL,72,NULL,NULL,NULL,72,..}
(4 rows)
```

Observe that in Example 7-25 we get a bunch of NULL fields in our arrays. We could work around this issue with some clever use of subselects, but most of those will be more verbose and slower than the FILTER alternative shown in Example 7-26.

Example 7-26. FILTER used with array_agg

```
SELECT student,
    array_agg(score) FILTER (WHERE subject ='algebra') As algebra,
    array_agg(score) FILTER (WHERE subject ='physics') As physics
FROM test_scores
GROUP BY student;

student | algebra | physics
--------+---------+--------
jojo    | {74,74} | {83,79}
jdoe    | {75,78} | {72,72}
robe    | {68,77} | {83,85}
lhsu    | {84,80} | {72,72}
```

FILTER works for all aggregate functions, not just aggregate functions built into PostgreSQL.

Percentiles and Mode

New in PostgreSQL 9.4 are statistical functions for computing percentile, median (aka .5 percentile), and mode. These functions are percentile_disc (percentile discrete), percentile_cont (percentile continuous), and mode.

The two percentile functions differ in how they handle even counts. For the discrete function, the first value encountered is taken, so the ordering of the data matters. For the continuous case, values within the same percentile are averaged.

Median is merely the .5 percentile; therefore, it does not deserve a separate function of its own. The mode function finds the most common value. Should there be more than one mode, the first one encountered is returned; therefore, ordering matters, as shown in Example 7-27.

Example 7-27. Compute median and mode scores

```
SELECT
    student,
    percentile_cont(0.5) WITHIN GROUP (ORDER BY score) As cont_median,
    percentile_disc(0.5) WITHIN GROUP (ORDER BY score) AS disc_median,
    mode() WITHIN GROUP (ORDER BY score) AS mode,
    COUNT(*) As num_scores
FROM test_scores
GROUP BY student
ORDER BY student;

student | cont_median | disc_median | mode | num_scores
--------+-------------+-------------+------+-----------
alex    |          78 |          77 |   74 |          8
leo     |          72 |          72 |   72 |          8
regina  |          76 |          76 |   68 |          9
sonia   |        73.5 |          72 |   72 |          8
(4 rows)
```

Example 7-27 computes both the discrete and the continuous median score, which could differ when students have an even number of scores.

The inputs of these functions differ from other aggregate functions. The column being aggregated is the column in the ORDER BY clauses of the WITHIN GROUP modifiers. The column is not direct input to the function, as we're used to seeing.

The percentile functions have another variant that accepts an array of percentiles, letting you retrieve multiple percentiles all in one call. Example 7-28 computes the median, the 60 percentile, and the highest score.

Example 7-28. Compute multiple percentiles

```
SELECT
    student,
    percentile_cont('{0.5,0.60,1}'::float[])
WITHIN GROUP (ORDER BY score) AS cont_median,
    percentile_disc('{0.5,0.60,1}'::float[])
WITHIN GROUP (ORDER BY score) AS disc_median,
COUNT(*) As num_scores
FROM test_scores
GROUP BY student
ORDER BY student;

student | cont_median    | disc_median | num_scores
--------+----------------+-------------+-----------
alex    | {78,79.2,84}   | {77,79,84}  |          8
```

```
leo       | {72,73.6,84}   | {72,72,84}  |          8
regina    | {76,76.8,90}   | {76,77,90}  |          9
sonia     | {73.5,75.6,86} | {72,75,86}  |          8
(4 rows)
```

As with all aggregates, you can combine these functions with modifiers. Example 7-29 combines WITHIN GROUP with FILTER.

Example 7-29. Compute median score for two subjects

```
SELECT
    student,
    percentile_disc(0.5) WITHIN GROUP (ORDER BY score)
        FILTER (WHERE subject = 'algebra') AS algebra,
    percentile_disc(0.5) WITHIN GROUP (ORDER BY score)
        FILTER (WHERE subject = 'physics') AS physics
FROM test_scores
GROUP BY student
ORDER BY student;

student | algebra | physics
--------+---------+--------
alex    |      74 |      79
leo     |      80 |      72
regina  |      68 |      83
sonia   |      75 |      72
(4 rows)
```

Window Functions

Window functions are a common ANSI SQL feature. A window function has the prescience to see and use data beyond the current row; hence the term *window*. A window defines which other rows need to be considered in addition to the current row. Windows let you add aggregate information to each row of your output where the aggregation involves other rows in the same window. Window functions such as row_number and rank are useful for ordering your data in sophisticated ways that use rows outside the selected results but within a window.

Without window functions, you'd have to resort to using joins and subqueries to poll neighboring rows. On the surface, window functions violate the set-based principle of SQL, but we mollify the purist by claiming that they are merely shorthand. You can find more details and examples in Window Functions (*http://bit.ly/1yUcnhM*).

Example 7-30 gives you a quick start. Using a window function, we can obtain both the detail data and the average value for all records with fact_type_id of 86 in one single SELECT. Note that the WHERE clause is always evaluated *before* the window function.

Example 7-30. The basic window

```
SELECT tract_id, val, AVG(val) OVER () as val_avg
FROM census.facts
WHERE fact_type_id = 86;

tract_id    | val      | val_avg
------------+----------+---------------------
25001010100 | 2942.000 | 4430.0602165087956698
25001010206 | 2750.000 | 4430.0602165087956698
25001010208 | 2003.000 | 4430.0602165087956698
25001010304 | 2421.000 | 4430.0602165087956698
:
```

The OVER sets the boundary of the window. In this example, because the parentheses contain no constraint, the window covers all the rows in our WHERE. So the average is calculated across all rows with fact_type_id = 86. The clause also morphed our conventional AVG aggregate function into a window aggregate function. For each row, PostgreSQL submits all the rows in the window to the AVG aggregation and outputs the value as part of the row. Because our window has multiple rows, the result of the aggregation is repeated. Notice that with window functions, we were able to perform an aggregation without GROUP BY. Furthermore, we were able to rejoin the aggregated result back with the other variables without using a formal join.

You can use all SQL aggregate functions as window functions. In addition, you'll find ROW, RANK, LEAD, and others listed in Window Functions (*http://bit.ly/1FUiJ2d*).

PARTITION BY

You can run a window function over rows containing particular values instead of using the whole table. This requires the addition of a PARTITION BY clause, which instructs PostgreSQL to take the aggregate over the indicated rows. In Example 7-31, we repeat what we did in Example 7-30 but partition our window by county code, which is always the first five characters of the tract_id column. Thus, the rows in each county code are averaged separately.

Example 7-31. Partitioning our window by county code

```
SELECT tract_id, val, AVG(val) OVER (PARTITION BY left(tract_id,5)) As val_avg_county
FROM census.facts
WHERE fact_type_id = 2 ORDER BY tract_id;

tract_id    | val      | val_avg_county
------------+----------+---------------------
25001010100 | 1765.000 | 1709.9107142857142857
25001010206 | 1366.000 | 1709.9107142857142857
25001010208 |  984.000 | 1709.9107142857142857
:
```

```
25003900100 | 1920.000 | 1438.2307692307692308
25003900200 | 1968.000 | 1438.2307692307692308
25003900300 | 1211.000 | 1438.2307692307692308
:
```

ORDER BY

Window functions also allow an ORDER BY in the OVER clause. Without getting too abstruse, the best way to think about this is that all the rows in the window will be ordered as indicated by ORDER BY, and the window function will consider only rows that range from the first row in the window up to and including the current row in the window or partition. The classic example uses the ROW_NUMBER function to sequentially number rows. In Example 7-32, we demonstrate how to number our census tracts in alphabetical order. To arrive at the row number, ROW_NUMBER counts all rows up to and including the current row based on the order dictated by the ORDER BY.

Example 7-32. Numbering using the ROW_NUMBER window function

```
SELECT ROW_NUMBER() OVER (ORDER BY tract_name) As rnum, tract_name
FROM census.lu_tracts
ORDER BY rnum LIMIT 4;

rnum | tract_name
-----+---------------------------------------------------
1    | Census Tract 1, Suffolk County, Massachusetts
2    | Census Tract 1001, Suffolk County, Massachusetts
3    | Census Tract 1002, Suffolk County, Massachusetts
4    | Census Tract 1003, Suffolk County, Massachusetts
```

In Example 7-32, we also have an ORDER BY for the entire query. Don't get confused between this and the ORDER BY that's specific to the window function.

You can combine ORDER BY with PARTITION BY, restarting the ordering for each partition. Example 7-33 returns to our example of county codes.

Example 7-33. Combining PARTITION BY and ORDER BY

```
SELECT tract_id, val,
    SUM(val) OVER (PARTITION BY left(tract_id,5) ORDER BY val) As sum_county_ordered
FROM census.facts
WHERE fact_type_id = 2
ORDER BY left(tract_id,5), val;

tract_id     | val     | sum_county_ordered
-------------+---------+-------------------
25001014100 | 226.000 |            226.000
25001011700 | 971.000 |           1197.000
```

```
25001010208 | 984.000 |        2181.000
:
25003933200 | 564.000 |         564.000
25003934200 | 593.000 |        1157.000
25003931300 | 606.000 |        1763.000
:
```

The key observation to make in the output is how the sum changes from row to row. The ORDER BY clause means that the sum will be taken only from the beginning of the partition to the current row, giving you a running total, where the location of the current row in the list is dictated by the ORDER BY clause. For instance, if your row is in the fifth row in the third partition, the sum will cover only the first five rows in the third partition. We put an ORDER BY left(tract_id,5), val at the end of the query so you can easily see the pattern, but keep in mind that the ORDER BY of the query is independent of the ORDER BY in each OVER clause.

You can explicitly control the rows under consideration by adding a RANGE or ROWS clause: ROWS BETWEEN CURRENT ROW AND 5 FOLLOWING.

PostgreSQL also supports window naming, which is useful if you have the same window for each of your window columns. Example 7-34 demonstrates how to name windows as well as how to use the LEAD and LAG window functions to show a record value before and after for a given partition.

Example 7-34. Naming windows, demonstrating LEAD and LAG

```
SELECT * FROM (
    SELECT
        ROW_NUMBER() OVER( wt ) As rnum, ❶
        substring(tract_id,1, 5) As county_code,
        tract_id,
        LAG(tract_id,2) OVER wt As tract_2_before,
        LEAD(tract_id) OVER wt As tract_after
    FROM census.lu_tracts
    WINDOW wt AS (PARTITION BY substring(tract_id,1, 5) ORDER BY tract_id) ❷
) As x
WHERE rnum BETWEEN 2 and 3 AND county_code IN ('25007','25025')
ORDER BY county_code, rnum;
```

rnum	county_code	tract_id	tract_2_before	tract_after
2	25007	25007200200		25007200300
3	25007	25007200300	25007200100	25007200400
2	25025	25025000201		25025000202
3	25025	25025000202	25025000100	25025000301

❶ Naming our window wt window.

❷ Using our window name instead of retyping.

Both LEAD and LAG take an optional step argument that defines how many rows to skip forward or backward; the step can be positive or negative. LEAD and LAG return NULL when trying to retrieve rows outside the window partition. This is a possibility that you always have to account for.

In PostgreSQL, any aggregate function you create can be used as a window function. Other databases tend to limit window functions to using built-in aggregates such as AVG, SUM, MIN, and MAX.

Common Table Expressions

Essentially, common table expressions (CTEs) allow you to define a query that can be reused in a larger query. CTEs act as temporary tables defined within the scope of the statement; they're gone once the enclosing statement has finished executing.

There are three ways to use CTEs:

Basic CTE
> This is your plain-vanilla CTE, used to make your SQL more readable or to encourage the planner to materialize a costly intermediate result for better performance.

Writable CTE
> This is an extension of the basic CTE with UPDATE, INSERT, and DELETE commands. A common final step in the CTE is to return changed rows.

Recursive CTE
> This puts an entirely new whirl on standard CTE. The rows returned by a recursive CTE vary during the execution of the query.

PostgreSQL allows you to have a CTE that is both writable and recursive.

Basic CTEs

The basic CTE looks like Example 7-35. The WITH keyword introduces the CTE.

Example 7-35. Basic CTE

```
WITH cte AS (
    SELECT
        tract_id, substring(tract_id,1, 5) As county_code,
        COUNT(*) OVER(PARTITION BY substring(tract_id,1, 5)) As cnt_tracts
    FROM census.lu_tracts
)
SELECT MAX(tract_id) As last_tract, county_code, cnt_tracts
```

```
FROM cte
WHERE cnt_tracts > 100
GROUP BY county_code, cnt_tracts;
```

cte is the name of the CTE in Example 7-35, defined using a SELECT statement to contain three columns: tract_id, county_code, and cnt_tracts. The main SELECT refers to the CTE.

You can stuff as many CTEs as you like, separated by commas, into the WITH clause, as shown in Example 7-36. The order of the CTEs matters in that CTEs defined later can call CTEs defined earlier, but not vice versa.

Example 7-36. Multiple CTEs

```
WITH
    cte1 AS (
        SELECT
            tract_id,
            substring(tract_id,1, 5) As county_code,
            COUNT(*) OVER (PARTITION BY substring(tract_id,1,5)) As cnt_tracts
        FROM census.lu_tracts
    ),
    cte2 AS (
        SELECT
            MAX(tract_id) As last_tract,
            county_code,
            cnt_tracts
        FROM cte1
        WHERE cnt_tracts < 8 GROUP BY county_code, cnt_tracts
    )
SELECT c.last_tract, f.fact_type_id, f.val
FROM census.facts As f INNER JOIN cte2 c ON f.tract_id = c.last_tract;
```

Writable CTEs

The writable CTE extends the CTE to allow for update, delete, and insert statements. We'll revisit our logs tables that we created in Example 6-3, adding another child table and populating it:

```
CREATE TABLE logs_2011_01_02 (
    PRIMARY KEY (log_id),
    CONSTRAINT chk
        CHECK (log_ts >= '2011-01-01' AND log_ts < '2011-03-01')
)
INHERITS (logs_2011);
```

In Example 7-37, we move data from our parent 2011 table to our new child Jan-Feb 2011 table. The ONLY keyword is described in "Restricting DELETE, UPDATE, and

SELECT from Inherited Tables" on page 175 and the RETURNING keyword in "Returning Affected Records to the User" on page 176.

Example 7-37. Writable CTE moving data from one branch to another

```
WITH t AS (
    DELETE FROM ONLY logs_2011 WHERE log_ts < '2011-03-01' RETURNING *
)
INSERT INTO logs_2011_01_02 SELECT * FROM t;
```

Recursive CTE

The official documentation for PostgreSQL (*http://www.postgresql.org/docs/current/ interactive/queries-with.html*) describes it best: "The optional RECURSIVE modifier changes CTE from a mere syntactic convenience into a feature that accomplishes things not otherwise possible in standard SQL." A more interesting CTE is one that uses a recursively defining construct to build an expression. PostgreSQL recursive CTEs utilize UNION ALL to combine tables, a kind of combination that can be done repeatedly as the query adds the tables over and over.

To turn a basic CTE to a recursive one, add the RECURSIVE modifier after the WITH. WITH RECURSIVE can contain a mix of recursive and nonrecursive table expressions. In most other databases, the RECURSIVE keyword is not necessary to denote recursion.

A common use of recursive CTEs is to represent message threads and other tree-like structures. We have an example of this in Recursive CTE to Display Tree Structures (*http://bit.ly/1yx9ggR*).

In Example 7-38, we query the system catalog to list the cascading table relationships we have in our database.

Example 7-38. Recursive CTE

```
WITH RECURSIVE tbls AS (
    SELECT
        c.oid As tableoid,
        n.nspname AS schemaname,
        c.relname AS tablename ❶
    FROM
        pg_class c LEFT JOIN
        pg_namespace n ON n.oid = c.relnamespace LEFT JOIN
        pg_tablespace t ON t.oid = c.reltablespace LEFT JOIN
        pg_inherits As th ON th.inhrelid = c.oid
    WHERE
        th.inhrelid IS NULL AND
        c.relkind = 'r'::"char" AND c.relhassubclass
    UNION ALL
    SELECT
```

```
        c.oid As tableoid,
        n.nspname AS schemaname,
        tbls.tablename || '->' || c.relname AS tablename  ❷ ❸
   FROM
        tbls INNER JOIN
        pg_inherits As th ON th.inhparent = tbls.tableoid INNER JOIN
        pg_class c ON th.inhrelid = c.oid LEFT JOIN
        pg_namespace n ON n.oid = c.relnamespace LEFT JOIN
    pg_tablespace t ON t.oid = c.reltablespace
)
SELECT * FROM tbls ORDER BY tablename;  ❹

tableoid | schemaname | tablename
---------+------------+-------------------------------------------
3152249  | public     | logs
3152260  | public     | logs->logs_2011
3152272  | public     | logs->logs_2011->logs_2011_01_02
```

❶   Get a list of all tables that have child tables but no parent table.

❷   This is the recursive part; it gets all children of tables in `tbls`.

❸   The names of the child tables start with the parental name.

❹   Return parents and all child tables. Because we sort by table name, which prepends the parent name, all child tables will follow their parents in their output.

Lateral Joins

LATERAL is a new ANSI SQL construction in version 9.3. Here's the motivation behind it: suppose you perform joins on two tables or subqueries; normally, the pair participating in the join are independent units and can't read data from each other. For example, the following interaction would generate an error because `l.yr = 2011` is not a column on the righthand side of the join:

```
SELECT *
    FROM
        census.facts L
        INNER JOIN
        (
            SELECT *
            FROM census.lu_fact_types
            WHERE category = CASE WHEN L.yr = 2011
    THEN 'Housing' ELSE category END
        ) R
    ON L.fact_type_id = R.fact_type_id;
```

Now add the LATERAL keyword, and the error is gone:

```
SELECT *
    FROM
        census.facts L INNER JOIN LATERAL
        (
            SELECT *
            FROM census.lu_fact_types
            WHERE category = CASE WHEN L.yr = 2011
THEN 'Housing' ELSE category END
        ) R
        ON L.fact_type_id = R.fact_type_id;
```

LATERAL lets you share data in columns across two tables in a FROM clause. However, it works only in one direction: the righthand side can draw from the lefthand side, but not vice versa.

There are situations when you should avail yourself of LATERAL to avoid extremely convoluted syntax. In Example 7-39, a column on the left serves as a parameter in the generate_series function on the right:

```
CREATE TABLE interval_periods(i_type interval);
INSERT INTO interval_periods (i_type)
VALUES ('5 months'), ('132 days'), ('4862 hours');
```

Example 7-39. Using LATERAL with generate_series

```
SELECT i_type, dt
FROM
    interval_periods CROSS JOIN LATERAL
    generate_series('2012-01-01'::date, '2012-12-31'::date, i_type) AS dt
WHERE NOT (dt = '2012-01-01' AND i_type = '132 days'::interval);

i_type      | dt
------------+-----------------------
 5 mons     | 2012-01-01 00:00:00-05
 5 mons     | 2012-06-01 00:00:00-04
 5 mons     | 2012-11-01 00:00:00-04
 132 days   | 2012-05-12 00:00:00-04
 132 days   | 2012-09-21 00:00:00-04
 4862:00:00 | 2012-01-01 00:00:00-05
 4862:00:00 | 2012-07-21 15:00:00-04
```

Lateral is also helpful for using values from the lefthand side to limit the number of rows returned from the righthand side. Example 7-40 uses LATERAL to return, for each superuser who has used our site within the last 100 days, the last five logins and what they were up to. Tables used in this example were created in "TYPE OF" on page 153 and "Basic Table Creation" on page 147.

Example 7-40. Using LATERAL to limit rows from a joined table

```
SELECT u.user_name, l.description, l.log_ts
FROM
    super_users AS u CROSS JOIN LATERAL (
    SELECT description, log_ts
    FROM logs
    WHERE
        log_ts > CURRENT_TIMESTAMP - interval '100 days' AND
        logs.user_name = u.user_name
    ORDER BY log_ts DESC LIMIT 5
    ) AS l;
```

Although you can achieve the same results by using window functions, lateral joins yield faster results with more succinct syntax.

You can use multiple lateral joins in your SQL and even chain them in sequence as you would when joining more than two subqueries. You can sometimes get away with omitting the LATERAL keyword; the query parser is smart enough to figure out a lateral join if you have a correlated expression. But we advise that you always include the keyword for the sake of clarity. Also, you'll get an error if you write your statement assuming the use of a lateral join but run the statement on a prelateral version PostgreSQL. Without the keyword, PostgreSQL might end up performing a join with unintended results.

Other database products also offer lateral joins, although they don't abide by the ANSI moniker. In Oracle, you'd use a table pipeline construct. In SQL Server, you'd use CROSS APPLY or OUTER APPLY.

WITH ORDINALITY

Introduced in version 9.4, the WITH ORDINALITY clause is an SQL ANSI standard construct. WITH ORDINALITY adds a sequential number column to a set-returning function result.

> Although you can't use WITH ORDINALITY with tables and subqueries, you can achieve the same result for those by using the window function ROW_NUMBER.

You'll find WITH ORDINALITY often used with functions like generate_series, unnest, and other functions that expand out composite types and arrays. It can be used with any set-returning function, including ones you create yourself.

Example 7-41 demonstrates WITH ORDINALITY used in conjunction with the temporal variant of the generate_series function.

Example 7-41. Numbering results from set-returning functions

```
SELECT dt.*
FROM generate_series('2016-01-01'::date,'2016-12-31'::date,interval '1 month')
WITH ORDINALITY As dt;
```

```
dt                       | ordinality
-------------------------+-----------
2016-01-01 00:00:00-05   |          1
2016-02-01 00:00:00-05   |          2
2016-03-01 00:00:00-05   |          3
2016-04-01 00:00:00-04   |          4
2016-05-01 00:00:00-04   |          5
2016-06-01 00:00:00-04   |          6
2016-07-01 00:00:00-04   |          7
2016-08-01 00:00:00-04   |          8
2016-09-01 00:00:00-04   |          9
2016-10-01 00:00:00-04   |         10
2016-11-01 00:00:00-04   |         11
2016-12-01 00:00:00-05   |         12
(12 rows)
```

WITH ORDINALITY always adds an additional column at the end of the result called *ordinality*, and WITH ORDINALITY can only appear in the FROM clause of an SQL statement. You are free to rename the ordinality column.

You'll often find WITH ORDINALITY paired with the LATERAL construct. In Example 7-42 we repeat the LATERAL in Example 7-39, but add on a sequential number to each set.

Example 7-42. Using WITH ORDINALITY with LATERAL

```
SELECT d.ord, i_type, d.dt
FROM
    interval_periods CROSS JOIN LATERAL
    generate_series('2012-01-01'::date, '2012-12-31'::date, i_type)
WITH ORDINALITY AS d(dt,ord)
WHERE NOT (dt = '2012-01-01' AND i_type = '132 days'::interval);
```

```
ord | i_type     | dt
----+------------+-----------------------
  1 | 5 mons     | 2012-01-01 00:00:00-05
  2 | 5 mons     | 2012-06-01 00:00:00-04
  3 | 5 mons     | 2012-11-01 00:00:00-04
  2 | 132 days   | 2012-05-12 00:00:00-04
  3 | 132 days   | 2012-09-21 00:00:00-04
  1 | 4862:00:00 | 2012-01-01 00:00:00-05
  2 | 4862:00:00 | 2012-07-21 15:00:00-04
(7 rows)
```

In Example 7-42, WITH ORDINALITY gets applied to the result of the set-returning function. It always gets applied before the WHERE condition. As a result, there is a gap in numbering in the final result (the number 1 is lacking for the 132 day interval), because the number was filtered out by our WHERE condition.

If we didn't have the WHERE condition excluding the 2012-01-01, 132 day record, we would have 8 rows with the 4th row being 1 | 132 days | 2012-01-01 00:00:00-04

GROUPING SETS, CUBE, ROLLUP

If you've ever tried to create a summary report that includes both totals and subtotals, you'll appreciate the capability to partition your data on the fly. Grouping sets let you do exactly that.

For our table of test scores, if we need to find both the overall average per student and the average per student by subject, we could write a query as shown in Example 7-43, taking advantage of grouping sets.

Example 7-43. Avg score for each student and student in subject

```
SELECT student, subject, AVG(score)::numeric(10,2)
FROM test_scores
WHERE student IN ('leo','regina')
GROUP BY GROUPING SETS ((student),(student,subject))
ORDER BY student, subject NULLS LAST;

 student |  subject  |  avg
---------+-----------+-------
 leo     | algebra   | 82.00
 leo     | calculus  | 65.50
 leo     | chemistry | 75.50
 leo     | physics   | 72.00
 leo     | NULL      | 73.75
 regina  | algebra   | 72.50
 regina  | calculus  | 64.50
 regina  | chemistry | 73.50
 regina  | economics | 90.00
 regina  | physics   | 84.00
 regina  | NULL      | 75.44
(11 rows)
```

In a single query, Example 7-43 gives us both the average of each student across all subjects and his or her average in each subject.

We can even include a total for each subject across all students by having multiple grouping sets as shown in Example 7-44.

Example 7-44. Avg score for each student, student in subject, and subject

```
SELECT student, subject, AVG(score)::numeric(10,2)
FROM test_scores
WHERE student IN ('leo','regina')
GROUP BY GROUPING SETS ((student,subject),(student),(subject))
ORDER BY student NULLS LAST, subject NULLS LAST;

 student |  subject  |  avg
---------+-----------+-------
 leo     | algebra   | 82.00
 leo     | calculus  | 65.50
 leo     | chemistry | 75.50
 leo     | physics   | 72.00
 leo     | NULL      | 73.75
 regina  | algebra   | 72.50
 regina  | calculus  | 64.50
 regina  | chemistry | 73.50
 regina  | economics | 90.00
 regina  | physics   | 84.00
 regina  | NULL      | 75.44
 NULL    | algebra   | 77.25
 NULL    | calculus  | 65.00
 NULL    | chemistry | 74.50
 NULL    | economics | 90.00
 NULL    | physics   | 78.00
(16 rows)
```

What if we wanted to have total breakdowns for student, student plus subject, and overall average? We could revise our query to add a universal grouping set GROUPING SETS ((student),(student, subject),()). This is equivalent to the shorthand ROLLUP (student, subject). See Example 7-45.

Example 7-45. Avg score for each student in subject, student, and overall

```
SELECT student, subject, AVG(score)::numeric(10,2)
FROM test_scores
WHERE student IN ('leo','regina')
GROUP BY ROLLUP (student,subject)
ORDER BY student NULLS LAST, subject NULLS LAST;

 student |  subject  |  avg
---------+-----------+-------
 leo     | algebra   | 82.00
 leo     | calculus  | 65.50
 leo     | chemistry | 75.50
 leo     | physics   | 72.00
 leo     | NULL      | 73.75
 regina  | algebra   | 72.50
 regina  | calculus  | 64.50
 regina  | chemistry | 73.50
```

```
regina  | economics | 90.00
regina  | physics   | 84.00
regina  | NULL      | 75.44
NULL    | NULL      | 74.65
(12 rows)
```

If we reverse the order of columns in ROLLUP, we get the score for each student/subject pair, average for each subject, and overall average as shown in Example 7-46.

Example 7-46. Avg score for each student in subject, subject, and overall

```
SELECT student, subject, AVG(score)::numeric(10,2)
FROM test_scores
WHERE student IN ('leo','regina')
GROUP BY ROLLUP (subject,student)
ORDER BY student NULLS LAST, subject NULLS LAST;

 student |  subject  |  avg
---------+-----------+-------
 leo     | algebra   | 82.00
 leo     | calculus  | 65.50
 leo     | chemistry | 75.50
 leo     | physics   | 72.00
 regina  | algebra   | 72.50
 regina  | calculus  | 64.50
 regina  | chemistry | 73.50
 regina  | economics | 90.00
 regina  | physics   | 84.00
 NULL    | algebra   | 77.25
 NULL    | calculus  | 65.00
 NULL    | chemistry | 74.50
 NULL    | economics | 90.00
 NULL    | physics   | 78.00
 NULL    | NULL      | 74.65
(15 rows)
```

If we also wanted to include subtotals for just the subject and just the student, we'd use GROUPING SETS ((student), (student, subject), (subject), ()), or the shorthand CUBE (student, subject) in Example 7-47.

Example 7-47. Avg score for each student, student in subject, subject, and overall

```
SELECT student, subject, AVG(score)::numeric(10,2)
FROM test_scores
WHERE student IN ('leo','regina')
GROUP BY  CUBE (student, subject)
ORDER BY student NULLS LAST, subject NULLS LAST;

 student |  subject  |  avg
---------+-----------+-------
 leo     | algebra   | 82.00
```

```
leo       | calculus  | 65.50
leo       | chemistry | 75.50
leo       | physics   | 72.00
leo       | NULL      | 73.75
regina    | algebra   | 72.50
regina    | calculus  | 64.50
regina    | chemistry | 73.50
regina    | economics | 90.00
regina    | physics   | 84.00
regina    | NULL      | 75.44
NULL      | algebra   | 77.25
NULL      | calculus  | 65.00
NULL      | chemistry | 74.50
NULL      | economics | 90.00
NULL      | physics   | 78.00
NULL      | NULL      | 74.65
(17 rows)
```

## CHAPTER 8

Writing Functions

In PostgreSQL, as in most databases, you can string a series of SQL statements together and treat them as a unit, even customizing each run by passing arguments. Different databases ascribe different names for this unit: stored procedures, user-defined functions, and so on. PostgreSQL simply refers to them as *functions*.

Aside from marshalling SQL statements, functions often add the capability to control the execution of the SQL using PLs. PostgreSQL offers a rich choice of languages for writing functions. SQL, C, PL/pgSQL, PL/Perl, and PL/Python are often packaged with installers. You'll also find PL/V8 (*http://code.google.com/p/plv8js/*), which allows you to write procedural functions in JavaScript. PL/V8 is a favorite for web developers and a darling companion to the built-in JSON and JSONB data types covered in "JSON" on page 120.

You can also install additional languages such as PL/R (*http://bit.ly/12sf8v9*), PL/Java (*http://bit.ly/1vUsHxX*), PL/sh (*http://bit.ly/1yUcwll*), PL/TSQL (*http://bit.ly/1q2gCHA*), and even experimental ones geared for high-end data processing and artificial intelligence, such as PL/Scheme (*http://bit.ly/1Iam4hw*) or PL/OpenCL (*http://bit.ly/1q2gFDe*). You can find a listing of available languages in Procedural Languages (*http://bit.ly/1vUsHxX*).

Anatomy of PostgreSQL Functions

PostgreSQL functions fall into the categories of basic function, aggregate function, window function, and trigger function. We'll start by detailing the basic anatomy of a function and then go into detail about how the various kinds of specialized function types extends from this.

Function Basics

Regardless of which languages you choose for writing functions, all functions share a similar structure, as shown in Example 8-1.

Example 8-1. Basic function structure

```
CREATE OR REPLACE FUNCTION func_name(arg1 arg1_datatype DEFAULT arg1_default)
RETURNS some type | set of some type | TABLE (..) AS
$$
BODY of function
$$
LANGUAGE language_of_function
```

Arguments can have default values, which allow the caller of the function to omit them. Optional arguments must be positioned after nonoptional arguments in the function definition.

Argument names are optional but are useful because they let you refer to an argument by name inside the function body. For example, think of a function that is defined to take three input arguments (two being optional):

```
big_elephant(ear_size numeric, skin_color text DEFAULT 'blue',
name text DEFAULT 'Dumbo')
```

You can refer to the arguments by name (`ear_size`, `skin_color`, etc.) inside the body of the function. If they are not named, you need to refer to the arguments inside the function by their order in the argument list: $1, $2, and $3.

If you name the arguments, you also have the option of using named notation when calling the function:

```
big_elephant(name => 'Wooly', ear_size => 1.2)
```

You can always use the positional notation `big_elephant(1.2, 'blue', 'Wooly')` even if function arguments are named. Named notation is useful if you have a function that takes several arguments and many of the arguments are optional. By using named notation, you can override a default value and keep other defaults regardless of the order in which the arguments are defined. You also don't need to state the arguments in the order they appear in the function definition. In the `big_elephant` example we were able to accept the default skin color of blue and override the default name, even though `name` appears last in the argument list. If we were to call the function simply by the order of arguments, we couldn't skip over `skin_color` if we wanted to override the `name` argument.

In PostgreSQL 9.5 and above, the named notation convention is `name => 'Wooly'`. In 9.4 and below you would use `name := 'Wooly'`. For backward compatibility, the old syntax of `arg1_name := arg1_value` is still supported in 9.5 and above, but may be removed in the future.

Functional definitions often include additional qualifiers to optimize execution and to enforce security:

LANGUAGE

The language must be one installed in your database. Obtain a list with the `SELECT lanname FROM pg_language;` query.

VOLATILITY

This setting clues the query planner as to whether outputs can be cached and used across multiple calls. Your choices are:

IMMUTABLE

The function will always return the same output for the same input. Think of arithmetic functions. Only immutable functions can be used in the definition of indexes.

STABLE

The function will return the same value for the same inputs within the same query.

VOLATILE

The function can return different values with each call, even with the same inputs. Think of functions that change data or depend on environment settings like system time. This is the default.

Keep in mind that the volatility setting is merely a hint to the planner. The default value of VOLATILE ensures that the planner will always recompute the result. If you use one of the other values, the planner can still choose to forgo caching should it decide that recomputing is more cost-effective.

STRICT

A function marked with this qualifier will always return NULL if any inputs are NULL. The planner skips evaluating the function altogether with any NULL inputs. When writing SQL functions, be cautious

when marking a function as STRICT, because it could prevent the planner from taking advantage of indexes. Read our article STRICT on SQL Functions (*http://bit.ly/1rX26C5*) for more details.

COST

This is a relative measure of computational intensiveness. SQL and PL/pgSQL functions default to 100 and C functions to 1. This affects the order that the planner will follow when evaluating the function in a WHERE clause, and the likelihood of caching. The higher you set the cost, the more computation the planner will assume the function needs.

ROWS

Applies only to functions returning sets of records. The value provides an estimate of how many rows will be returned. The planner will take this value into consideration when coming up with the best strategy.

SECURITY DEFINER

This causes execution to take place within the security context of the owner of the function. If omitted, the function executes under the context of the user calling the function. This qualifier is useful for giving people rights to update a table via a function when they do not have direct update privileges.

PARALLEL

New in PostgreSQL 9.6. This qualifier allows the planner to run in parallel mode. By default, a function is marked as PARALLEL UNSAFE, which prevents any queries containing the function from being distributed into separate work processes. Refer to Parallel Safety (*https://www.postgresql.org/docs/9.6/static/parallel-safety.html*). Your choices are:

SAFE

This allows parallel use, and is generally a safe choice for IMMUTABLE functions or functions that don't update data or change transaction state or other variables.

UNSAFE

Functions that change nontemp table data, access sequences, or state should be marked as UNSAFE. They prevent the query from being run in parallel mode and therefore risking the corruption of the tables or other system state.

RESTRICTED

You may want to use this value for functions that use temporary tables, prepared statements, or client connection state. This value does not prevent a query from running in parallel mode, but processing of these functions can happen only on the lead query.

In many of the examples in this chapter, we'll be including PARALLEL mode options. If you are running lower than version 9.6, leave out the parallel clauses.

Triggers and Trigger Functions

No worthy database should lack triggers, which automatically detect and handle changes in data. PostgreSQL allows you to attach triggers to tables, views, and even DDL events like creation of a new table.

Triggers can actuate at both the statement level and the row level. Statement triggers run once per SQL statement, whereas row triggers run for each row affected by the SQL. For example, if you execute an UPDATE statement that affects 1,500 rows, a statement-level update trigger will fire only once, whereas the row-level trigger can fire up to 1,500 times.

You can further refine the timing of the trigger by making a distinction between BEFORE, AFTER, and INSTEAD OF triggers. A BEFORE trigger fires prior to the execution of the statement, giving you a chance to cancel or back up data before the change. An AFTER trigger fires after statement execution, giving you a chance to retrieve the new data values. AFTER triggers are often used for logging or replication purposes. INSTEAD OF triggers execute in lieu of the statement. You can attach BEFORE and AFTER triggers only to tables and events, and INSTEAD OF triggers only to views.

Trigger functions that change values of a row should be called only in the BEFORE event, because in the AFTER event, all updates to the NEW record will be ignored.

You can also adorn a trigger with a WHEN condition to control which rows being updated will fire the trigger, or an UPDATE OF *columns_list* clause to have the trigger fire only if certain columns are updated. To gain a more nuanced understanding of the interplay between triggers and the underlying statement, see the official documentation: Overview of Trigger Behavior (*http://bit.ly/1vUsXgq*). We also demonstrated a view-based trigger in Example 7-5.

PostgreSQL offers specialized functions to handle triggers. These are called *trigger functions* and behave like any other function and have the same basic structure. Where they differ is in the input parameter and the output type. A trigger function never takes an argument, because internally the function already has access to the data and can modify it.

A trigger function always outputs a data type called a trigger. Because PostgreSQL trigger functions are no different from any other function, you can reuse the same trigger function across different triggers. This is usually not the case for other databases, where each trigger is wedded to its own handler code.

In PostgreSQL, each trigger must have exactly one associated triggering function to handle the firing. To apply multiple triggering functions, you must create multiple triggers against the same event. The alphabetical order of the trigger name determines the order of firing. Each trigger will have access to the revised data from the previous trigger. If any trigger issues a rollback, all data amended by earlier triggers fired by the same event will roll back.

You can use almost any language to create trigger functions, with SQL being the notable exception. PL/pgSQL is by far the most popular language. We demonstrate writing trigger functions using PL/pgSQL in "Writing Trigger Functions in PL/pgSQL" on page 210.

Aggregates

Most other databases limit you to ANSI SQL built-in aggregate functions such as MIN, MAX, AVG, SUM, and COUNT. In PostgreSQL, you don't have this limitation. If you need a more esoteric aggregate function, you're welcome to write your own. Because you can use any aggregate function in PostgreSQL as a window function (see "Window Functions" on page 184), you get twice the use out of any aggregate function that you author.

You can write aggregates in almost any language, SQL included. An aggregate is generally comprised of one or more functions. It must have at least a state transition function to perform the computation; usually this function runs repeatedly to create one output row from two input rows. You can also specify optional functions to manage initial and final states. You can also use a different language for each of the subfunctions. We have various examples of building aggregates using PL/pgSQL, PL/Python, and SQL in the article PostgreSQL Aggregates (*http://bit.ly/1CNAd3Y*).

Regardless of which language you use to code the functions, the glue that brings them all together is the CREATE AGGREGATE command:

```
CREATE AGGREGATE my_agg (input data type) (
SFUNC=state function name,
STYPE=state type,
FINALFUNC=final function name,
INITCOND=initial state value, SORTOP=sort_operator
);
```

The final function is optional, but if specified, it must take as input the result of the state function. The state function always takes a data type as the input along with the result of the last call to the state function. Sometimes this result is what you want as the result of the aggregate function, and sometimes you want to run a final function to massage the result. The initial condition is also optional. When the initial condition value is present, the command uses it to initialize the state value.

The optional sort operator can serve as the associated sort operator for a MIN- or MAX-like aggregate. It is used to take advantage of indexes. It is just an operator name such as > and <. It should be used only when the two following statements are equivalent:

```
SELECT agg(col) FROM sometable;
```

```
SELECT col FROM sometable ORDER BY col USING sortop LIMIT 1;
```

The PostgreSQL 9.4 CREATE AGGREGATE structure was expanded to include support for creating moving aggregates, which are useful with window functions that move the window. See PostgreSQL 9.4: CREATE AGGREGATE (*http://bit.ly/12IFIRA*) for details.

In PostgreSQL 9.6, aggregates were expanded to include support for parallelization. This was accomplished through the parallel property, which can take the values of safe, unsafe, or restric ted. If the parallel property is left out, the aggregate is marked as parallel unsafe. In addition to the parallel setting, combinefunc, serialfunc, and deserialfunc properties were added to support parallel aggregates. Refer to SQL Create Aggregate (*https:// www.postgresql.org/docs/9.6/static/sql-createaggregate.html*) for details.

Aggregates need not depend on a single column. If you need more than one column for your aggregate (an example is a built-in covariance function), see How to Create Multi-Column Aggregates (*http://bit.ly/1s2pEQD*) for guidance.

SQL language functions are easy to write. You don't have fancy control flow commands to worry about, and you probably have a good grasp of SQL to begin with. When it comes to writing aggregates, you can get pretty far with the SQL language alone. We demonstrate aggregates in "Writing SQL Aggregate Functions" on page 208.

Trusted and Untrusted Languages

Function languages can be either trusted or untrusted. Many—but not all—languages offer both a trusted and untrusted version. The term *trusted* connotes that the language can do no harm to the underlying operating system by denying it access to the key OS operations. In short:

Trusted
A trusted language lacks access to the server's filesystem beyond the data cluster. It therefore cannot execute OS commands. Users of any level can create functions in a trusted language. Languages such as SQL, PL/pgSQL, PL/Perl, and PL/V8 are trusted.

Untrusted
An untrusted language can interact with the OS. It can execute OS functions and call web services. Only superusers have the privilege of authoring functions in an untrusted language. However, a superuser can grant permission to another role

to run an untrusted function. By convention, languages that are untrusted end in the letter U (PL/PerlU, PL/PythonU, etc.). But ending in U is not a requirement. For example, PL/R is such an exception.

Writing Functions with SQL

Although SQL is mostly a language for issuing queries, it can also be used to write functions. In PostgreSQL, using an existing piece of SQL for the function is fast and easy: take your existing SQL statements, add a functional header and footer, and you're done. But the ease comes at a price. You can't use control features like conditional branches, looping, or defining variables. More restrictively, you can't run dynamic SQL statements that you assemble on the fly using arguments passed into the function.

On the positive side, the query planner can peek into an SQL function and optimize execution—a process called inlining. Query planners treat other languages as black boxes. Only SQL functions can be inlined, which lets them take advantage of indexes and collapse repetitive computations.

Basic SQL Function

Example 8-2 shows a primitive SQL function that inserts a row into a table and returns a scalar value.

Example 8-2. SQL function that returns the identifier of an inserted record

```
CREATE OR REPLACE FUNCTION write_to_log(param_user_name varchar,
param_description text)
RETURNS integer AS
$$
INSERT INTO logs(user_name, description) VALUES($1, $2)
RETURNING log_id;
$$
LANGUAGE 'sql' VOLATILE;
```

To call the function, execute something like:

```
SELECT write_to_log('alex', 'Logged in at 11:59 AM.') As new_id;
```

Similarly, you can update data with an SQL function and return a scalar or void, as shown in Example 8-3.

Example 8-3. SQL function to update a record

```
CREATE OR REPLACE FUNCTION
update_logs(log_id int, param_user_name varchar, param_description text)
RETURNS void AS
```

```
$$
UPDATE logs SET user_name = $2, description = $3
, log_ts = CURRENT_TIMESTAMP WHERE log_id = $1;
$$
LANGUAGE 'sql' VOLATILE;
```

To execute:

```
SELECT update_logs(12, 'alex', 'Fell back asleep.');
```

Functions, in almost all languages, can return sets. SQL functions are no exception. There are three common approaches to doing this: the ANSI SQL standard RETURNS TABLE syntax, OUT parameters, and composite data types. The RETURNS TABLE approach is closest to what you'll find in other database products. In Example 8-4, we demonstrate how to write the same function three ways.

Example 8-4. Examples of function returning sets

Using RETURNS TABLE:

```
CREATE OR REPLACE FUNCTION select_logs_rt(param_user_name varchar)
RETURNS TABLE (log_id int, user_name varchar(50),
description text, log_ts timestamptz) AS
$$
SELECT log_id, user_name, description, log_ts FROM logs WHERE user_name = $1;
$$
LANGUAGE 'sql' STABLE PARALLEL SAFE;
```

Using OUT parameters:

```
CREATE OR REPLACE FUNCTION select_logs_out(param_user_name varchar, OUT log_id int
, OUT user_name varchar, OUT description text, OUT log_ts timestamptz)
RETURNS SETOF record AS
$$
SELECT * FROM logs WHERE user_name = $1;
$$
LANGUAGE 'sql' STABLE PARALLEL SAFE;
```

Using a composite type:

```
CREATE OR REPLACE FUNCTION select_logs_so(param_user_name varchar)
RETURNS SETOF logs AS
$$
SELECT * FROM logs WHERE user_name = $1;
$$
LANGUAGE 'sql' STABLE PARALLEL SAFE;
```

Call all these functions using:

```
    SELECT * FROM select_logs_xxx('alex');
```

Writing SQL Aggregate Functions

Yes! In PostgreSQL you are able to author your own aggregate functions to expand beyond the usual aggregates MIN, MA, COUNT, AVG, etc. We demonstrate by creating an aggregate function to compute the geometric mean. A *geometric mean* (*http://www.buzzardsbay.org/geomean.htm*) is the *n*th root of a product of *n* positive numbers $((x1*x2*x3...xn)^{(1/n)})$. It has various uses in finance, economics, and statistics. A geometric mean substitutes for the more common arithmetic mean when the numbers range across vastly different scales. A more suitable computational formula uses logarithms to transform a multiplicative process to an additive one (`EXP(SUM(LN(x))/n)`). We'll be using this method in our example.

To build our geometric mean aggregate, we need two subfunctions: a state transition function to sum the logs (see Example 8-5) and a final function to exponentiate the logs. We'll also specify an initial condition of zero when we assemble everything together.

Example 8-5. Geometric mean aggregate: state function

```
CREATE OR REPLACE FUNCTION geom_mean_state(prev numeric[2], next numeric)
RETURNS numeric[2] AS
$$
SELECT
  CASE
    WHEN $2 IS NULL OR $2 = 0 THEN $1
    ELSE ARRAY[COALESCE($1[1],0) + ln($2), $1[2] + 1]
  END;
$$
LANGUAGE sql IMMUTABLE PARALLEL SAFE;
```

Our state transition function takes two inputs: the previous state passed in as an array with two elements, and the next added in the summation. If the next argument evaluates to NULL or zero, the state function returns the prior state. Otherwise, it returns a new array in which the first element is the sum of the logs and the second element is the running count.

We also need a final function, shown in Example 8-6, that divides the sum from the state transition by the count.

Example 8-6. Geometric mean aggregate: final function

```
CREATE OR REPLACE FUNCTION geom_mean_final(numeric[2])
RETURNS numeric AS
$$
SELECT CASE WHEN $1[2] > 0 THEN exp($1[1]/$1[2]) ELSE 0 END;
$$
LANGUAGE sql IMMUTABLE PARALLEL SAFE;
```

Now we stitch all the subfunctions together in our aggregate definition, as shown in Example 8-7. (Note that our aggregate has an initial condition that is the same data type as the one returned by our state function.)

Example 8-7. Geometric mean aggregate: assembling the pieces

```
CREATE AGGREGATE geom_mean(numeric) (
SFUNC=geom_mean_state,
STYPE=numeric[],
FINALFUNC=geom_mean_final,
PARALLEL = safe,
INITCOND='{0,0}'
);
```

Let's take our new function for a test drive. In Example 8-8, we compute a heuristic rating for racial diversity and list the top five most racially diverse counties in Massachusetts.

Example 8-8. Top five most racially diverse counties using geometric mean

```
SELECT left(tract_id,5) As county, geom_mean(val) As div_county
FROM census.vw_facts
WHERE category = 'Population' AND short_name != 'white_alone'
GROUP BY county
ORDER BY div_county DESC LIMIT 5;
```

```
county |      div_county
-------+--------------------
25025  | 85.1549046212833364
25013  | 79.5972921427888918
25017  | 74.7697097102419689
25021  | 73.8824162064128504
25027  | 73.5955049035237656
```

Let's go into overdrive and engage our new function as a window aggregate, as shown in Example 8-9.

Example 8-9. Top five most racially diverse census tracts with averages

```
WITH X AS (SELECT
  tract_id,
  left(tract_id,5) As county,
  geom_mean(val) OVER (PARTITION BY tract_id) As div_tract,
  ROW_NUMBER() OVER (PARTITION BY tract_id) As rn,
  geom_mean(val) OVER(PARTITION BY left(tract_id,5)) As div_county
FROM census.vw_facts WHERE category = 'Population' AND short_name != 'white_alone'
)
SELECT tract_id, county, div_tract, div_county
FROM X
```

```
WHERE rn = 1
ORDER BY div_tract DESC, div_county DESC LIMIT 5;

 tract_id    | county |       div_tract       |       div_county
-------------+--------+-----------------------+----------------------
 25025160101 | 25025  | 302.6815688785928786  | 85.1549046212833364
 25027731900 | 25027  | 265.6136902148147729  | 73.5955049035237656
 25021416200 | 25021  | 261.9351057509603296  | 73.8824162064128504
 25025130406 | 25025  | 260.3241378371627137  | 85.1549046212833364
 25017342500 | 25017  | 257.4671462282508267  | 74.7697097102419689
```

Writing PL/pgSQL Functions

When your functional needs outgrow SQL, turning to PL/pgSQL is a common practice. PL/pgSQL surpasses SQL in that you can declare local variables using DECLARE and you can incorporate control flow.

Basic PL/pgSQL Function

To demonstrate syntax differences from SQL, in Example 8-10 we rewrite Example 8-4 as a PL/pgSQL function.

Example 8-10. Function to return a table using PL/pgSQL

```
CREATE FUNCTION select_logs_rt(param_user_name varchar)
RETURNS TABLE (log_id int, user_name varchar(50),
description text, log_ts timestamptz) AS
$$
BEGIN
        RETURN QUERY
    SELECT log_id, user_name, description, log_ts FROM logs
      WHERE user_name = param_user_name;
END;
$$
LANGUAGE 'plpgsql' STABLE;
```

Writing Trigger Functions in PL/pgSQL

Because you can't write trigger functions in SQL, PL/pgSQL is your next best bet. In this section, we'll demonstrate how to write a basic trigger function in PL/pgSQL.

We proceed in two steps. First, we write the trigger function. Second, we explicitly attach the trigger function to the appropriate trigger. The second step is a powerful feature of PostgreSQL that decouples the function handling the trigger from the trigger itself. You can attach the same trigger function to multiple triggers, adding another level of reuse not found in other databases. Because each trigger function can stand on its own, you have your choice of languages, and mixing is completely OK. For a single triggering event, you can set up multiple triggers, each with functions written in a different language. For example, you can have a trigger email a client written in PL/PythonU or PL/PerlU and another trigger write to a log table with PL/pgSQL.

A basic trigger function and accompanying trigger is demonstrated in Example 8-11.

Example 8-11. Trigger function to timestamp new and changed records

```
CREATE OR REPLACE FUNCTION trig_time_stamper() RETURNS trigger AS ❶
$$
BEGIN
    NEW.upd_ts := CURRENT_TIMESTAMP;
    RETURN NEW;
END;
$$
LANGUAGE plpgsql VOLATILE;

CREATE TRIGGER trig_1
BEFORE INSERT OR UPDATE OF session_state, session_id ❷
ON web_sessions
FOR EACH ROW EXECUTE PROCEDURE trig_time_stamper();
```

❶ Defines the trigger function. This function can be used on any table that has a `upd_ts` column. It updates the `upd_ts` field to the current time before returning the changed record.

❷ This is a new feature introduced in version 9.0 that allows us to limit the firing of the trigger so it happens only if specified columns have changed. Prior to version 9.0, the trigger would fire on any update and you would need to perform a column-wise comparison using `OLD.some_column` and `NEW.some_column` to determine what changed. (This feature is not supported for `INSTEAD OF` triggers.)

Writing PL/Python Functions

Python is a slick language with a vast number of available libraries. PostgreSQL is the only database we know of that lets you compose functions using Python. PostgreSQL supports both Python 2 and Python 3.

 Although you can install both `plpython2u` and `plpython3u` in the same database, you can't use both during the same session. This means that you can't write a query that calls both `plpython2u` and `plpython3u` functions. You may encounter a third extension called `plpythonu`; this is an alias for `plpython2u` and is left around for backward compatibility.

In order to use PL/Python, you first need to install Python on your server. For Windows and Mac, Python installers are available. For Linux/Unix systems, Python binaries are usually available via the various distributions. For details, see PL/Python (*http://bit.ly/1zvCawf*). After installing Python, install the PostgreSQL Python extension:

```
CREATE EXTENSION plpython2u;
CREATE EXTENSION plpython3u;
```

Make absolutely sure that you have Python properly running on your server before attempting to install the extension, or else you will run into errors that could be difficult to troubleshoot.

The extensions are compiled against a specific minor version of Python. You should install the minor version of Python that matches what your `plpythonu` extensions were compiled against. For example, if your `plpython2u` was compiled against Python 2.7, you should install Python 2.7.

Basic Python Function

PostgreSQL automatically converts PostgreSQL data types to Python data types and back. PL/Python is capable of returning arrays and composite types. You can use PL/Python to write triggers and create aggregate functions. We've demonstrated some of these in the Postgres OnLine Journal, in PL/Python Examples (*http://bit.ly/12IG0rC*).

Python allows you to perform feats that aren't possible in PL/pgSQL. In Example 8-12, we demonstrate how to write a PL/Python function to do a text search of the online PostgreSQL document site.

Example 8-12. Searching PostgreSQL documents using PL/Python

```
CREATE OR REPLACE FUNCTION postgresql_help_search(param_search text)
RETURNS text AS
$$
import urllib, re ❶
response = urllib.urlopen(
    'http://www.postgresql.org/search/?u=%2Fdocs%2Fcurrent%2F&q=' + param_search
) ❷
raw_html = response.read() ❸
result =
        raw_html[raw_html.find("<!-- docbot goes here -->") :
        raw_html.find("<!-- pgContentWrap -->") - 1] ❹
result = re.sub('<[^<]+?>', '', result).strip() ❺
return result ❻
$$
LANGUAGE plpython2u SECURITY DEFINER STABLE;
```

❶ Imports the libraries we'll be using.

---

❷   Performs a search after concatenating the search term.

❸   Reads the response and saves the retrieved HTML to a variable called `raw_html`.

❹   Saves the part of the `raw_html` that starts with `<!-- docbot goes here -->` and ends just before the beginning of `<!-- pgContentWrap -->` into a new variable called `result`.

❺   Removes leading and trailing HTML symbols and whitespace.

❻   Returns `result`.

Calling Python functions is no different from calling functions written in other languages. In Example 8-13, we use the function we created in Example 8-12 to output the result with three search terms.

Example 8-13. Using Python functions in a query

```
SELECT search_term, left(postgresql_help_search(search_term),125) AS result
FROM (VALUES ('regexp_match'),('pg_trgm'),('tsvector')) As x(search_term);
```

Recall that PL/Python is an untrusted language, without a trusted counterpart. This means only superusers can write functions using PL/Python, and the function can interact with the filesystem of the OS. Example 8-14 takes advantage of the untrusted nature of PL/Python to retrieve file listings from a directory. Keep in mind that from the perspective of the OS, a PL/Python function runs under the context of the post gres user account created during installation, so you need to be sure that this account has adequate access to the relevant directories.

Example 8-14. Listing files in directories

```
CREATE OR REPLACE FUNCTION list_incoming_files()
RETURNS SETOF text AS
$$
import os
return os.listdir('/incoming')
$$
LANGUAGE 'plpython2u' VOLATILE SECURITY DEFINER;
```

Run the function in Example 8-14 with the following query:

```
SELECT filename
FROM list_incoming_files() As filename
WHERE filename ILIKE '%.csv'
```

Writing PL/V8, PL/CoffeeScript, and PL/LiveScript Functions

PL/V8 (*http://code.google.com/p/plv8js/wiki/PLV8*) (aka PL/JavaScript) is a trusted language built atop the Google V8 (*http://code.google.com/p/v8/*) engine. It allows you to write functions in JavaScript and interface with the JSON data type. It is not part of the core PostgreSQL offering, so you won't find it in all popular PostgreSQL distributions. You can always compile it from source. For Windows, we've built PL/V8 extension windows binaries (*http://bit.ly/1u09x5B*). You can download them from our Postgres OnLine Journal site for PostgreSQL 9.6 (*http://www.postgresonline.com/jour nal/archives/367-PLV8*) (both 32-bit and 64-bit).

When you add PL/V8 binaries to your PostgreSQL setup, you get not one, but three JavaScript-related languages:

PL/V8 (plv8)
This is the basic language that serves as the basis for the other two JavaScript languages.

PL/CoffeeScript (plcoffee)
This language lets you write functions in CoffeeScript (*http://coffeescript.org/*). CoffeeScript is JavaScript with a more succinct syntax structure that resembles Python. Like Python, it relies on indentation to impart context but does away with annoying curly braces.

PL/LiveScript (plls)
PL/LiveScript allows you to write functions in LiveScript (*http://livescript.net/*), a fork of CoffeeScript. LiveScript is similar to CoffeeScript but with some added syntactic condiments. This article promotes LiveScript as a superior alternative to CoffeeScript: 10 Reasons to Switch from CoffeeScript to LiveScript (*http://bit.ly/ 1BltJrs*). If anything, LiveScript does have more Python, F#, and Haskell features than CoffeeScript. If you're looking for a language that has a lighter footprint than PL/Python and is trusted, you might want to give LiveScript a try.

PL/CoffeeScript and PL/LiveScript are compiled using the same PL/V8 library. Their functionality is therefore identical to that of PL/V8. In fact, you can easily convert back to PL/V8 if they don't suit your taste buds. All three languages are trusted. This means they can't access OS filesystems, but they can be used by nonsuperusers to create functions.

Example 8-15 has the commands to install the three languages using extensions. For each database where you'd like to install the support, you must run these lines. You need not install all three if you choose not to.

Example 8-15. Installing PL/V8 family of languages

```
CREATE EXTENSION plv8;
CREATE EXTENSION plcoffee;
CREATE EXTENSION plls;
```

The PL/V8 family of languages has many key qualities that make them stand apart from PL/pgSQL, some of which you'll find only in other high-end procedural languages like PL/R:

- Generally faster numeric processing than SQL and PL/pgSQL.
- The ability to create window functions. You can't do this using SQL, PL/pgSQL, or PL/Python. (You can in PL/R and C, though.)
- The ability to create triggers and aggregate functions.
- Support for prepared statements, subtransactions, inner functions, classes, and try-catch error handling.
- The ability to dynamically generate executable code using an eval function.
- JSON support, allowing for looping over and filtering of JSON objects.
- Access to functions from DO commands.
- Compatibility with Node.js (*http://nodejs.org*). Node.js users, and other users who want to use Javascript for building network applications, will appreciate that PL/V8 and Node.js are built on the same Google V8 engine and that many of the libraries available for Node.js will work largely unchanged when used in PL/V8. There is an extension called plv8x (*https://github.com/clkao/plv8x*) that makes using Node.js modules and modules you build easier to reuse in PL/V8.

You can find several examples on our site of PL/V8 use. Some involved copying fairly large bodies of JavaScript code that we pulled from the web and wrapped in a PL/V8 wrapper, as detailed in Using PLV8 to Build JSON Selectors (*http://bit.ly/1Blrkgm*). The PL/V8 family mates perfectly with web applications because much of the same client-side JavaScript logic can be reused. More important, it makes a great all-purpose language for developing numeric functions, updating data, and so on.

Basic Functions

One of the great benefits of PL/V8 is that you can use any JavaScript function in your PL/V8 functions with minimal change. For example, you'll find many JavaScript examples on the web to validate email addresses. We arbitrarily picked one and made a PL/V8 out of it in Example 8-16.

Example 8-16. Using PL/V8 to validate an email address

```
CREATE OR REPLACE FUNCTION
validate_email(email text) returns boolean as
$$
 var re = /\S+@\S+\.\S+/;
 return re.test(email);
$$ LANGUAGE plv8 IMMUTABLE STRICT PARALLEL SAFE;
```

Our code uses a JavaScript regex object to check the email address. To use the function, see Example 8-17.

Example 8-17. Calling the PL/V8 email validator

```
SELECT email, validate_email(email) AS is_valid
 FROM (VALUES ('alexgomezq@gmail.com')
 ,('alexgomezqgmail.com'),('alexgomezq@gmailcom')) AS x (email);
```

which outputs:

```
      email          | is_valid
---------------------+----------
 alexgomezq@gmail.com | t
 alexgomezqgmail.com  | f
 alexgomezq@gmailcom  | f
```

Although you can code the same function using PL/pgSQL and PostgreSQL's own regular expression support, we guiltlessly poached someone else's time-tested code and wasted no time of our own. If you're a web developer and find yourself having to validate data on both the client side and the database side, using PL/V8 could halve your development efforts, pretty much by cutting and pasting.

You can store a whole set of these validation functions in a modules table. You can then inject results onto the page but also use the validation functions directly in the database, as described in Andrew Dunstan's "Loading Useful Modules in PLV8" (*http://bit.ly/1q2htrz*). This is possible because the eval function is part of the PL/V8 JavaScript language. The built-in function allows you to compile functions at startup for later use.

We fed Example 8-17 through an online converter (*http://js2coffee.org*) and added a return statement to generate its CoffeeScript counterpart in Example 8-18.

Example 8-18. PL/Coffee validation of email function

```
CREATE OR REPLACE FUNCTION
validate_email(email text) returns boolean as
$$
    re = /\S+@\S+\.\S+/
    return re.test email
```

```
$$
LANGUAGE plcoffee IMMUTABLE STRICT PARALLEL SAFE;
```

CoffeeScript doesn't look all that different from JavaScript, except for the lack of parentheses, curly braces, and semicolons. The LiveScript version looks exactly like the CoffeeScript except with a LANGUAGE plls specifier.

Writing Aggregate Functions with PL/V8

In Examples 8-19 and 8-20, we reformulate the state transition and final function of the geometric mean aggregate function (see "Writing SQL Aggregate Functions" on page 208) using PL/V8.

Example 8-19. PL/V8 geometric mean aggregate: state transition function

```
CREATE OR REPLACE FUNCTION geom_mean_state(prev numeric[2], next numeric)
RETURNS numeric[2] AS
$$
    return (next == null || next == 0) ? prev :
    [(prev[0] == null)? 0: prev[0] + Math.log(next), prev[1] + 1];
$$
LANGUAGE plv8 IMMUTABLE PARALLEL SAFE;
```

Example 8-20. PL/V8 geometric mean aggregate: final function

```
CREATE OR REPLACE FUNCTION geom_mean_final(in_num numeric[2])
RETURNS numeric AS
$$
  return in_num[1] > 0 ? Math.exp(in_num[0]/in_num[1]) : 0;
$$
LANGUAGE plv8 IMMUTABLE PARALLEL SAFE;
```

The final CREATE AGGREGATE puts all the pieces together and looks more or less the same in all languages. Our PL/V8 variant is shown in Example 8-21.

Example 8-21. PL/V8 geometric mean aggregate: putting all the pieces together

```
CREATE AGGREGATE geom_mean(numeric) (
  SFUNC=geom_mean_state,
  STYPE=numeric[],
  FINALFUNC=geom_mean_final,
  PARALLEL = safe,
  INITCOND='{0,0}'
);
```

When you run Example 8-9, calling our new PL/V8 function, you get the same answers as the version written in SQL, but the PL/V8 version is two to three times faster. Generally, for mathematical operations, you'll find that PL/V8 functions are 10 to 20 times faster than their SQL counterparts.

Writing Window Functions in PL/V8

PostgreSQL has many built-in window functions, as discussed in "Window Functions" on page 184. Any aggregate function, including the ones you create, can be used as window aggregate functions. These two points alone make PostgreSQL stand out from most other relational databases. Even more impressive is that PostgreSQL allows you to create your own window functions.

The only caveat is that most PLs you can install in PostgreSQL will not allow you to create window functions. If you need to write a window function in PostgreSQL, you cannot do it with built-in PL/PGSQL or SQL languages. Nor can you do it in other popular PLs like PL/Python or PL/Perl. You can do it in C, but that requires compilation. You can also to some extent do it in a language like PL/R. PL/V8, on the other hand, fully supports writing window functions and is fairly efficient (in many cases just as fast as a window function written in C), but unlike C, doesn't require compilation of your function code.

What makes writing window functions in PL/V8 possible is that PL/V8 comes packaged with a plv8.window_object() helper function that returns a handle to the current window object. This object includes methods for inspecting and accessing elements within the window.

In Example 8-22, we'll create a window function that, for each row, returns true if it's the beginning of a run, and false otherwise. Runs, or streaks, are sequences of identical outcome. The function lets the caller decide how many rows constitute a "run" through the ofs argument.

Example 8-22. PL/V8 window function to flag repeating data values

```
CREATE FUNCTION run_begin(arg anyelement, ofs int) RETURNS boolean AS $$
  var winobj = plv8.get_window_object();
  var result = true;
  /** Get current value **/
  var cval = winobj.get_func_arg_in_partition(0,
                                              0,
                                              winobj.SEEK_CURRENT,
                                              false);
  for (i = 1; i < ofs; i++){
      /** get next value **/
      nval = winobj.get_func_arg_in_partition(0,
                                              i,
                                              winobj.SEEK_CURRENT,
                                              false);
      result = (cval == nval) ? true : false;
```

```
        if (!result){
            break;
        }
        /** next current value is our last value **/
        cval = nval;

    }
  return result;
$$ LANGUAGE plv8 WINDOW;
```

To declare a function as a window function, it must have a `WINDOW` designator in the function envelope as in the last line of Example 8-22.

The body of the function must inspect elements of the window set of data and use them. PL/V8 has a handle to this window and helper methods outlined in the PL/V8 documentation PL/V8 Window function API (*http://pgxn.org/dist/plv8/doc/plv8.html#Window.function.API*). Our function needs to look forward in the window for values from the current position in the window through `ofs` values. If these values are all the same, it will return true, otherwise false. The function method that PL/V8 provides for scanning values of a window is `get_func_arg_in_partition`. We use that to look forward and exit with false, as soon as the pattern of equality fails or we've reached the last value.

We'll use this function to find the winner in a simple game of coin toss. Each player gets four tosses, and the winner must have a run of three heads, as shown in Example 8-23.

Example 8-23. PL/V8 window function example usage

```
SELECT id, player, toss,
 run_begin(toss,3) OVER (PARTITION BY player ORDER BY id) AS rb
    FROM coin_tosses
ORDER BY player, id;
```

```
 id | player | toss | rb
----+--------+------+----
  4 | alex   | H    | t
  8 | alex   | H    | t
 12 | alex   | H    | f
 16 | alex   | H    | f
  2 | leo    | T    | f
  6 | leo    | H    | f
 10 | leo    | H    | f
 14 | leo    | T    | f
  1 | regina | H    | f
  5 | regina | H    | f
  9 | regina | T    | f
 13 | regina | T    | f
  3 | sonia  | T    | t
```

```
 7 | sonia | T  | t
11 | sonia | T  | f
15 | sonia | T  | f
(16 rows)
```

For other examples of writing PL/V8 functions in PL/V8, check out the PL/V8 window regression script (*https://github.com/plv8/plv8/blob/master/sql/window.sql*), which demonstrates how to create many of the built-in PostgreSQL window functions (lead, lag, row_number, cume_dist, and first_value, last_value) in PL/V8.

## CHAPTER 9

Query Performance Tuning

Sooner or later, we'll all face a query that takes just a bit longer to execute than we have patience for. The best and easiest fix is to perfect the underlying SQL, followed by adding indexes and updating planner statistics. To guide you in these pursuits, PostgreSQL comes with a built-in explainer that tells you how the query planner is going to execute your SQL. Armed with your knack for writing flawless SQL, your instinct to sniff out useful indexes, and the insight of the explainer, you should have no trouble getting your queries to run as fast as your hardware budget will allow.

EXPLAIN

The easiest tools for targeting query performance problems are the EXPLAIN and EXPLAIN (ANALYZE) commands. EXPLAIN has been around since the early years of PostgreSQL. Over time the command has matured into a full-blown tool capable of reporting highly detailed information about the query execution. Along the way, it added more output formats. EXPLAIN can even dump the output to XML, JSON, or YAML.

Perhaps the most exciting enhancement for the casual user came several years back when pgAdmin introduced graphical explain. With a hard and long stare, you can identify where the bottlenecks are in your query, which tables are missing indexes, and whether the path of execution took an unexpected turn.

EXPLAIN Options

To use the nongraphical version of EXPLAIN, simply preface your SQL with the word EXPLAIN, qualified by some optional arguments:

- EXPLAIN by itself will just give you an idea of how the planner intends to execute the query without running it.

- Adding the `ANALYZE` argument, as in `EXPLAIN (ANALYZE)`, will execute the query and give you a comparative analysis of expected versus actual behavior.

- Adding the `VERBOSE` argument, as in `EXPLAIN (VERBOSE)`, will report the planner's activities down to the columnar level.

- Adding the `BUFFERS` argument, which must be used in conjunction with `ANALYZE`, as in `EXPLAIN (ANALYZE, BUFFERS)`, will report *share hits*. The higher this number, the more records were already in memory from prior queries, meaning that the planner did not have to go back to disk to reretrieve them.

An `EXPLAIN` that provides all details, including timing, output of columns, and buffers, would look like `EXPLAIN (ANALYZE, VERBOSE, BUFFERS) your_query_here;`.

To see the results of `EXPLAIN (ANALYZE)` on a data-changing statement such as `UPDATE` or `INSERT` without making the actual data change, wrap the statement in a transaction that you abort: place `BEGIN` before the statement and `ROLLBACK` after it.

You can use graphical explain with a GUI such as pgAdmin. After launching pgAdmin, compose your query as usual, but instead of executing it, choose `EXPLAIN` or `EXPLAIN (ANALYZE)` from the drop-down menu.

Sample Runs and Output

Let's try an example. First, we'll use the `EXPLAIN (ANALYZE)` command with a table we created in Examples 4-1 and 4-2.

In order to ensure that the planner doesn't use an index, we first drop the primary key from our table:

```
ALTER TABLE census.hisp_pop DROP CONSTRAINT IF EXISTS hisp_pop_pkey;
```

Dropping all indexes lets us see the most basic of plans in action, the sequential scan strategy. See Example 9-1.

Example 9-1. EXPLAIN (ANALYZE) of a sequential scan

```
EXPLAIN (ANALYZE)
SELECT tract_id, hispanic_or_latino
FROM census.hisp_pop
WHERE tract_id = '25025010103';
```

Using EXPLAIN alone gives us estimated plan costs. Using EXPLAIN in conjunction with ANALYZE gives us both estimated and actual costs to execute the plan. Example 9-2 shows the output of Example 9-1.

Example 9-2. EXPLAIN (ANALYZE) output

```
Seq Scan on hisp_pop
    (cost=0.00..33.48 rows=1 width=16)
    (actual time=0.213..0.346 rows=1 loops=1)
    Filter: ((tract_id)::text = '25025010103'::text)
    Rows Removed by Filter: 1477
Planning time: 0.095 ms
Execution time: 0.381 ms
```

In EXPLAIN plans, you'll see a breakdown by steps. Each step has a reported cost that looks something like cost=0.00..33.48, as shown in Example 9-2. In this case we have 0.00, which is the estimated startup cost, and the second number, 33.48, which is the total estimated cost of the step. The startup is the time before retrieval of data and could include scanning of indexes, joins of tables, etc. For sequential scan steps, the startup cost is zero because the planner mindlessly pulls all data; retrieval begins right away.

Keep in mind that the cost measure is reported in arbitrary units, which varies based on hardware and configuration cost settings. As such, it's useful only as an estimate when comparing different plans on the same server. The planner's job is to pick the plan with the lowest estimated overall costs.

Because we opted to include the ANALYZE argument in Example 9-1, the planner will run the query, and we're blessed with the actual timings as well.

From the plan in Example 9-2, we can see that the planner elected a sequential scan because it couldn't find any indexes. The additional tidbit of information Rows Removed by Filter: 1477 shows the number of rows that the planner examined before excluding them from the output.

If you are running PostgreSQL 9.4 or above, the output makes a distinction between planning time and execution time. Planning time is the amount of time it takes for the planner to come up with the execution plan, whereas the execution time is everything that follows.

Let's now add back our primary key:

```
ALTER TABLE census.hisp_pop ADD CONSTRAINT hisp_pop_pkey PRIMARY KEY(tract_id);
```

Now we'll repeat Example 9-1, with the plan output in Example 9-3.

Example 9-3. EXPLAIN (ANALYZE) output of index strategy plan

```
Index Scan using idx_hisp_pop_tract_id_pat on hisp_pop
    (cost=0.28..8.29 rows=1 width=16)
    (actual time=0.018..0.019 rows=1 loops=1)
    Index Cond: ((tract_id)::text = '25025010103'::text)
```

```
Planning time: 0.110 ms
Execution time: 0.046 ms
```

The planner concludes that using the index is cheaper than a sequential scan and switches to an index scan. The estimated overall cost drops from 33.48 to 8.29. The startup cost is no longer zero, because the planner first scans the index, then pulls the matching records from data pages (or from memory if in shared buffers already). You'll also notice that the planner no longer needed to scan 1,477 records. This greatly reduced the cost.

More complex queries, such as in Example 9-4, include additional steps referred to as subplans, with each subplan having its own cost and all adding up to the total cost of the plan. The parent plan is always listed first, and its cost and time is equal to the sum of all its subplans. The output indents the subplans.

Example 9-4. EXPLAIN (ANALYZE) with GROUP BY and SUM

```
EXPLAIN (ANALYZE)
SELECT left(tract_id,5) AS county_code, SUM(white_alone) As w
FROM census.hisp_pop
WHERE tract_id BETWEEN '25025000000' AND '25025999999'
GROUP BY county_code;
```

The output of Example 9-4 is shown in Example 9-5, consisting of a grouping and sum.

Example 9-5. EXPLAIN (ANALYZE) output of HashAggregate strategy plan

```
HashAggregate
    (cost=29.57..32.45 rows=192 width=16)
    (actual time=0.664..0.664 rows=1 loops=1)
    Group Key: "left"((tract_id)::text, 5)
    -> Bitmap Heap Scan on hisp_pop
        (cost=10.25..28.61 rows=192 width=16)
        (actual time=0.441..0.550 rows=204 loops=1)
        Recheck Cond:
            (((tract_id)::text >= '25025000000'::text) AND
            ((tract_id)::text <= '25025999999'::text))
        Heap Blocks: exact=15
        -> Bitmap Index Scan on hisp_pop_pkey
            (cost=0.00..10.20 rows=192 width=0)
            (actual time=0.421..0.421 rows=204 loops=1)
            Index Cond:
                (((tract_id)::text >= '25025000000'::text) AND
                ((tract_id)::text <= '25025999999'::text))
Planning time: 4.835 ms
Execution time: 0.732 ms
```

The parent of Example 9-5 is the HashAggregate. It contains a subplan of Bitmap Heap Scan, which in turn contains a subplan of Bitmap Index Scan. In this example, because this is the first time we're running this query, our planning time greatly over-shadows the execution time. However, PostgreSQL caches plans and data, so if we were to run this query or a similar one within a short period of time, we should be rewarded with a much reduced planning time and also possibly reduced execution time if much of the data it needs is already in memory. Because of caching, our second run has these stats:

```
Planning time: 0.200 ms
Execution time: 0.635 ms
```

Graphical Outputs

If reading the output is giving you a headache, see Figure 9-1 for the graphical EXPLAIN (ANALYZE) of Example 9-4.

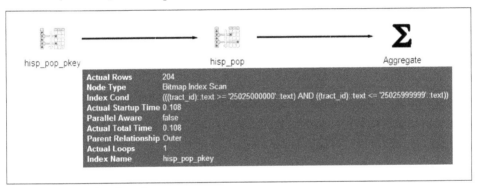

Figure 9-1. Graphical explain output

You can get more detailed information about each part by mousing over the node in the display.

Before wrapping up this section, we must pay homage to the tabular explain plan (*http://explain.depesz.com*) created by Hubert Lubaczewski. Using his site, you can copy and paste the text output of your EXPLAIN output, and it will show you a beauti-fully formatted table, as shown in Figure 9-2.

HTML TEXT **STATS** Did it help? Consider supporting us

Per node type stats

node type	count	sum of times	% of query
Bitmap Heap Scan	1	0.129 ms	19.4 %
Bitmap Index Scan	1	0.421 ms	63.4 %
HashAggregate	1	0.114 ms	17.2 %

Per table stats

Table name	Scan count	Total time	% of query
scan type	count	sum of times	% of table
hisp_pop	1	0.129 ms	19.4 %
Bitmap Heap Scan	1	0.129 ms	100.0 %

Figure 9-2. Online EXPLAIN statistics

In the HTML tab, you'll see a nicely reformatted color-coded table of the plan, with problem areas highlighted in vibrant colors, as shown in Figure 9-3. It has columns for exclusive time (time consumed by the parent step) and inclusive time (the time of the parent step plus its child steps).

#	exclusive	inclusive	rows x	rows	loops	node
1.	0.114	0.664	↑ 192.0	1	1	→ HashAggregate (cost=29.57..32.45 rows=192 width=16) (actual time=0.664..0.664 rows=1 loops=1) Group Key: "left"((tract_id)::text, 5)
2.	0.129	0.550	↓ 1.1	204	1	→ Bitmap Heap Scan on hisp_pop (cost=10.25..28.61 rows=192 width=16) (actual time=0.441..0.550 rows=204 loops=1) Recheck Cond: (((tract_id)::text >= '25025000000'::text) AND ((tract_id)::text <= '25025999999'::text)) Heap Blocks: exact=15
3.	0.421	0.421	↓ 1.1	204	1	→ Bitmap Index Scan on hisp_pop_pkey (cost=0.00..10.20 rows=192 width=0) (actual time=0.421..0.421 rows=204 loops=1) Index Cond: (((tract_id)::text >= '25025000000'::text) AND ((tract_id)::text <= '25025999999'::text))

Figure 9-3. Tabular explain output

Although the HTML table in Figure 9-3 provides much the same information as our plain-text output, the color coding and the breakout of numbers makes it easier to digest. For example, yellow, brown, and red highlight potential bottlenecks.

The *rows x* column is the expected number of rows, while the *rows* column shows the actual number after execution. This reveals that, although our planner's final step was expecting 192 records, we ended up with just one. Bad row estimates are often caused by out-of-date table statistics. It's always a good habit to analyze tables frequently to update the statistics, especially right after an extensive update or insert.

Gathering Statistics on Statements

The first step in optimizing performance is to determine which queries are bottle-necks. One monitoring extension useful for getting a handle on your most costly queries is pg_stat_statements (*http://bit.ly/1IanI2K*). This extension provides metrics on running queries, the most frequently run queries, and how long each takes. Studying these metrics will help you determine where you need to focus your optimization efforts.

pg_stat_statements comes packaged with most PostgreSQL distributions but must be preloaded on startup to initiate its data-collection process:

1. In *postgresql.conf*, change `shared_preload_libraries = ''` to `shared_pre load_libraries = 'pg_stat_statements'`.

2. In the customized options section of *postgresql.conf*, add the lines:

   ```
   pg_stat_statements.max = 10000
   pg_stat_statements.track = all
   ```

3. Restart your `postgresql` service.

4. In any database you want to use for monitoring, enter `CREATE EXTENSION pg_stat_statements;`.

The extension provides two key features:

- A view called `pg_stat_statements`, which shows all the databases to which the currently connected user has access.

- A function called `pg_stat_statements_reset`, which flushes the query log. This function can be run only by superusers.

The query in Example 9-6 lists the five most costly queries in the `postgresql_book` database.

Example 9-6. Expensive queries in database

```
SELECT
    query, calls, total_time, rows,
    100.0*shared_blks_hit/NULLIF(shared_blks_hit+shared_blks_read,0) AS hit_percent
FROM pg_stat_statements As s INNER JOIN pg_database As d On d.oid = s.dbid
WHERE d.datname = 'postgresql_book'
ORDER BY total_time DESC LIMIT 5;
```

Writing Better Queries

The best and easiest way to improve query performance is to start with well-written queries. Four out of five queries we encounter are not written as efficiently as they could be.

There appear to be two primary causes for all this bad querying. First, we see people reuse SQL patterns without thinking. For example, if they successfully write a query using a left join, they will continue to use left join when incorporating more tables instead of considering the sometimes more appropriate inner join. Unlike other programming languages, the SQL language does not lend itself well to blind reuse.

Second, people don't tend to keep up with the latest developments in their dialect of SQL. Don't be oblivious to all the syntax-saving (and sanity-saving) addenda that have come along in new versions of PostgreSQL.

Writing efficient SQL takes practice. There's no such thing as a wrong query as long as you get the expected result, but there is such a thing as a slow query. In this section, we point out some of the common mistakes we see people make. Although this book is about PostgreSQL, our recommendations are applicable to other relational databases as well.

Overusing Subqueries in SELECT

A classic newbie mistake is to think of subqueries as independent entities. Unlike conventional programming languages, SQL doesn't take kindly to black-boxing—writing a bunch of subqueries independently and then assembling them mindlessly to get the final result. You have to treat each query holistically. How you piece together data from different views and tables is every bit as important as how you go about retrieving the data in the first place.

The unnecessary use of subqueries, as shown in Example 9-7, is a common symptom of piecemeal thinking.

Example 9-7. Overusing subqueries

```
SELECT tract_id,
    (SELECT COUNT(*) FROM census.facts As F
WHERE F.tract_id = T.tract_id) As num_facts,
    (SELECT COUNT(*)
    FROM census.lu_fact_types As Y
    WHERE Y.fact_type_id IN (
        SELECT fact_type_id
        FROM census.facts F
        WHERE F.tract_id = T.tract_id
    )
```

```
    ) As num_fact_types
FROM census.lu_tracts As T;
```

Example 9-7 can be more efficiently written as Example 9-8. This query, consolidating selects and using a join, is not only shorter than the prior one, but faster. If you have a larger dataset or weaker hardware, the difference could be even more pronounced.

Example 9-8. Overused subqueries simplified

```
SELECT T.tract_id,
    COUNT(f.fact_type_id) As num_facts,
    COUNT(DISTINCT fact_type_id) As num_fact_types
FROM census.lu_tracts As T LEFT JOIN census.facts As F ON T.tract_id = F.tract_id
GROUP BY T.tract_id;
```

Figure 9-4 shows the graphical plan for Example 9-7 (we'll save you the eyesore of seeing the gnarled output of the text EXPLAIN), while Figure 9-5 shows the tabular output from *http://explain.depesz.com*, revealing a great deal of inefficiency.

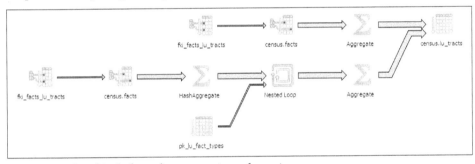

Figure 9-4. Graphical plan when overusing subqueries

exclusive	inclusive	rows x	rows	loops	node
10.709	1292.135	↑ 1.0	1478	1	→ Seq Scan on lu_tracts t (cost=0.00..615535.37 rows=1478 width=12) (actual time
					SubPlan (forSeq Scan)
63.554	264.562	↑ 1.0	1	1478	→ Aggregate (cost=207.86..207.87 rows=1 width=0) (ac
153.712	201.008	↑ 1.0	68	1478	→ Bitmap Heap Scan on facts f (cost=4.79..207.69 rows=68 width=0) (actual time
					Recheck Cond: ((tract_id)::text = (t.tract_id)::text)
47.296	47.296	↑ 1.0	68	1478	→ Bitmap Index Scan on fki_facts_lu_tracts (cost=0.00..4.78 rows=68 width=0) (actual tim
					Index Cond: ((tract_id)::text = (t.tract_id)::text)
59.120	1010.864	↑ 1.0	1	1478	→ Aggregate (cost=208.56..208.57 rows=1 width=0) (ac
314.814	957.744	↑ 1.0	68	1478	→ Nested Loop (cost=207.86..208.39 rows=68 width=0) (actual ti
155.190	341.418	↓ 68.0	68	1478	→ HashAggregate (cost=207.86..207.87 rows=1 width=4) (actua
141.888	186.228	↑ 1.0	68	1478	→ Bitmap Heap Scan on facts f (cost=4.79..207.69 rows=68 width=4) (act
					Recheck Cond: ((tract_id)::text = (t.tract_ic
44.340	44.340	↑ 1.0	68	1478	→ Bitmap Index Scan on fki_facts_lu_tra((cost=0.00..4.78 rows=68 width=0) (ac
					Index Cond: ((tract_id)::text = (t.tract_i)
301.512	301.512	↑ 1.0	1	100504	→ Index Scan using pk_lu_fact_types on lu_fact (cost=0.00..0.50 rows=1 width=4) (actual time
					Index Cond: (fact_type_id = f.fact_type_id)

Figure 9-5. Tabular plan when overusing subqueries

Figure 9-6 shows the graphical plan of Example 9-8, demonstrating how much less work goes on in it.

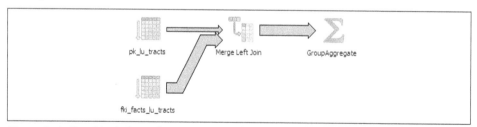

Figure 9-6. Graphical plan after removing subqueries

Keep in mind that we're not asking you to avoid subqueries entirely. We're only asking you to use them judiciously. When you do use them, pay extra attention to how you incorporate them into the main query. Finally, remember that a subquery should work with the main query, not independently of it.

Avoid SELECT *

SELECT * is wasteful. It's akin to printing out a 1,000-page document when you need only 10 pages. Besides the obvious downside of adding to network traffic, there are two other drawbacks that you might not think of.

First, PostgreSQL stores large blob and text objects using TOAST (The Oversized-Attribute Storage Technique). TOAST maintains side tables for PostgreSQL to store this extra data and may chunk a single text field into multiple rows. So retrieving a large field means that TOAST must assemble the data from several rows of a side TOAST table. Imagine the extra processing if your table contains text data the size of *War and Peace* and you perform an unnecessary SELECT *.

Second, when you define views, you often will include more columns than you'll need. You might even go so far as to use SELECT * inside a view. This is understandable and perfectly fine. PostgreSQL is smart enough to let you request all the columns you want in your view definition and even include complex calculations or joins without incurring penalty, as long as no user runs a query referring to individual columns.

To drive home our point, let's wrap our census in a view and use the slow subquery example from Example 9-7:

```
CREATE OR REPLACE VIEW vw_stats AS
SELECT tract_id,
    (SELECT COUNT(*)
      FROM census.facts As F
      WHERE F.tract_id = T.tract_id) As num_facts,
    (SELECT COUNT(*)
      FROM census.lu_fact_types As Y
      WHERE Y.fact_type_id IN (
        SELECT fact_type_id
        FROM census.facts F
        WHERE F.tract_id = T.tract_id
    )
    ) As num_fact_types
FROM census.lu_tracts As T;
```

Now we query our view with this query:

```
SELECT tract_id FROM vw_stats;
```

Execution time is about 21 ms on our server because it doesn't run any computation for certain fields such as num_facts and num_fact_types, fields we did not ask for. If you looked at the plan, you may be startled to find that it never even touches the facts table because it's smart enough to know it doesn't need to. But suppose we enter:

```
SELECT * FROM vw_stats;
```

Our execution time skyrockets to 681 ms, and the plan is just as we had in Figure 9-4. Although our results in this example suffer the loss of just milliseconds, imagine tables with tens of millions of rows and hundreds of columns. Those milliseconds could translate into overtime at the office waiting for a query to finish.

Make Good Use of CASE

We're always surprised how frequently people forget about using the ANSI SQL CASE expression. In many aggregate situations, a CASE can obviate the need for inefficient subqueries. We'll demonstrate the point with two equivalent queries and their corresponding plans. Example 9-9 uses subqueries.

Example 9-9. Using subqueries instead of CASE

```
SELECT T.tract_id, COUNT(*) As tot, type_1.tot AS type_1
FROM
    census.lu_tracts AS T LEFT JOIN
    (SELECT tract_id, COUNT(*) As tot
        FROM census.facts
        WHERE fact_type_id = 131
        GROUP BY tract_id
    ) As type_1 ON T.tract_id = type_1.tract_id LEFT JOIN
    census.facts AS F ON T.tract_id = F.tract_id
GROUP BY T.tract_id, type_1.tot;
```

Figure 9-7 shows the graphical plan of Example 9-9.

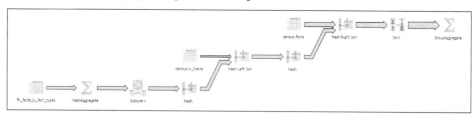

Figure 9-7. Graphical plan when using subqueries instead of CASE

We now rewrite the query using CASE. You'll find that the economized query, shown in Example 9-10, is generally faster and much easier to read.

Example 9-10. Using CASE instead of subqueries

```
SELECT T.tract_id, COUNT(*) As tot,
    COUNT(CASE WHEN F.fact_type_id = 131 THEN 1 ELSE NULL END) AS type_1
FROM census.lu_tracts AS T LEFT JOIN census.facts AS F
ON T.tract_id = F.tract_id
GROUP BY T.tract_id;
```

Figure 9-8 shows the graphical plan of Example 9-10.

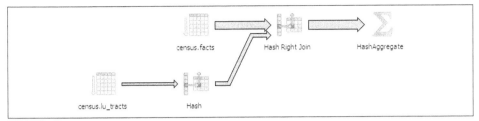

Figure 9-8. Graphical explain when using CASE

Even though our rewritten query still doesn't use the `fact_type` index, it's faster than using subqueries because the planner scans the `facts` table only once. A shorter plan is generally not only easier to comprehend but also often performs better than a longer one, although not always.

Using FILTER Instead of CASE

PostgreSQL 9.4 introduced the `FILTER` construct, which we introduced in "FILTER Clause for Aggregates" on page 181. `FILTER` can often replace `CASE` in aggregate expressions. Not only is this syntax more pleasant to look at, but in many situations it performs better. We repeat Example 9-10 with the equivalent filter version in Example 9-11.

Example 9-11. Using FILTER instead of subqueries

```
SELECT T.tract_id, COUNT(*) As tot,
    COUNT(*) FILTER (WHERE F.fact_type_id = 131) AS type_1
FROM census.lu_tracts AS T LEFT JOIN census.facts AS F
ON T.tract_id = F.tract_id
GROUP BY T.tract_id;
```

For this particular example, the `FILTER` performance is only about a millisecond faster than our `CASE` version, and the plans are more or less the same.

Parallelized Queries

A parallelized query is one whose execution is distributed by the planner among multiple backend processes. By so doing, PostgreSQL is able to utilize multiple processor cores so that work completes in less time. Depending on the number of processor cores in your hardware, the time savings could be significant. Having two cores could halve your time; four could quarter your time, etc.

Parallelization was introduced in version 9.6. The kinds of queries available for parallelization are limited, usually consisting only of the most straightforward select statements. But with each new release, we expect the range of parallelizable queries to expand.

The kinds of queries that cannot be parallelized as of version 10.0 are:

- Any data modifying queries, such as updates, inserts, and deletes.
- Any data definition queries, such as the creation of new tables, columns, and indexes.
- Queries called by cursors or for loops.
- Some aggregates. Common ones like COUNT and SUM are parallelizable, but aggregates that include DISTINCT or ORDER BY are not.
- Functions of your own creation. By default they are PARALLEL UNSAFE, but you can enable parallelization through the PARALLEL setting of the function as described in "Anatomy of PostgreSQL Functions" on page 199.

The following setting requirements are needed to enable the use of parallelism:

- dynamic_shared_memory_type cannot be set to none.
- max_worker_processes needs to be greater than zero.
- max_parallel_workers, a new setting in PostgreSQL 10, needs to be greater than zero and less than or equal to max_worker_processes.
- max_parallel_workers_per_gather needs to be greater than zero and less than or equal to max_worker_processes. For PostgreSQL 10, this setting must also be less than or equal to max_parallel_workers. You can apply this particular setting at the session or function level.

What Does a Parallel Query Plan Look Like?

How do you know if your query is a beneficiary of parallelization? Look in the plan. Parallelization is done by a part of the planner called a gather node. So if you see a gather node in your query plan, you have some kind of parallelization. A gather node contains exactly one plan, which it divides amongst what are called workers. Each worker runs as separate backend processes, each process working on a portion of the overall query. The results of workers are collected by a worker acting as the leader. The leader does the same work as other workers but has the added responsibility of collecting all the answers from fellow workers. If the gather node is the root node of a plan, the whole query will be run in parallel. If it's lower down, only the subplan it encompasses will be parallelized.

For debugging purposes, you can invoke a setting called force_parallel_mode. When true, it will encourage the planner to use parallel mode if a query is parallelizable even when the planner concludes it's not cost-effective to do so. This setting is useful during debugging to figure out why a query is not parallelized. Don't switch on this setting in a production environment, though!

The queries you've seen thus far in this chapter will not trigger a parallel plan because the cost of setting up the background workers outweighs the benefit. To confirm that our query takes longer when forced to be parallel, try the following:

```
set force_parallel_mode = true;
```

And then run Example 9-4 again. The output of the new plan is shown in Example 9-12.

Example 9-12. EXPLAIN (ANALYZE) output of Parallel plan

```
Gather
    (cost=1029.57..1051.65 rows=192 width=64)
    (actual time=12.881..13.947 rows=1 loops=1)
    Workers Planned: 1
    Workers Launched: 1
    Single Copy: true
    -> HashAggregate
        (cost=29.57..32.45 rows=192 width=64)
        (actual time=0.230..0.231 rows=1 loops=1)
        Group Key: "left"((tract_id)::text, 5)
        -> Bitmap Heap Scan on hisp_pop
            (cost=10.25..28.61 rows=192 width=36)
            (actual time=0.127..0.184 rows=204 loops=1)
            Recheck Cond:
                (((tract_id)::text >= '25025000000'::text) AND
                ((tract_id)::text <= '25025999999'::text))
                -> Bitmap Index Scan on hisp_pop_pkey
                    (cost=0.00..10.20 rows=192 width=0)
                    (actual time=0.106..0.106 rows=204 loops=1)
                    Index Cond:
                        (((tract_id)::text >= '25025000000'::text) AND
                        ((tract_id)::text <= '25025999999'::text))
Planning time: 0.416 ms
Execution time: 16.160 ms
```

The cost of organizing additional workers (even one) significantly increases the total time of the query.

Generally, parallelization is rarely worthwhile for queries that finish in a few milliseconds. But for queries over a ginormous dataset that normally take seconds or minutes to complete, parallelization is worth the initial setup cost.

To illustrate the benefit of parallelization, we downloaded a table from the US Bureau of Labor Statistics with 6.5 million rows of data and ran the query in Example 9-13.

Example 9-13. Group by with parallelization

```
set max_parallel_workers_per_gather=4;
EXPLAIN ANALYZE VERBOSE
SELECT COUNT(*), area_type_code
FROM labor
GROUP BY area_type_code
ORDER BY area_type_code;

Finalize GroupAggregate
    (cost=104596.49..104596.61 rows=3 width=10)
    (actual time=500.440..500.444 rows=3 loops=1)
    Output: COUNT(*), area_type_code
    Group Key: labor.area_type_code
    -> Sort
        (cost=104596.49..104596.52 rows=12 width=10)
        (actual time=500.433..500.435 rows=15 loops=1)
        Output: area_type_code, (PARTIAL COUNT(*))
        Sort Key: labor.area_type_code
        Sort Method: quicksort  Memory: 25kB
        -> Gather
            (cost=104595.05..104596.28 rows=12 width=10)
            (actual time=500.159..500.382 rows=15 loops=1)
            Output: area_type_code, (PARTIAL COUNT(*))
            Workers Planned: 4
            Workers Launched: 4
            -> Partial HashAggregate
                (cost=103595.05..103595.08 rows=3 width=10)
                (actual time=483.081..483.082 rows=3 loops=5)
                Output: area_type_code, PARTIAL count(*)
                Group Key: labor.area_type_code
                Worker 0: actual time=476.705..476.706 rows=3 loops=1
                Worker 1: actual time=480.704..480.705 rows=3 loops=1
                Worker 2: actual time=480.598..480.599 rows=3 loops=1
                Worker 3: actual time=478.000..478.000 rows=3 loops=1
                -> Parallel Seq Scan on public.labor
                    (cost=0.00..95516.70 rows=1615670 width=2)
                    (actual time=1.550..282.833 rows=1292543 loops=5)
                    Output: area_type_code
                    Worker 0: actual time=0.078..282.698 rows=1278313 loops=1
                    Worker 1: actual time=3.497..282.068 rows=1338095 loops=1
                    Worker 2: actual time=3.378..281.273 rows=1232359 loops=1
                    Worker 3: actual time=0.761..278.013 rows=1318569 loops=1
Planning time: 0.060 ms
Execution time: 512.667 ms
```

To see the cost and timing without parallelization, set `max_parallel_work ers_per_gather=0`, and compare the plan, as shown in Example 9-14.

Example 9-14. Group by without parallelization

```
set max_parallel_workers_per_gather=0;
EXPLAIN ANALYZE VERBOSE
SELECT COUNT(*), area_type_code
FROM labor
GROUP BY area_type_code
ORDER BY area_type_code;

Sort
    (cost=176300.24..176300.25 rows=3 width=10)
    (actual time=1647.060..1647.060 rows=3 loops=1)
    Output: (COUNT(*)), area_type_code
    Sort Key: labor.area_type_code
    Sort Method: quicksort  Memory: 25kB
    -> HashAggregate
        (cost=176300.19..176300.22 rows=3 width=10)
        (actual time=1647.025..1647.025 rows=3 loops=1)
        Output: count(*), area_type_code
        Group Key: labor.area_type_code
        -> Seq Scan on public.labor
            (cost=0.00..143986.79 rows=6462679 width=2)
            (actual time=0.076..620.563 rows=6462713 loops=1)
            Output: series_id, year, period, value, footnote_codes, area_type_code
Planning time: 0.054 ms
Execution time: 1647.115 ms
```

In both cases, the output is the following:

```
count   | area_type_code
--------+---------------
3718937 | M
2105205 | N
 638571 | S
(3 rows)
```

In the parallel plan, four workers each take about 280 ms to accomplish their portion of the task.

Parallel Scans

A parallel query has a particular scan strategy for partitioning the set of data among workers. In PostgreSQL 9.6, only a sequential scan is parallelizable. PostgreSQL 10 is also able to parallelize bitmap heap scans, index scans, and index-only scans. However, for index and index-only scans, only B-Tree indexes will parallelize. No such limitation exists for bitmap heap scans: for them, any index type will qualify. But in the bitmap heap scan, the building of the bitmap index is not parallelizable, so workers must wait for the bitmap index to be fully built.

Parallel Joins

Joins also benefit from parallelization. In PostgreSQL 9.6, nested loops and hash joins are parallelizable.

In nested loops, each worker matches its subset of data against a complete reference set of data shared by all workers.

In hash joins, each worker builds a separate copy of the hash table and joins this with their partitioned share of other tables. Thus, in a hash join, workers are doing redundant work by doing a full hash. So in cases where creating the hash table is expensive, a parallel hash join is less efficient than a nonparallel join.

In PostgreSQL 10, merge joins are parallelizable. Merge joins have a similar limitation to hash joins, in that one side of the join is repeated in its entirety by each worker.

Guiding the Query Planner

The planner's behavior is driven by the presence of indexes, cost settings, strategy settings, and its general perception of the distribution of data. In this section, we'll go over various approaches for optimizing the planner's behavior.

Strategy Settings

Although the PostgreSQL query planner doesn't accept index hints as some other database products do, you can disable various strategy settings on a per-query or permanent basis to dissuade the planner from going down an unproductive path. All planner optimizing settings are documented in the section Planner Method Configuration (*http://www.postgresql.org/docs/current/static/runtime-config-query.html*) of the manual. By default, all strategy settings are enabled, arming the planner with maximum flexibility. You can disable various strategies if you have some prior knowledge of the data. Keep in mind that disabling doesn't necessarily mean that the planner will be barred from using the strategy. You're only making a polite request to the planner to avoid it.

Two settings that we occasionally disable are `enable_nestloop` and `enable_seqscan`. The reason is that these two strategies tend to be the slowest, though not in all cases. Although you can disable them, the planner can still use them when it has no viable alternative. When you do see them being used, it's a good idea to double-check that the planner is using them out of efficiency, and not out of ignorance. One quick way to check is to disable them. If they are used by default but not used when you disable them, compare the actual costs between the two cases to confirm that using them is more efficient than not using them.

How Useful Is Your Index?

When the planner decides to perform a sequential scan, it loops through all the rows of a table. It opts for this route when it finds no index that could satisfy a query condition, or it concludes that using an index is more costly than scanning the table. If you disable the sequential scan strategy, and the planner still insists on using it, this means that indexes are missing or that the planner can't use the indexes you have in place for the particular query. Two common mistakes people make are to leave useful indexes out of their tables or to put in indexes that can't be used by their queries. An easy way to check whether your indexes are being used is to query the `pg_stat_user_indexes` and `pg_stat_user_tables` views. To target slow queries, use the `pg_stat_statements` extension described in "Gathering Statistics on Statements" on page 227.

Let's start off with a query against the table we created in Example 7-22. We'll add a GIN index on the array column. GIN indexes are among the few indexes you can use to index arrays:

```
CREATE INDEX idx_lu_fact_types ON census.lu_fact_types USING gin (fact_subcats);
```

To test our index, we'll execute a query to find all rows with subcats containing "White alone" or "Asian alone." We explicitly enabled sequential scan even though it's the default setting, just to be sure. The accompanying EXPLAIN output is shown in Example 9-15.

Example 9-15. Allow planner to choose sequential scan

```
set enable_seqscan = true;
EXPLAIN (ANALYZE)
SELECT *
FROM census.lu_fact_types
WHERE fact_subcats && '{White alone, Black alone}'::varchar[];

Seq Scan on lu_fact_types
    (cost=0.00..2.85 rows=2 width=200)
    actual time=0.066..0.076 rows=2 loops=1)
        Filter: (fact_subcats
&& '{"White alone","Black alone"}'::character varying[])
        Rows Removed by Filter: 66
Planning time: 0.182 ms
Execution time: 0.108 ms
```

Observe that when `enable_seqscan` is enabled, our index is not being used and the planner has chosen to do a sequential scan. This could be because our table is so small or because the index we have is no good for this query. If we repeat the query but turn off sequential scan beforehand, as shown in Example 9-16, we can see that we have succeeded in forcing the planner to use the index.

Example 9-16. Disable sequential scan, coerce index use

```
set enable_seqscan = false;
EXPLAIN (ANALYZE)
SELECT *
FROM census.lu_fact_types
WHERE fact_subcats && '{White alone, Black alone}'::varchar[];

Bitmap Heap Scan on lu_fact_types
        (cost=12.02..14.04 rows=2 width=200)
    (actual time=0.058..0.058 rows=2 loops=1)
        Recheck Cond: (fact_subcats
&& '{"White alone","Black alone"}'::character varying[])
        Heap Blocks: exact=1
            -> Bitmap Index Scan on idx_lu_fact_types
        (cost=0.00..12.02 rows=2 width=0)
        (actual time=0.048..0.048 rows=2 loops=1)
        Index Cond: (fact_subcats
&& '{"White alone","Black alone"}'::character varying[])
Planning time: 0.230 ms
Execution time: 0.119 ms
```

From this plan, we learn that our index can be used but ends up making the query take longer because the cost is more than doing a sequential scan. Therefore, under normal circumstances, the planner will opt for the sequential scan. As we add more data to our table, we'll probably find that the planner changes strategies to an index scan.

In contrast to the previous example, suppose we were to write a query of the form:

```
SELECT * FROM census.lu_fact_types WHERE 'White alone' = ANY(fact_subcats);
```

We would discover that, regardless of how we set `enable_seqscan`, the planner will always perform a sequential scan because the index we have in place can't service this query. So it is important to consider which indexes will be useful and to write queries to take advantage of them. And experiment, experiment, experiment!

Table Statistics

Despite what you might think or hope, the query planner is not a magician. Its decisions follow prescribed logic that's far beyond the scope of this book. The rules that the planner follows depend heavily on the current state of the data. The planner can't possibly scan all the tables and rows prior to formulating its plan. That would be self-defeating. Instead, it relies on aggregated statistics about the data.

Therefore, having accurate and current stats is crucial for the planner to make the right decision. If stats differ greatly from reality, the planner will often come up with bad plans, the most detrimental of these being unnecessary sequential table scans. Generally, only about 20 percent of the entire table is sampled to produce stats. This percentage could be even lower for very large tables. You can control the number of rows sampled on a column-by-column basis by setting the STATISTICS value.

To get a sense of the information culled and used by the planner, query the pg_stats table, as illustrated in Example 9-17.

Example 9-17. Data distribution histogram

```
SELECT
    attname As colname,
    n_distinct,
    most_common_vals AS common_vals,
    most_common_freqs As dist_freq
FROM pg_stats
WHERE tablename = 'facts'
ORDER BY schemaname, tablename, attname;

colname      | n_distinct | common_vals       | dist_freq
-------------+------------+-------------------+-----------------------------
fact_type_id |        68  | {135,113...       | {0.0157,0.0156333,...
perc         |       985  | {0.00,...         | {0.1845,0.0579333,0.056...
tract_id     |      1478  | {25025090300...   | {0.00116667,0.00106667,0.0...
val          |      3391  | {0.000,1.000,2... | {0.2116,0.0681333,0...
yr           |         2  | {2011,2010}       | {0.748933,0.251067}
```

pg_stats gives the planner a sense of how actual values are dispersed within a given column and lets it plan accordingly. The pg_stats table is constantly updated as a background process. After a large data load or a major deletion, you should manually update the stats by executing VACUUM ANALYZE. VACUUM permanently removes deleted rows from tables; ANALYZE updates the stats.

For columns that participate often in joins and are used heavily in WHERE clauses, consider increasing the number of sampled rows:

```
ALTER TABLE census.facts ALTER COLUMN fact_type_id SET STATISTICS 1000;
```

Version 10 introduced support for multicolumn stats via the new CREATE STATISTICS (*https://www.postgresql.org/docs/10/static/sql-createstatistics.html*) DDL construct. This feature allows you to create stats against a combination of columns. A multicolumn stat is useful if you have columns that are correlated in value. Say, for example, that you have a particular kind of data for only one year and not other years. In that case, you might want to create a compound stat for fact_type_id and yr as shown in Example 9-18.

Example 9-18. Multicolumn stats

```
CREATE STATISTICS census.stats_facts_type_yr_dep_dist (dependencies, ndistinct)
            ON fact_type_id, yr FROM census.facts;
ANALYZE census.facts;
```

A CREATE STATISTICS statement must specify two or more columns in a single table. Example 9-18 creates stats on the columns `fact_type_id` and `yr` in the `census.facts` table. The statistics should also be named, although that is optional. If you specify a schema as part of the name, the statistics will be created in that schema; otherwise, they get created in the default schema.

You can collect two kinds of statistics, and must specify one or both in your statement:

- The `dependencies` statistic catalogs dependencies between columns. For example, zip code 02109 is seen only with Boston in the `city` column. `dependencies` statistics are used only to optimize queries with equalities, such as a query specifying `city = 'Boston'` and `zip = '02109'`.

- The `ndistinct` statistic catalogs how often column values are seen together and tries to catalog statistics for each group of columns. `ndistinct` statistics are only used for improving GROUP BY clauses. Specifically, they are useful only on queries that group by all the columns in your statistic.

Statistics created using CREATE STATISTICS are stored in the table `pg_statis tic_ext` and can be dropped using DROP STATISTICS. Similar to other statistics, they are computed during an ANALYZE run, which happens during the system vacuum analyze process. After creating a table, it's a good idea to run an ANALYZE on it so the new stats can be used immediately.

Random Page Cost and Quality of Drives

Another setting that influences the planner is the `random_page_cost` (RPC) ratio, which is the relative cost of disk access when retrieving a record using a sequential read versus random access. Generally, the faster (and more expensive) the physical disk, the lower the ratio. The default value for RPC is 4, which works well for most mechanical hard drives on the market today. The use of solid-state drives (SSDs), high-end storage area networks (SANs), or cloud storage makes it worth tweaking this value.

You can set the RPC ratio per database, per server, or per tablespace. At the server level, it makes most sense to set the ratio in the *postgresql.conf* file. If you have different kinds of disks, you can set the values at the `tablespace` level using the ALTER TABLESPACE (*http://bit.ly/1AvAsf1*) command:

```
ALTER TABLESPACE pg_default SET (random_page_cost=2);
```

Details about this setting can be found at Random Page Cost Revisited (*http://bit.ly/ 15SZdrT*). The article suggests the following settings:

- High-end NAS/SAN: 2.5 or 3.0
- Amazon EBS and Heroku: 2.0
- iSCSI and other mediocre SANs: 6.0, but varies widely
- SSDs: 2.0 to 2.5
- NvRAM (or NAND): 1.5

Caching

If you execute a complex query that takes a while to run, subsequent runs are often much faster. Thank caching. If the same query executes in sequence, by the same user or different users, and no changes have been made to the underlying data, you should get back the same result. As long as there's space in memory to cache the data, the planner can skip replanning or reretrieving. Using common table expressions and immutable functions in your queries encourages caching.

How do you check what's in the current cache? You can install the pg_buffercache extension:

```
CREATE EXTENSION pg_buffercache;
```

You can then run a query against the pg_buffercache view, as shown in Example 9-19.

Example 9-19. Are my table rows in the buffer cache?

```
SELECT
    C.relname,
    COUNT(CASE WHEN B.isdirty THEN 1 ELSE NULL END) As dirty_buffers,
    COUNT(*) As num_buffers
FROM
    pg_class AS C INNER JOIN
    pg_buffercache B ON C.relfilenode = B.relfilenode INNER JOIN
    pg_database D ON B.reldatabase = D.oid AND D.datname = current_database()
WHERE C.relname IN ('facts','lu_fact_types')
GROUP BY C.relname;
```

Example 9-19 returns the number of buffered pages of the facts and lu_fact_types tables. Of course, to actually see buffered rows, you need to run a query. Try this one:

```
SELECT T.fact_subcats[2], COUNT(*) As num_fact
FROM
```

```
        census.facts As F
        INNER JOIN
        census.lu_fact_types AS T ON F.fact_type_id = T.fact_type_id
    GROUP BY T.fact_subcats[2];
```

The second time you run the query, you should notice at least a 10% performance speed increase and should see the following cached in the buffer:

```
relname       | dirty_buffers | num_buffers
--------------+---------------+------------
facts         |            0 |         736
lu_fact_types |            0 |           4
```

The more onboard memory you have dedicated to the cache, the more room you'll have to cache data. You can set the amount of dedicated memory by changing the shared_buffers setting in *postgresql.conf*. Don't go overboard; raising shared_buf fers too much will bloat your cache, leading to more time wasted scanning the cache.

Nowadays, there's no shortage of onboard memory. You can take advantage of this by precaching commonly used tables using an extension called pg_prewarm. pg_pre-warm lets you prime your PostgreSQL by loading data from commonly used tables into memory so that the first user to hit the database can experience the same performance boost offered by caching as later users. A good article that describes this feature is Prewarming Relational Data (*http://bit.ly/1FUkmNa*).

## CHAPTER 10

Replication and External Data

PostgreSQL has a number of options for sharing data with external servers or data sources. The first option is the built-in replication options of PostgreSQL, which allow you to create a copy of your server ready to run on another PostgreSQL server. The second option is to use third-party add-ons, many of which are freely available and time-tested. The third option is to use a foreign data wrapper (FDW). FDWs give you the flexibility to query from a wide array of external data sources. Since version 9.3, some FDWs also permit updating: these include postgres_fdw (*http://bit.ly/ 1z3iIIZ*), hadoop_fdw (*http://bit.ly/1yxbFIn*), and ogr_fdw (*https://github.com/pram sey/pgsql-ogr-fdw*) (see "Querying Other Tabular Formats with ogr_fdw" on page 259).

Replication Overview

The reasons for replicating your databases distill down to two: availability and scalability. Availability is assured by providing a redundant server so that, if your main server goes down, you have another that can immediately assume its role. For small databases, you could just make sure you have another physical server ready and restore the database onto it. But for large databases (in the terabytes), the restore itself could take hours, if not days. To avoid downtime, you'll need to replicate.

The other motivation for replications is scalability. Suppose you set up a database to breed fancy elephant shrews (*http://en.wikipedia.org/wiki/elephant_shrew*) for profit. After a few years of breeding, you now have thousands of elephant shrews. People all over the world come to your site to gawk and purchase. You're overwhelmed by the traffic, but replication comes to your aid. You arrange a read-only slave server to replicate with your main server. Then you direct the countless gawkers to the slave, and let only serious buyers onto the master server to finalize their purchases.

Replication Jargon

Before we get too carried away, we should introduce some common lingo in PostgreSQL replication:

Master

The master server is the database server sourcing the data being replicated and where all updates take place. You're allowed only one master when using the built-in server replication features of PostgreSQL. Plans are in place to support multimaster replication scenarios. Watch for it in future releases. You may also hear the term publisher used to mean the provider of the data. Publisher/subscriber terminology gains more traction in PostgreSQL 10 for built-in logical replication.

Slave

A slave server consumes the replicated data and provides a replica of the master. More aesthetically pleasing terms such as *subscriber* and *agent* have been bandied about, but *slave* is still the most apropos. PostgreSQL built-in replication supports only read-only slaves at this time.

Write-ahead log (WAL)

WAL is the log that keeps track of all transactions, often referred to as the transaction log in other database products. To stage replication, PostgreSQL simply makes the logs available to the slaves. Once slaves have pulled the logs, they just need to execute the transactions therein.

Synchronous replication

A transaction on the master will not be considered complete until at least one synchronous slave listed in `synchronous_standby_names` updates and reports back. Prior to version 9.6, if any synchronous slave responds, the transaction is complete. In version 9.6 and higher, the number of standbys that must respond is configurable using the `synchronous_standby_names` postgresql.conf configuration variable. Version 10 introduced the keywords FIRST and ANY that can be added to the `synchronous_standby_names` configuration variable that dictates which nodes need to report back. FIRST is the default behavior if not specified and the behavior of 9.6.

Asynchronous replication

A transaction on the master will commit even if no slave updates. This is expedient for distant servers where you don't want transactions to wait because of network latency, but the downside is that your dataset on the slave might lag behind. Should the lag be severe, the slave might need to be reinitialized if the transaction it needs to continue has already been removed from the WAL logs.

To minimize the risk of WALs being removed before all slaves have used them, version 9.4 introduced replication slots. A replication slot is a contract between a slave and its master whereby the master will not wipe out any WAL logs that are still needed by any replication slots. The hazard is that if a slave holding a replication slot fails or loses communication for a long time, the master will keep the WALS indefinitely and run out of disk space and shut down.

Streaming replication
  The slave does not require direct file access between master and slaves. Instead, it relies on the PostgreSQL connection protocol to transmit the WALs.

Cascading replication
  Slaves can receive logs from nearby slaves instead of directly from the master. This allows a slave to behave like a master for replication purposes. The slave remains read-only. When a slave acts both as a receiver and a sender, it is called a *cascading standby*.

Logical replication
  This is a new replication option in version 10 that allows the replication of individual tables instead of requiring the whole server cluster to be replicated. It relies on a feature called *logical decoding*, which extracts changes to a database table from the WAL logs in an easy-to-understand format without detailed knowledge of the database's internal state. Logical decoding has existed since 9.4 and has been used by some extensions for auditing and providing replication. This new feature comes with the new DDL commands `CREATE PUBLICATION` and `CREATE SUBSCRIPTION` for designating what tables to replicate and what servers and corresponding database to send data to.

  To use this feature, you must set `wal_level` to `logical`.

  Refer to Logical Replication in PostgreSQL 10 (*https://blog.2ndquadrant.com/logical-replication-postgresql-10/*) for an example of its use.

Remastering
  Remastering promotes a slave to be the master. Version 9.3 introduced streaming-only remastering, which eliminates the need for remastering to consult a WAL archive; it can be done via streaming, and slaves no longer need to be recloned. As of version 9.4, though, a restart is still required. This may change in future releases.

PostgreSQL binary replication replicates only changes that are transactional. Because any DDL command is transactional, the creation of tables, views, and installation of extensions can be replicated as well. But because unlogged table inserts and updates are not transactional, they cannot be replicated. When installing extensions, you should make sure all slaves have the binaries for the extension and version of extension you are installing; otherwise, replication will fail when the `CREATE EXTENSION` command is executed on the master.

Evolution of PostgreSQL Replication

PostgreSQL's stock replication relies on WAL shipping. Streaming replication slaves should be running the same OS and bitness (32-bit/64-bit) as the master. It is also recommended that all servers be running the same minor version as the master, though running the same patch level (microversion) is not required. Though not recommended, the slave and master can be running a different minor version. In this case, it's preferable for the slave to be running a newer minor version than the master.

Support for built-in replication improved over the following PostgreSQL releases:

- Version 9.4 added replication slots. A replication slot is a contract between a master and a slave that requires the master to hold on to WALs until a slave is done processing them.

- Version 9.5 added several functions for monitoring the progress of replication: refer to Replication Progress Tracking (*https://www.postgresql.org/docs/current/static/replication-origins.html*) in the documentation.

- Version 9.6 introduced multiple standby servers in synchronous replication for increased reliability.

- Version 10 introduced built-in logical replication, which allows the replication of individual tables. The other benefit of logical replication is that a slave can have databases and tables of its own that are not part of replication and that can be updated on the slave. Version 10 also introduced temporary replication slots, which allow a process to create a replication slot on a one-time basis and have it disappear after the session is over. This is particularly useful for initializing a new copy of the server via pg_basebackup.

  Although logical replication is built into PostgreSQL for the first time in version 10, you can use logical replication in PostgreSQL 9.4 and higher versions of PostgreSQL 9 through the open source PostgreSQL extension pglogical (*https://2ndquadrant.com/en/resources/pglogical/release-notes/*). If you need to replicate between version 10 and versions 9.4–9.6, you'll need to have pglogical installed on both version 10 and the lower-versioned server. For logical replication between version 10 and future versions of PostgreSQL, you can use the built-in logical replication feature.

Third-Party Replication Options

As alternatives to PostgreSQL's built-in replication, common third-party options abound. Slony (*http://slony.info/*) and Bucardo (*http://bucardo.org/wiki/Bucardo*) are two popular open source ones. Although PostgreSQL is improving replication with each new release, Slony, Bucardo, and other third-party replication options still offer more flexibility. Slony and Bucardo allow you to replicate individual databases or even tables instead of the entire server. They also don't require that all masters and slaves run the same PostgreSQL version and OS. Both also support multimaster scenarios. However, both rely on additional triggers and possible addition of columns to tables to initiate the replication and often don't replicate DDL commands for rare actions such as creating new tables, installing extensions, and so on. Thus, they require more manual intervention, such as the addition of triggers, additional table fields, or views.

We urge you to consult a comparison matrix of popular third-party options (*http:// bit.ly/1vUu5AP*) before deciding what to use.

Setting Up Full Server Replication

Let's go over the steps to replicate the whole server cluster. We'll take advantage of streaming replication. Recall that streaming replication only requires connections at the PostgreSQL database level between the master and slaves.

Configuring the Master

The steps for setting up the master are:

1. Create a replication account:

   ```
   CREATE ROLE pgrepuser REPLICATION LOGIN PASSWORD 'woohoo';
   ```

2. Alter the following configuration settings in *postgresql.auto.conf*. These can be done using ALTER SYSTEM set variable=value followed by SELECT pg_reload_conf(); without the need to touch the physical config file:

   ```
   listen_addresses = *
   wal_level = hot_standby
   archive_mode = on
   max_wal_senders = 5
   wal_keep_segments = 10
   ```

If you want to use logical replication to do partial replication of only some tables, you'll need to set wal_level = logical. Logical does more logging than hot_standby so will also work for doing full server replication.

These settings are described in Server Configuration: Replication (*http://bit.ly/ 1z3iXUq*). You may want to set wal_keep_segments higher if your servers are far apart and your production server has a lot of transactions. If you are running version 9.6 or above, you should use replica instead of hot_standby for the wal_level. `hot_standby` is still accepted in 9.6 for backward compatibility, but will be read as `replica`.

3. Add the `archive_command` configuration directive to *postgresql.auto.conf* or use `ALTER SYSTEM` to indicate where the WALs will be saved. With streaming, you're free to choose any directory. More details on this setting can be found in the PostgreSQL PGStandby (*http://bit.ly/1yxbOvw*) documentation.

On Linux/Unix, your `archive_command` line should look something like:

```
archive_command = 'cp %p ../archive/%f'
```

You can also use `rsync` instead of `cp` if you want to store the WALs on a different server:

```
archive_command = 'rsync -av %p postgres@192.168.0.10:archive/%f'
```

On Windows:

```
archive_command = 'copy %p ..\\archive\\%f'
```

4. Add a rule to *pg_hba.conf* allowing the slaves to replicate. As an example, the following rule will allow a PostgreSQL account named `pgrepuser` on a server on your private network with an IP address in the range 192.168.0.1 to 192.168.0.254 to replicate using an md5 password:

```
host replication pgrepuser 192.168.0.0/24 md5
```

5. Restart the PostgreSQL service for the settings to take effect.

Use the `pg_basebackup` (*https://www.postgresql.org/docs/current/interactive/app-pgbasebackup.html*) utility, found in the *bin* folder of your PostgreSQL installation, to create a cluster backup. This will create a copy of the data cluster files in the specified directory.

When using pg_basebackup, use the `--xlog-method-stream` switch to also copy over the WAL logs and the `-R` switch to automatically create a config file. The command `--xlog-method-stream` will spawn another database connection for copying the WALs.

 In version 10 and above, the *pg_xlog* directory is *pg_wal*.

In the following example, we are on the slave server and performing a streaming basebackup from our master server (192.168.0.1):

```
pg_basebackup -D /target_dir -h 192.168.0.1 \
--port=5432 --checkpoint=fast
--xlog-method=stream -R
```

If you are using pg_basebackup primarily for backup purposes, you can use the tar-red/compressed form, which will create a *tar.gz* file in the *target_dir* folder for each table space. -X is shorthand for --xlog-method. The tarred/compression format does not support streaming logs, so you have to resort to fetching the logs with that format:

```
pg_basebackup -Z9 -D /target_dir/ -h 192.168.0.1 -Ft -Xfetch
```

For backup, you will want to augment your backup to include transaction log shipping backup using pg_receivexlog (*https://www.postgresql.org/docs/9.6/static/app-pgreceivexlog.html*) for versions prior to 10. For versions 10 and above, pg_receivexlog was renamed to pg_receivewal (*https://www.postgresql.org/docs/10/static/app-pgreceivewal.html*). This you'll want to keep running as a cronjob or service to continually make log backups.

Configuring the Slaves for Full Server Cluster Replication

This part is not needed for logical replication. To minimize headaches, slaves should have the same configuration as the master, especially if you'll be using them for fail-over. They must also have the same set of PostgreSQL extensions installed in binary; otherwise, when CREATE EXTENSION is played back, it will fail and stop restore. In order for the server to be a slave, it must be able to play back the WAL transactions of the master. The steps for creating a slave are as follows:

1. Create a new instance of PostgreSQL with the same version (preferably even microversions) as your master server. For PostgreSQL, keeping servers identical for microversions is not a requirement, and you're welcome to experiment and see how far you can deviate.

2. Shut down PostgreSQL on the new slave.

3. Overwrite the data folder files with those you generated with pg_basebackup.

4. Add the following configuration setting to the *postgresql.auto.conf* file:

   ```
   hot_standby = on
   max_connections = 20 #set to higher or equal to master
   ```

5. You don't need to run the slaves on the same port as the master, so you can optionally change the port either via *postgresql.auto.conf, postgresql.conf,* or via some other OS-specific startup script that sets the PGPORT environment variable before startup.

6. Create a new file in the *data* folder called *recovery.conf* with the following contents, but substitute the actual hostname, IP address, and port of your master on

the second line. This file is automatically created if you used pg_basebackup. You will have to add the trigger_file line though.

The application_name is optional but useful if you want to track the replica in postgresql system views:

```
standby_mode = 'on'
primary_conninfo = 'host=192.168.0.1 port=5432 user=pgrepuser ↵
password=woohoo application_name=replica1'
trigger_file = 'failover.now'
```

7. If you find that the slave can't play back WALs fast enough, you can specify a location for caching. In that case, add to the *recovery.conf* file a line such as the following, which varies depending on the OS.

On Linux/Unix:

```
restore_command = 'cp %p ../archive/%f'
```

On Windows:

```
restore_command = 'copy %p ..\\archive\\%f'
```

In this example, the *archive* folder is where we're caching.

Initiating the Streaming Replication Process

After you have made the basebackup with pg_basebackup and put it in place, verify that the settings in the *recovery.conf* look right. Then start up the slave server.

You should now be able to connect to both servers. Any changes you make on the master, even structural changes such as installing extensions or creating tables, should trickle down to the slave. You should also be able to query the slave.

When and if the time comes to liberate a chosen slave, create a blank file called *failover.now* in the data folder of the slave. PostgreSQL will then complete playback of the WAL and rename the *recovery.conf* file to *recover.done*. At that point, your slave will be unshackled from the master and continue life on its own with all the data from the last WAL. Once the slave has tasted freedom, there's no going back. In order to make it a slave again, you'll need to go through the whole process from the beginning.

Replicating Only Some Tables or Databases with Logical Replication

New in version 10 is the ability to replicate only some of the tables or some of the databases in your master using an approach called logical replication. One big benefit of logical replication is you can use it to replicate between a PostgreSQL 10 database and future versions of PostgreSQL and even replicate when OS platforms or architectures are different. For example, you can use it to replicate between a Linux server and a Windows server.

In logical replication, the server providing the data is called the `publisher` and the server receiving the data is called the `subscriber`. You use `CREATE PUBLICATION` on the publishing server in the database with tables you want to publish to dictate what tables to replicate and CREATE SUBSCRIPTION on the subscriber database denoting the server and publication name it should subscribe to. The main caveat with logical replication is that DDL is not replicated, so in order to replicate a table, the table structure must exist on both the publisher database and the subscriber database.

We have two PostgreSQL 10 servers running on our server. The publisher is on port 5447 and the subscriber is on port 5448. The process is the same if clusters are on separate servers. To replicate:

1. Make sure the following configuration setting is set on the publisher:

   ```
   SHOW wal_level
   ```

   If anything other than `logical`, do:

   ```
   ALTER SYSTEM SET wal_level = logical;
   ```

   And then restart the postgres service.

   This can be set on the subscription server as well, especially if in some cases the subscription server will act as a publisher for some tables or databases.

2. On the database where you will be replicating data, create the table structures for tables you will be replicating. If you have a lot of tables or want to replicate a whole database, as we will be doing, use pg_dump on the publishing database to create backup structure of tables. For example, for the postgresql_book database, we would dump out the structure:

   ```
   pg_dump -U postgres -p5447 -Fp --section pre-data --section post-data \
   -f pub_struct.sql postgresql_book
   ```

   And then use psql on the subscriber server to create our subscription database with structures as follows:

   ```
   CREATE DATABASE book_sub;
   \connect book_sub;
   \i pub_struct.sql
   ```

3. We then create a publication on the publisher database of items we want to replicate. For this exercise, we'll replicate all the tables in the database using CREATE PUBLICATION (*http://bit.ly/2kDdFR3*). Note that this command will also replicate future tables created, though we've had to create the structure on the subscription databases:

   ```
   CREATE PUBLICATION full_db_pub
       FOR ALL TABLES;
   ```

4. In order to use the publication, we need to subscribe to it. We do this by executing this command when connected to the subscriber database book_sub:

```
\connect book_sub;
 CREATE SUBSCRIPTION book_sub
    CONNECTION 'host=localhost port=5447 dbname=postgresql_book \
user=postgres'
    PUBLICATION full_db_pub;
```

When you inspect the tables on the book_sub database, you should find that all the tables are full of data collected during the initial synchronization. If you add data to the postgresql_book database, you should see the new records appear on the book_sub database.

If you no longer need a subscription or publication, you can drop them from the publisher with DROP SUBSCRIPTION and DROP PUBLICATION.

Foreign Data Wrappers

FDWs are an extensible, standard-compliant method for your PostgreSQL server to query other data sources, both other PostgreSQL servers and many types of non-PostgreSQL data sources. At the center of the architecture is a foreign table, a table that you can query like other tables in your PostgreSQL database but that resides on another database, perhaps even on another physical server. Once you put in the effort to establish foreign tables, they persist in your database and you're forever free from having to worry about the intricate protocols of communicating with alien data sources. You can also find the status of popular FDWs and examples of usage at PostgreSQL Wiki FDW (*https://wiki.postgresql.org/wiki/Foreign_data_wrappers*). You can find a catalog of some FDWs for PostgreSQL at PGXN FDW (*http://pgxn.org/tag/fdw/*) and PGXN Foreign Data Wrapper (*http://bit.ly/1z3j9D3*). You'll find the source code for many of these and for additional ones on GitHub by searching for PostgreSQL Foreign Data Wrappers (*http://bit.ly/2tnWdRf*). If you need to wrap foreign data sources, start by visiting these links to see whether someone has already done the work of creating wrappers. If not, try creating one yourself. If you succeed, be sure to share it with others.

Most PostgreSQL installs provide two FDWs; you can install file_fdw (*http://www.postgresql.org/docs/current/interactive/file-fdw.html*) and postgres_fdw (*http://www.postgresql.org/docs/current/interactive/postgres-fdw.html*) using the CREATE EXTENSION command.

Up through PostgreSQL 9.2, you could use FDWs only to read from foreign sources. Version 9.3 introduced an API feature to update foreign tables as well. postgres_fdw supports updates.

In this section, we'll demonstrate how to register foreign servers, foreign users, and foreign tables, and finally, how to query foreign tables. Although we use SQL to create and delete objects in our examples, you can perform the exact same commands using pgAdmin.

Querying Flat Files

The file_fdw wrapper is packaged as an extension. To install it, use the following SQL:

```
CREATE EXTENSION file_fdw;
```

Although file_fdw can read only from file paths accessible by your local server, you still need to define a server for it for the sake of consistency. Issue the following command to create a "faux" foreign server in your database:

```
CREATE SERVER my_server FOREIGN DATA WRAPPER file_fdw;
```

Next, you must register the tables. You can place foreign tables in any schema you want. We usually create a separate schema to house foreign data. For this example, we'll use our staging schema, as shown in Example 10-1.

Here are a few initial lines of the pipe-delimited file we are linking to, to show the format of the data we are taking in:

```
Dev|Company
Tom Lane|Crunchy Data
Bruce Momjian|EnterpriseDB
```

Example 10-1. Make a foreign table from a delimited file

```
CREATE FOREIGN TABLE staging.devs (developer VARCHAR(150), company VARCHAR(150))
SERVER my_server
OPTIONS (
    format 'csv',
    header 'true',
    filename '/postgresql_book/ch10/devs.psv',
    delimiter '|',
    null ''
);
```

In our example, even though we're registering a pipe-delimited file, we still use the csv option. A CSV file, as far as FDW is concerned, represents a file delimited by any specified character.

When the setup is finished, you can finally query your pipe-delimited file directly:

```
SELECT * FROM staging.devs WHERE developer LIKE 'T%';
```

Once you no longer need the foreign table, drop it using:

```
DROP FOREIGN TABLE staging.devs;
```

Querying Flat Files as Jagged Arrays

Often, flat files have a different number of columns on each line and could include multiple header and footer rows. Our favorite FDW for handling these files is file_textarray_fdw. This wrapper can handle any kind of delimited flat file, even if the number of elements vary from row to row, by treating each row as a text array (text[]).

Unfortunately, file_textarray_fdw is not part of the core PostgreSQL, so you'll need to compile it yourself. First, install PostgreSQL with PostgreSQL development headers. Then download the file_textarray_fdw source code from the Adunstan GitHub site (*https://github.com/adunstan/file_text_array_fdw*). There is a different branch for each version of PostgreSQL, so make sure to pick the right one. Once you've compiled the code, install it as an extension, as you would any other FDW.

If you are on Linux/Unix, it's an easy compile if you have the postgresql-dev package installed. We did the work of compiling for Windows; you can download our binaries from one of the following links: one for Windows 32/64 9.4 FDWs (*http://bit.ly/2occRB6*), and another for Windows 32/64 9.5 and 32/64 9.6 FDWs (*http://bit.ly/2oRDY6X*).

The first step to perform after you have installed an FDW is to create an extension in your database:

```
CREATE EXTENSION file_textarray_fdw;
```

Then create a foreign server as you would with any FDW:

```
CREATE SERVER file_taserver FOREIGN DATA WRAPPER file_textarray_fdw;
```

Next, register the tables. You can place foreign tables in any schema you want. In Example 10-2, we use our staging schema again.

Example 10-2. Make a file text array foreign table from a delimited file

```
CREATE FOREIGN TABLE staging.factfinder_array (x text[])
SERVER file_taserver
OPTIONS (
    format 'csv',
    filename '/postgresql_book/ch10/DEC_10_SF1_QTH1_with_ann.csv',
    header 'false',
    delimiter ',',
    quote '"',
    encoding 'latin1',
    null ''
);
```

Our example CSV begins with eight header rows and has more columns than we care to count. When the setup is finished, you can finally query our delimited file directly.

The following query will give us the names of the header rows where the first column of the header is GEO.id:

```
SELECT unnest(x) FROM staging.factfinder_array WHERE x[1] = 'GEO.id'
```

This next query will give us the first two columns of our data:

```
SELECT x[1] As geo_id, x[2] As tract_id
FROM staging.factfinder_array WHERE x[1] ~ '[0-9]+';
```

Querying Other PostgreSQL Servers

The PostgreSQL FDW, postgres_fdw (*http://bit.ly/1z3iIIZ*), is packaged with most distributions of PostgreSQL since PostgreSQL 9.3. This FDW allows you to read as well as push updates to other PostgreSQL servers, even different versions.

Start by installing the FDW for the PostgreSQL server in a new database:

```
CREATE EXTENSION postgres_fdw;
```

Next, create a foreign server:

```
CREATE SERVER book_server
FOREIGN DATA WRAPPER postgres_fdw
OPTIONS (host 'localhost', port '5432', dbname 'postgresql_book');
```

If you need to change or add connection options to the foreign server after creation, you can use the ALTER SERVER command. For example, if you needed to change the server you are pointing to, you could enter:

```
ALTER SERVER book_server OPTIONS (SET host 'prod');
```

 Changes to connection settings such as the host, port, and database do not take effect until a new session is created. This is because the connection is opened on first use and is kept open.

Next, create a user, mapping its public role to a role on the foreign server:

```
CREATE USER MAPPING FOR public SERVER book_server
OPTIONS (user 'role_on_foreign', password 'your_password');
```

The role you map to must exist on the foreign server and have login rights. Anyone who can connect to your database will be able to access the foreign server as well.

Now you are ready to create a foreign table. This table can have a subset of columns of the table it connects to. In Example 10-3, we create a foreign table that maps to the census.facts table.

Example 10-3. Defining a PostgreSQL foreign table

```
CREATE FOREIGN TABLE ft_facts (
    fact_type_id int NOT NULL,
    tract_id varchar(11),
    yr int, val numeric(12,3),
    perc numeric(6,2)
)
SERVER book_server OPTIONS (schema_name 'census', table_name 'facts');
```

This example includes only the most basic options for the foreign table. By default, all PostgreSQL foreign tables are updatable, unless the remote account you use doesn't have update access. The `updatable` setting is a Boolean setting that can be changed at the foreign table or the foreign server definition. For example, to make your table read-only, execute:

```
ALTER FOREIGN TABLE ft_facts OPTIONS (ADD updatable 'false');
```

You can set the table back to `updatable` by running:

```
ALTER FOREIGN TABLE ft_facts OPTIONS (SET updatable 'true');
```

The `updatable` property at the table level overrides the foreign server setting.

In addition to changing `OPTIONS`, you can also add and drop columns with the `ALTER FOREIGN TABLE .. DROP COLUMN` statement.

PostgreSQL 9.5 introduced the `IMPORT FOREIGN SCHEMA` command, which saves a great deal of time by automatically creating the foreign tables for you. Not all FDWs support IMPORT FOREIGN SCHEMA. Each FDW can also support a custom set of server options when importing. `postgres_fdw` supports the following custom options:

import_collate
> This copies the collation settings from the foreign server for the foreign tables. The default for this setting is `true`.

import_default
> This controls whether default values for columns should be included. The default for the option is `false`, so columns on the local server have no defaults. But default values are useful during inserts: if you neglect to specify the value of a column, PostgreSQL automatically inserts the default. Be careful, though—the behavior of default could be unexpected if you're relying on a sequence for auto-numbering. The next assigned value from the sequence could be different between the foreign server and the local server.

import_not_null
> This controls whether NOT NULL constraints are imported. The default is `true`.

In Example 10-4, we import all tables in our books.public schema.

Example 10-4. Use IMPORT FOREIGN SCHEMA to link all tables in a schema

```
CREATE SCHEMA remote_census;
IMPORT FOREIGN SCHEMA public
FROM SERVER book_server
INTO remote_census
OPTIONS (import_default 'true');
```

The IMPORT FOREIGN SCHEMA, as shown in Example 10-4, will create foreign tables with the same names as those in the foreign schema and create them in the designated schema `remote_census`.

To bring in only a subset of tables, use LIMIT TO or EXCEPT modifiers. For example, to bring in just the facts and lu_fact_types tables, we could have written:

```
IMPORT FOREIGN SCHEMA census
    LIMIT TO (facts, lu_fact_types)
    FROM SERVER book_server INTO remote_census;
```

If a table specified in the LIMIT TO does not exist on the remote server, no error will be thrown. You might want to verify after the import that you have all the foreign tables you expected.

A companion clause to LIMIT TO is the EXCEPT clause. Instead of bringing in tables listed, it brings in tables not listed.

If you take advantage of PostgreSQL extensions, you'll want to use the performance enhancement foreign server option introduced in version 9.6, called *extensions*. To utilize it, add the option to an existing postgres_fdw server as we do in the following example:

```
ALTER SERVER census(OPTION ADD extensions 'btree_gist, pg_trgm');
```

The *extensions* option is a comma-separated list of extensions installed on the foreign server. When PostgreSQL runs a query involving any of the types or functions defined in the extension in a WHERE clause, it will try to push the function calls to the remote server for improved performance. If the *extensions* option is not specified, all extension functions will be run locally, which may require transferring more data.

Querying Other Tabular Formats with ogr_fdw

There are many FDWs for querying other relational databases or flat file formats. Most FDWs target a specific kind of data source. For example, you can find the MongoDB FDW for querying MongoDb data, Hadoop FDW for querying Hadoop datasources, and MySQL FDW for querying MySQL data sources.

There are two FDWs we are aware of that bundle many formats. Multicorn FDW is really an FDW API that allows you to write your own FDW in Python. There are some ready-made drivers available, but the Multicorn FDW currently has no offering on Windows and is often tricky to get working on Linux.

ogr_fdw is another FDW that supports many formats, and the one we'll demonstrate in this section. ogr_fdw supports many tabular formats, such as spreadsheets, Dbase files, and CSVs, as well as other relational databases. It is also a spatial database driver that transforms spatial columns from other databases like SQL Server or Oracle into the PostGIS PostgreSQL spatial geometry type.

Several packages that distribute PostGIS also offer the ogr_fdw extension. For instance, the PostGIS Bundle for Windows found on the stack builder includes the ogr_fdw extension, ogr_fdw for CentOS/RHEL is available via yum.postgresql.org, and BigSQL Linux/Mac/Windows PostgreSQL distribution (*http://www.bigsql.org*) also offers ogr_fdw. If you need or want to compile it yourself, the source for ogr_fdw is on GitHub (*https://github.com/pramsey/pgsql-ogr-fdw*).

Underneath the hood, ogr_fdw relies on the Geospatial Data Abstraction Library (GDAL) to do the heavy lifting. Therefore, you need to have GDAL compiled and installed before being able to compile or use ogr_fdw. GDAL has undergone quite a few evolutions, and its capabilities vary according to the dependencies it was compiled with. So be warned that your GDAL may not be our GDAL. GDAL is generally installed as part of PostGIS, the spatial extension for PostgreSQL. So to make GDAL use easier, we recommend always installing the latest version of PostGIS.

Many GDAL instances come with support for Excel, LibreOffice Calc, ODBC, and various Spatial web services. You will find support for Microsoft Access on Windows, but rarely on Linux/Mac distributions.

After you have installed the ogr_fdw binaries, to enable the ogr_fdw in a particular database, connect to the database and run:

```
CREATE EXTENSION ogr_fdw;
```

Foreign servers take on different meanings depending on the type of data source. For example, a folder of CSV files would be considered a server, with each file being a separate table. A Microsoft Excel or LibreOffice Calc workbook would be considered a server, with each sheet in the workbook being a separate table. An SQLite database would be considered a server and each table a foreign table.

The following example links a LibreOffice workbook as a server and corresponding spreadsheets as foreign tables:

```
CREATE SERVER ogr_fdw_wb
FOREIGN DATA WRAPPER ogr_fdw
OPTIONS (
    datasource '/fdw_data/Budget2015.ods',
```

```
     format 'ODS'
);

CREATE SCHEMA wb_data;
IMPORT FOREIGN SCHEMA ogr_all
FROM SERVER ogr_fdw_wb INTO wb_data;
```

The `ogr_all` schema is a catch-all that imports all tables in the foreign server regardless of schema. Some datasources schemas and some don't. To accommodate all inputs, ogr_fdw (in place of ogr_all) accepts the initial characters of a table name as the schema. So, for example, if you wanted to import just a subset of worksheets where the worksheet name begins with "Finance," you would replace *ogr_all* with "*Finance*":

```
CREATE SCHEMA wb_data;
IMPORT FOREIGN SCHEMA "Finance"
FROM SERVER ogr_fdw_wb INTO wb_data;
```

The schema is case-sensitive, so if the name of a worksheet contains uppercase characters or nonstandard characters, it needs to be quoted.

This next example will create a server pointing to a folder of CSV files. Create a schema *ff* to house foreign tables for the CSV server. The FDW will then create foreign tables linked to CSV files where the CSV filename begins with *Housing* in schema *ff*:

```
CREATE SERVER ogr_fdw_ff
FOREIGN DATA WRAPPER ogr_fdw
OPTIONS (datasource '/fdw_data/factfinder', format 'CSV');
CREATE SCHEMA ff;
IMPORT FOREIGN SCHEMA "Housing"
FROM SERVER ogr_fdw_ff INTO ff;
```

In the aforementioned example CSV files named *Housing_2015.csv* and *Housing_2016.csv* will be linked in as foreign tables in schema *ff* with names *housing_2015* and *housing_2016*.

ogr_fdw by default launders table names and column names: all uppercase table names and column names are converted to lowercase. If you don't want this behavior, you can pass in settings in IMPORT FOREIGN SCHEMA to keep table names and column names as they were named in the foreign table. For example:

```
IMPORT FOREIGN SCHEMA "Housing"
    FROM SERVER ogr_fdw_ff INTO ff
      OPTIONS(launder_table_names 'false', launder_column_names 'false');
```

This creates the tables with names *Housing_2015* and *Housing_2016*, where the column names of the tables would appear in the same case as they are in the header of the files.

Querying Nonconventional Data Sources

The database world does not appear to be getting more homogeneous. Exotic databases are spawned faster than virile elephants. Some are fads and quickly drown in their own hype. Some aspire to dethrone relational databases altogether. Some could hardly be considered databases. The introduction of FDWs is in part a response to the growing diversity. FDW assimilates without compromising the PosgreSQL core.

In this next example, we'll demonstrate how to use the www_fdw FDW to query web services. We borrowed the example from www_fdw Examples (*http://bit.ly/12sggyN*).

The www_fdw FDW is not generally packaged with PostgreSQL. If you are on Linux/ Unix, it's an easy compile if you have the postgresql-dev package installed and can download the latest source (*https://github.com/cyga/www_fdw*). We did the work of compiling for some Windows platforms; you can download our binaries from Windows-32 9.1 FDWs (*http://bit.ly/1FUkLPQ*) and Windows-64 9.3 FDWs (*http:// bit.ly/1yn3cne*).

Now create an extension to hold the FDW:

```
CREATE EXTENSION www_fdw;
```

Then create your Google foreign data server:

```
CREATE SERVER www_fdw_server_google_search
    FOREIGN DATA WRAPPER www_fdw
    OPTIONS (uri 'http://ajax.googleapis.com/ajax/services/search/web?v=1.0');
```

The default format supported by www_fdw is JSON, so we didn't need to include it in the OPTIONS modifier. The other supported format is XML. For details on additional parameters that you can set, refer to the www_fdw documentation (*https://github.com/ cyga/www_fdw/wiki/Documentation*). Each FDW is different and comes with its own API settings.

Next, establish at least one user for your FDW. All users that connect to your server should be able to access the Google search server, so here we create one for the entire public group:

```
CREATE USER MAPPING FOR public SERVER www_fdw_server_google_search;
```

Now create your foreign table, as shown in Example 10-5. Each field in the table corresponds to a GET parameter in the URL that Google creates for a search.

Example 10-5. Make a foreign table from Google

```
CREATE FOREIGN TABLE www_fdw_google_search (
    q text,
    GsearchResultClass text,
    unescapedUrl text,
```

```
    url text,
    visibleUrl text,
    cacheUrl text,
    title text,
    content text
) SERVER www_fdw_server_google_search;
```

The user mapping doesn't assign any rights. You still need to grant rights before being able to query the foreign table:

```
GRANT SELECT ON TABLE www_fdw_google_search TO public;
```

Now comes the fun part. We search with the term `New in PostgreSQL 9.4` and mix in a bit of regular expression goodness to strip off HTML tags:

```
SELECT regexp_replace(title,E'(?x)(< [^>]*? >)','','g') As title
FROM www_fdw_google_search
WHERE q = 'New in PostgreSQL 10'
LIMIT 2;
```

Voilà! We have our response:

```
title
--------------------
PostgreSQL 10 Roadmap
PostgreSQL: Roadmap
(2 rows)
```

Installing PostgreSQL

Windows and Desktop Linux

EnterpriseDB (*http://www.EnterpriseDB.com*) builds installers for Windows and desktop versions of Linux. They offer both 32-bit and 64-bit versions for each OS.

The installers are easy to use. They come packaged with PgAdmin (PostgreSQL 9.6+ come with pgAdmin4 while older versions come with pgAdmin3) and a stack builder from which you can install add-ons like JDBC, .NET drivers, Ruby, PostGIS, phpPgAdmin, and pgAgent.

EnterpriseDB has two PostgreSQL offerings: the official, open source edition of PostgreSQL, dubbed the Community Edition; and its proprietary edition, called Advanced Plus. The proprietary fork offers Oracle compatibility and enhanced management features. Don't get confused between the two when you download installers. In this book, we focused on the official PostgreSQL, not Postgres Plus Advanced Server; however, much of the material applies to Postgres Plus Advanced Server.

BigSQL (*http://www.bigsql.org*) is an open source PostgreSQL distribution, largely funded by the company OpenSCG (*http://www.openscg.com/*). The BigSQL distribution is similar to EnterpriseDB and has installers for 64-bit versions of Windows, Mac, and Linux.

It is newer than the EnterpriseDB distribution and targets interoperability, DevOps, and Big Data. As such, it includes extensions you wouldn't commonly find in other distributions. It is packaged with *pgTSQL*, a procedural language that emulates Microsoft SQL Server's Transact-SQL stored procedure language, and lots of goodies for benchmarking and monitoring like pgBadger.

You'll also find other enhancements like *PostGIS* (including ogr_fdw), many other FDWs such as *hadoop_fdw*, *cassandra_fdw*, *oracle_fdw*, and various PLs.

Like EnterpriseDB, BigSQL has its own installer system. The installer can be triggered via a web interface or via the shell command-line tool they call `pgc`, which stands for "pretty good command-line." The pgc package management tool follows the same pattern as Linux yum, apt-get, etc., even on Windows. So to install new packages, start by opening up a shell prompt and changing the directory to the folder where you installed BigSQL.

To update your local list of packages and see list of packages:

```
pgc update
pgc list
```

The output will show something like:

Category	Component	Version	ReleaseDt	Status	Cur?
PostgreSQL	pg92	9.2.21-1	2017-05-11		1
PostgreSQL	pg93	9.3.17-1	2017-05-11		1
PostgreSQL	pg94	9.4.12-1	2017-05-11		1
PostgreSQL	pg95	9.5.7-1	2017-05-11		1
PostgreSQL	pg96	9.6.3-1	2017-05-11	Installed	1
Extensions	cassandra_fdw3-pg96	3.0.1-1	2016-11-08		1
Extensions	hadoop_fdw2-pg96	2.5.0-1	2016-09-01		1
Extensions	oracle_fdw1-pg96	1.5.0-1	2016-09-01		1
Extensions	orafce3-pg96	3.3.1-1	2016-09-23		1
Extensions	pgaudit11-pg96	1.1.0-2	2017-05-18		1
Extensions	pgpartman2-pg96	2.6.4-1	2017-04-15		1
Extensions	pldebugger96-pg96	9.6.0-1	2016-12-28		1
Extensions	plprofiler3-pg96	3.2-1	2017-04-15		1
Extensions	postgis23-pg96	2.3.2-3	2017-05-18	Installed	1
Extensions	setuser1-pg96	1.2.0-1	2017-02-23		1
Extensions	tds_fdw1-pg96	1.0.8-1	2016-11-23		1
Servers	pgdevops	1.4-1	2017-05-18	Installed	1
Applications	backrest	1.18	2017-05-18		1
Applications	ora2pg	18.1	2017-03-23		1
Applications	pgadmin3	1.23.0a	2016-10-20	Installed	1
Applications	pgagent	3.4.1-1	2017-02-23		1
Applications	pgbadger	9.1	2017-02-09		1
Frameworks	java8	8u121	2017-02-09		1
Frameworks	perl5	5.20.3.3	2016-03-14		1
Frameworks	python2	2.7.12-1	2016-10-20	Installed	0
Frameworks	tcl86	8.6.4-1	2016-03-11		1

To install the binaries for a package:

```
pgc install pgdevops
```

The pgdevops package is a web-based administration tool that includes pgadmin4 and the ability to install and monitor bigsql packages.

After you install it, you would do:

```
pgc init pgdevops
pgc start pgdevops
```

The default port it installs on is *http://localhost:8051*.

To upgrade an existing package, use `pgc upgrade` instead of `pgc install`.

 To help you try out different versions of PostgreSQL on the same machine or run it from a USB device, both EnterpriseDB and BigSQL offer standalone setups. Read Starting PostgreSQL in Windows without Install (*http://bit.ly/1yxcuAY*) for guidance on EnterpriseDB. For BigSQL, read Installing pgDevOps (*https://www.openscg.com/2017/05/installing-pgdevops/*).

CentOS, Fedora, Red Hat, Scientific Linux

Most Linux/Unix distributions offer PostgreSQL in their main repositories, although the version might be outdated. To compensate, many people use backports, which are alternative package repositories offering newer versions.

For adventurous Linux users, download the latest PostgreSQL, including the developmental versions, by going to the PostgreSQL Yum repository (*http://yum.postgresql.org*). Not only will you find the core server, but you can also retrieve popular add-ons. PostgreSQL developers maintain this repository and release patches and updates as soon as they are available. The PostgreSQL Yum repository generally maintains updated packages for the newest stable PostgreSQL for 2–4 versions of CentOS, RedHat EL, Fedora, Scientific Linux, Amazon AMI, and Oracle Enterprise. If you have older versions of the OS or still need older PostgreSQL versions that have reached EOL, check the documentation to see what repository still maintains. For detailed installation instructions using YUM, refer to the Yum section (*http://www.postgresonline.com/journal/categories/53-yum*) of our PostgresOnLine journal site.

Debian, Ubuntu

You can install the latest stable and development versions of PostgreSQL on both Debian and Ubuntu from the apt-postgresql (*https://wiki.postgresql.org/wiki/Apt*) repository. apt_postgresql is a repository, similar to yum postgresql, that is maintained by the PostgreSQL development group. The latest stable version is generally also available via the default Ubuntu and Debian repos. A typical installation command looks like:

```
sudo apt-get install postgresql-9.6
```

If you plan to compile add-ons you don't find listed in the repo, you need to also install the postgresql-server-dev:

```
sudo apt-get install postgresql-server-dev-9.6
```

If your repository doesn't have the latest version of PostgreSQL, try visiting the Apt PostgreSQL packages (*http://apt.postgresql.org*) for the latest stable and beta releases. It also offers additional packages such as PL/V8 and PostGIS. It generally supports the latest two or three versions of Debian and Ubuntu.

FreeBSD

FreeBSD is a popular platform for PostgreSQL. You can find the latest versions of PostgreSQL at FreeBSD (*http://www.freebsd.org/ports/databases.html*) and install it via the FreeBSD ports package management system.

macOS

We've seen a variety of ways to install PostgreSQL on Macs. Both EnterpriseDB and BigSQL offer an installer. The Homebrew package manager is gaining popularity and attracts advanced Mac users. Postgres.app is a variant distributed by Heroku that is very popular with novice users. The long-standing MacPorts and Fink distributions are still around. We do advise against mixing installers for Mac users. For instance, if you installed PostgreSQL using BigSQL, don't go to EnterpriseDB to get add-ons.

The following list describes each of these options:

- EnterpriseDB (*http://www.EnterpriseDB.com*) maintains an easy-to-use, one-step installer for macOS. PgAdmin comes as part of the installer. For add-ons, EnterpriseDB offers a stack builder program, from which you can install popular extensions, drivers, languages, and administration tools.

- BigSQL (*http://www.bigsql.org*) maintains an easy-to-use, one-step installer for macOS 64-bit users. For add-ons, BigSQL offers a command-line tool called *pgc* and a pgDevops web browser interface, which we covered in "Windows and Desktop Linux" on page 265 and from which you can install popular extensions, drivers, languages, and administration tools. BigSQL currently includes PL/V8 for non-Windows.

- Homebrew (*http://brew.sh*) is a macOS package manager for many things PostgreSQL. PostgreSQL, Homebrew, and You (*http://bit.ly/2ujEaxH*) provides instructions for installing PostgreSQL using Homebrew. You'll find other articles at the Homebrew PostgreSQL Wiki (*https://wiki.postgresql.org/wiki/Homebrew*).

- Postgres.app (*http://postgresapp.com/*), distributed by Heroku, is a free desktop distribution touted as the easiest way to get started with PostgreSQL on the Mac. It usually maintains the latest version of PostgreSQL bundled with popular extensions such as PostGIS, PL/Python, and PLV8. Postgres.app runs as a standalone application that you can stop and start as needed, making it suitable for development or single users.

- MacPorts (*http://www.macports.org*) is a macOS package distribution for compiling, installing, and upgrading many open source packages. It's the oldest of the macOS distribution systems that carries PostgreSQL.

- Fink (*http://www.finkproject.org*) is a macOS/Darwin packagedistribution based on the Debian apt-get installation framework.

PostgreSQL Packaged Command-Line Tools

This appendix summarizes indispensable command-line tools packaged with PostgreSQL server. We discussed them at length in the book. Here we list their help messages. We hope to save you a bit of time with their inclusion and perhaps make this book a not-so-strange bedfellow.

Database Backup Using pg_dump

Use pg_dump (*http://www.postgresql.org/docs/current/interactive/app-pgdump.html*) to back up all or part of a database. Backup file formats available are TAR, compressed (PostgreSQL custom format), plain text, and plain-text SQL. Plain-text backup can copy psql-specific commands; therefore, restore by running the file within psql. A plain-text SQL backup is merely a file with standard SQL CREATE and INSERT commands. To restore, you can run the file using psql or pgAdmin. Example B-1 shows the pg_dump help output. For full coverage of pg_dump usage, see "Selective Backup Using pg_dump" on page 51.

Example B-1. pg_dump help

```
pg_dump --help

pg_dump dumps a database as a text file or to other formats.
Usage:
pg_dump [OPTION]... [DBNAME]

General options:
-f, --file=FILENAME        output file or directory name
-F, --format=c|d|t|p       output file format (custom, directory, tar, plain
text)
-j, --jobs=NUM             use this many parallel jobs to dump
-v, --verbose              verbose mode
```

```
-Z, --compress=0-9          compression level for compressed formats
--lock-wait-timeout=TIMEOUT fail after waiting TIMEOUT for a table lock
--no-sync                   do not wait for changes to be written safely to disk ❶
--help                      show this help, then exit
--version                   output version information, then exit
Options controlling the output content:
-a, --data-only             dump only the data, not the schema
-b, --blobs                 include large objects in dump
-B, --no-blobs              exclude large objects in dump  ❷
-c, --clean                 clean (drop) database objects before recreating
-C, --create                include commands to create database in dump
-E, --encoding=ENCODING     dump the data in encoding ENCODING
-n, --schema=SCHEMA         dump the named schema(s) only
-N, --exclude-schema=SCHEMA do NOT dump the named schema(s)
-o, --oids                  include OIDs in dump
-O, --no-owner              skip restoration of object ownership in
plain-text format
-s, --schema-only           dump only the schema, no data
-S, --superuser=NAME        superuser user name to use in plain-text format
-t, --table=TABLE           dump the named table(s) only
-T, --exclude-table=TABLE   do NOT dump the named table(s)
-x, --no-privileges         do not dump privileges (grant/revoke)
--binary-upgrade            for use by upgrade utilities only
--column-inserts            dump data as INSERT commands with column names
--disable-dollar-quoting    disable dollar quoting, use SQL standard quoting
--disable-triggers          disable triggers during data-only restore
--enable-row-security        enable row security (dump only content user has
                              access to) ❸
--exclude-table-data=TABLE  do NOT dump data for the named table(s)
--if-exists                  use IF EXISTS when dropping objects
--inserts                   dump data as INSERT commands, rather than COPY
--no-publications            do not dump publications ❹
--no-security-labels        do not dump security label assignments
--no-subscriptions           do not dump subscriptions ❺
--no-synchronized-snapshots do not use synchronized snapshots in parallel jobs
--no-tablespaces            do not dump tablespace assignments
--no-unlogged-table-data    do not dump unlogged table data
--quote-all-identifiers     quote all identifiers, even if not key words
--section=SECTION           dump named section (pre-data, data, or post-data)
--serializable-deferrable   wait until the dump can run without anomalies
--snapshot=SNAPSHOT          use given snapshot for the dump  ❻
--strict-names               require table and/or schema include patterns to
                              match at least one entity each ❼
--use-set-session-authorization
use SET SESSION AUTHORIZATION commands instead of
ALTER OWNER commands to set ownership
Connection options:
-d, --dbname=DBNAME         database to dump
-h, --host=HOSTNAME         database server host or socket directory
-p, --port=PORT             database server port number
-U, --username=NAME         connect as specified database user
-w, --no-password           never prompt for password
```

```
-W, --password            force password prompt (should happen automatically)
--role=ROLENAME           do SET ROLE before dump
```

❶❷❸   New features introduced in PostgreSQL 10.

❹   New features introduced in PostgreSQL 9.6.

❺❻   New features introduced in PostgreSQL 9.5.

❼   New features introduced in PostgreSQL 9.4.

Server Backup: pg_dumpall

Use pg_dump_all (*http://bit.ly/1q2iRdW*) to back up all databases on your server onto
a single plain-text or plain-text SQL file. The backup routine will automatically
include server-level objects such as roles and tablespaces. Example B-2 shows the
pg_dumpall help output. See "Systemwide Backup Using pg_dumpall" on page 53 for
the full discussion.

Example B-2. pg_dumpall help

```
pg_dumpall --help

pg_dumpall extracts a PostgreSQL database cluster into an SQL script file.
Usage:
pg_dumpall [OPTION]...

General options:
-f, --file=FILENAME       output file name
-v, --verbose             verbose mode
-V, --version             output version information, then exit
--lock-wait-timeout=TIMEOUT  fail after waiting TIMEOUT for a table lock
-?, --help                show this help, then exit

Options controlling the output content:
  -a, --data-only         dump only the data, not the schema
  -c, --clean             clean (drop) databases before recreating
  -g, --globals-only      dump only global objects, no databases
  -o, --oids              include OIDs in dump
  -O, --no-owner          skip restoration of object ownership
  -r, --roles-only        dump only roles, no databases or tablespaces
  -s, --schema-only       dump only the schema, no data
  -S, --superuser=NAME    superuser user name to use in the dump
  -t, --tablespaces-only  dump only tablespaces, no databases or roles
  -x, --no-privileges     do not dump privileges (grant/revoke)
  --binary-upgrade        for use by upgrade utilities only
  --column-inserts        dump data as INSERT commands with column names
  --disable-dollar-quoting  disable dollar quoting, use SQL standard quoting
  --disable-triggers      disable triggers during data-only restore
```

```
    --inserts                    dump data as INSERT commands, rather than COPY
    --no-publications            do not dump publications ❶
    --no-security-labels         do not dump security label assignments
    --no-subscriptions           do not dump subscriptions ❷
    --no-sync                    do not wait for changes to be written safely to disk ❸
    --no-tablespaces             do not dump tablespace assignments
    --no-unlogged-table-data     do not dump unlogged table data
    --no-role-passwords          do not dump passwords for roles ❹
    --quote-all-identifiers      quote all identifiers, even if not keywords
    --use-set-session-authorization
use SET SESSION AUTHORIZATION commands instead o
ALTER OWNER commands to set ownership

Connection options:
  -d, --dbname=CONNSTR     connect using connection string
  -h, --host=HOSTNAME      database server host or socket directory
  -l, --database=DBNAME    alternative default database
  -p, --port=PORT          database server port number
  -U, --username=NAME      connect as specified database user
  -w, --no-password        never prompt for password
  -W, --password           force password prompt (should happen automatically)
  --role=ROLENAME          do SET ROLE before dump
```

If -f/--file is not used, then the SQL script will be written to the standard
output.

❶❷❸❹ New in PostgreSQL 10.

Database Restore: pg_restore

Use pg_restore to restore backup files in tar, custom, or directory formats created
using pg_dump. Example B-3 shows the pg_restore help output. See "Restoring Data"
on page 53 for more examples.

Example B-3. pg_restore help

```
pg_restore --help

pg_restore restores a PostgreSQL database from an archive created by pg_dump.
Usage:
  pg_restore [OPTION]... [FILE]

General options:
  -d, --dbname=NAME        connect to database name
  -f, --file=FILENAME      output file name
  -F, --format=c|d|t       backup file format (should be automatic)
  -l, --list               print summarized TOC of the archive
  -v, --verbose            verbose mode
  -V, --version            output version information, then exit
  -?, --help               show this help, then exit
```

```
Options controlling the restore:
  -a, --data-only           restore only the data, no schema
  -c, --clean               clean (drop) database objects before recreating
  -C, --create              create the target database
  -e, --exit-on-error       exit on error, default is to continue
  -I, --index=NAME          restore named index
  -j, --jobs=NUM            use this many parallel jobs to restore
  -L, --use-list=FILENAME   use table of contents from this file for
                            selecting/ordering output
  -n, --schema=NAME         restore only objects in this schema
  -N, --exclude-schema=NAME do not restore objects in this schema ❶
  -O, --no-owner            skip restoration of object ownership
  -P, --function=NAME(args) restore named function
  -s, --schema-only         restore only the schema, no data
  -S, --superuser=NAME      superuser user name to use for disabling triggers
  -t, --table=NAME          restore named relation (table, view, etc.) ❷
  -T, --trigger=NAME        restore named trigger
  -x, --no-privileges       skip restoration of access privileges (grant/revoke)
  -1, --single-transaction  restore as a single transaction
  --enable-row-security     enable row security ❸
  --disable-triggers        disable triggers during data-only restore
  --no-data-for-failed-tables do not restore data of tables that could not be
                            created
  --no-publications         do not restore publications ❹
  --no-security-labels      do not restore security labels
  --no-subscriptions        do not restore subscriptions ❺
  --no-tablespaces          do not restore tablespace assignments
  --section=SECTION         restore named section (pre-data, data, or post-data)
  --strict-names            require table and/or schema include patterns to
                            match at least one entity each ❻
  --use-set-session-authorization
                            use SET SESSION AUTHORIZATION commands instead of
                            ALTER OWNER commands to set ownership

Connection options:
  -h, --host=HOSTNAME       database server host or socket directory
  -p, --port=PORT           database server port number
  -U, --username=NAME       connect as specified database user
  -w, --no-password         never prompt for password
  -W, --password            force password prompt (should happen automatically)
  --role=ROLENAME           do SET ROLE before restore
```

❶❷❸ New features introduced in PostgreSQL 10.

❹❺ New features introduced in PostgreSQL 9.6. Prior to 9.6, the -t option matched only tables. In 9.6 it was changed to also match foreign tables, views, materialized views, and sequences.

❻ New features introduced in PostgreSQL 9.5.

psql Interactive Commands

Example B-4 lists commands available in psql when you launch an interactive session. For examples of usage, see "Environment Variables" on page 59 and "Interactive versus Noninteractive psql" on page 60.

Example B-4. Getting a list of interactive psql commands

```
\?
General
  \copyright              show PostgreSQL usage and distribution terms
  \errverbose             show most recent error message at maximum verbosity ❶
  \g [FILE] or ;          execute query (and send results to file or |pipe)
  \gexec                  execute query, then execute each value in its result ❷
  \gset [PREFIX]          execute query and store results in psql variables
  \h [NAME]               help on syntax of SQL commands, * for all commands
  \gx [FILE]              as \g, but forces expanded output mode ❸
  \q                      quit psql
  \crosstabview [COLUMNS] execute query and display results in crosstab ❹
  \watch [SEC]            execute query every SEC seconds
Help
  \? [commands]           show help on backslash commands
  \? options              show help on psql command-line options
  \? variables            show help on special variables
  \h [NAME]               help on syntax of SQL commands, * for all commands
Query Buffer
  \e [FILE] [LINE]        edit the query buffer (or file) with external editor
  \ef [FUNCNAME [LINE]]   edit function definition with external editor
  \ev [VIEWNAME [LINE]]   edit view definition with external editor ❺
  \p                      show the contents of the query buffer
  \r                      reset (clear) the query buffer
  \w FILE                 write query buffer to file
Input/Output
  \copy ...               perform SQL COPY with data stream to the client host
  \echo [STRING]          write string to standard output
  \i FILE                 execute commands from file
  \ir FILE                as \i, but relative to location of current script
  \o [FILE]               send all query results to file or |pipe
  \qecho [STRING]         write string to query output stream (see \o)
Conditional ❻
  \if EXPR                begin conditional block
  \elif EXPR              alternative within current conditional block
  \else                   final alternative within current conditional block
  \endif                  end conditional block
Informational
  (options: S = show system objects, + = additional detail)
  \d[S+]                  list tables, views, and sequences
  \d[S+]   NAME           describe table, view, sequence, or index
  \da[S]   [PATTERN]      list aggregates
  \dA[+]   [PATTERN]      list access methods ❼
```

```
\db[+]    [PATTERN]        list tablespaces
\dc[S]    [PATTERN]        list conversions
\dC       [PATTERN]        list casts
\dd[S]    [PATTERN]        show comments on objects
\ddp      [PATTERN]        list default privileges
\dD[S]    [PATTERN]        list domains
\det[+]   [PATTERN]        list foreign tables
\des[+]   [PATTERN]        list foreign servers
\deu[+]   [PATTERN]        list user mappings
\dew[+]   [PATTERN]        list foreign-data wrappers
\df[antw][S+] [PATRN]      list [only agg/normal/trigger/window] functions
\dF[+]    [PATTERN]        list text search configurations
\dFd[+]   [PATTERN]        list text search dictionaries
\dFp[+]   [PATTERN]        list text search parsers
\dFt[+]   [PATTERN]        list text search templates
\dg[S+]   [PATTERN]         list roles
\di[S+]   [PATTERN]        list indexes
\dl                        list large objects, same as \lo_list
\dL[S+]   [PATTERN]        list procedural languages
\dm[S+]   [PATTERN]        list materialized views
\dn[S+]   [PATTERN]        list schemas
\do[S]    [PATTERN]        list operators
\dO[S+]   [PATTERN]        list collations
\dp       [PATTERN]        list table, view, and sequence access privileges
\drds [PATRN1 [PATRN2]] list per-database role settings ❽
\dRp[+]   [PATTERN]        list replication publications ❽
\dRs[+]   [PATTERN]        list replication subscriptions ❾
\ds[S+]   [PATTERN]        list sequences
\dt[S+]   [PATTERN]        list tables
\dT[S+]   [PATTERN]        list data types
\du[S+]   [PATTERN]         list roles
\dv[S+]   [PATTERN]        list views
\dE[S+]   [PATTERN]        list foreign tables
\dx[+]    [PATTERN]        list extensions
\dy       [PATTERN]        list event triggers
\l[+]                      list databases
\sf[+] FUNCNAME            show a function's definition
\sv[+]  VIEWNAME           show a view's definition ❿
\z        [PATTERN]        same as \dp
Formatting
 \a                        toggle between unaligned and aligned output mode
 \C [STRING]               set table title, or unset if none
 \f [STRING]               show or set field separator for unaligned query output
 \H                        toggle HTML output mode (currently off)
 \pset NAME [VALUE]        set table output option
                           (NAME := {format|border|expanded|fieldsep|fieldsep_zero
              | footer|null|
           numericlocale|recordsep|tuples_only|title|tableattr|pager
           |unicode_border_linestyle|unicode_column_linestyle
           |unicode_header_linestyle ⓫
           })
 \t [on|off]               show only rows (currently off)
```

```
  \T [STRING]            set HTML <table> tag attributes, or unset if none
  \x [on|off]            toggle expanded output (currently off)
Connection
  \c[onnect] {[DBNAME|- USER|- HOST|- PORT|-] | conninfo}
                         connect to new database (currently "postgres")
  \encoding [ENCODING]   show or set client encoding
  \password [USERNAME]   securely change the password for a user
  \conninfo              display information about current connection
Operating System
  \cd [DIR]              change the current working directory
\setenv NAME [VALUE]     set or unset environment variable
  \timing [on|off]       toggle timing of commands (currently off)
  \! [COMMAND]           execute command in shell or start interactive shell
```

❶❷❸ New features introduced in PostgreSQL 10. All conditional options are new.

❹❺❻❼❽❾❿ New features introduced in PostgreSQL 9.6.

⓫ New feature introduced in PostgreSQL 9.5.

psql Noninteractive Commands

Example B-5 shows the noninteractive commands help screen. Examples of their usage are covered in "Interactive versus Noninteractive psql" on page 60.

Example B-5. psql basic help screen

```
psql --help

psql is the PostgreSQL interactive terminal.
Usage:
psql [OPTION]... [DBNAME [USERNAME]]

General options:
-c, --command=COMMAND   run only single command (SQL or internal) and exit
-d, --dbname=DBNAME     database name to connect to
-f, --file=FILENAME     execute commands from file, then exit
-l, --list              list available databases, then exit
-v, --set=, --variable=NAME=VALUE
                          set psql variable NAME to VALUE
                          (e.g., -v ON_ERROR_STOP=1)
-X, --no-psqlrc         do not read startup file (~/.psqlrc)
-1 ("one"), --single-transaction
execute command file as a single transaction
  -?, --help[=options]  show this help, then exit
    --help=commands     list backslash commands, then exit ❶
    --help=variables    list special variables, then exit ❷
--version               output version information, then exit

Input and output options:
```

```
-a, --echo-all          echo all input from script
-b, --echo-errors       echo failed commands  ❸
-e, --echo-queries      echo commands sent to server
-E, --echo-hidden       display queries that internal commands generate
-L, --log-file=FILENAME send session log to file
-n, --no-readline       disable enhanced command-line editing (readline)
-o, --output=FILENAME   send query results to file (or |pipe)
-q, --quiet             run quietly (no messages, only query output)
-s, --single-step       single-step mode (confirm each query)
-S, --single-line       single-line mode (end of line terminates SQL command)


Output format options:
-A, --no-align          unaligned table output mode
-F, --field-separator=STRING
set field separator (default: "|")
-H, --html              HTML table output mode
-P, --pset=VAR[=ARG]    set printing option VAR to ARG (see \pset command)
-R, --record-separator=STRING
set record separator (default: newline)
-t, --tuples-only       print rows only
-T, --table-attr=TEXT   set HTML table tag attributes (e.g., width, border)
-x, --expanded          turn on expanded table output
-z, --field-separator-zero
                        set field separator to zero byte
-0, --record-separator-zero
                        set record separator to zero byte


Connection options:
-h, --host=HOSTNAME     database server host or socket directory
-p, --port=PORT         database server port (default: "5432")
-U, --username=USERNAME database user name
-w, --no-password       never prompt for password
-W, --password          force password prompt (should happen automatically)
```

For more information, type "\?" (for internal commands) or "\help" (for SQL commands) from within psql, or consult the psql section in the PostgreSQL documentation.

❶❷❸ These items are new features introduced in PostgreSQL 9.5.

Index

RETURNING predicate, 176, 189
RETURNS TABLE clause, 207
REVOKE command, 43
rights (see privileges)
roles
    about, 23, 34
    backing up, 53
    group, 34-38
    login, 34-35
    organizing schemas by, 39
ROLLUP operator, 16, 196
row-level security, 17
rows (records)
    converting to JSON objects, 122
    partitioned tables and, 150
    returning affected records to users, 176
    row numbers in returned sets, 18
    unnesting arrays to, 113
ROWS FROM clause, 18
ROWS qualifier, 202
row_number function, 184, 186
row_to_json function, 122
rpad function, 102
RPC (random page cost) ratio, 242
rtrim function, 102
Ruby language, 19
rules, 13, 169
RUM index method type, 159

S

scans, parallel, 237
scheduling jobs, 94-98
schemas
    about, 8
    creating to house extensions, 9, 40, 48
    index names and, 157
    ogr_all, 261
    usage considerations, 39-41
searches
    ANY operator and, 174
    case-insensitive, 173
    full text, 12, 15, 130-141
SECURITY DEFINER qualifier, 202
security, row-level, 17
SELECT command
    avoiding *, 231
    embedding functions within, 33
    overusing subqueries in, 228-230
    restricting from inherited tables, 175

set-returning functions in, 174
sequences
    about, 12
    serial data types and, 100
serial data type, 100, 148
session_user global variable, 36
\set command, 63, 64
set force_parallel_mode setting, 235
SET ROLE command, 36-38
SET SESSION AUTHORIZATION command,
    36-38
set-returning functions, 174, 193, 207
sets
    grouping, 16, 195-197
    row numbers in returned, 18
setweight function, 135
shared_buffers network setting, 28, 29, 58
shell commands, executing, 65
shorthand casting, 172
SHOW ALL command, 26
SHOW command, 26
similar to operator (~), 105
single table views, 166
SKIP LOCKED clause, 33
slave servers, 246, 251
sort operator, 204
SP-GIST indexes, 159
split_part function, 103
SQL language
    about, 206
    basic functions, 206-207
    dynamic execution, 67-68
    writing aggregate functions, 208-209
state function, 204
statement_timeout setting, 33
statistics
    computing percentiles, median, mode,
        182-184
    gathering on statements, 227
    table, 240-242
storage
    command history, 65
    managing with tablespaces, 55
streaming replication, 247, 252
STRICT qualifier, 201
strings (see characters and strings)
string_agg function, 72, 102, 119, 181
string_to_array function, 103, 112
strip function, 140

U

Ubuntu platform, 267
unique constraints, 155, 162
Unix platform
    archive_command directive and, 250
    crontab command, 94
    installing PostgreSQL, 267
    psql tool and, 62
    restore_command directive and, 252
    retrieving command history, 65
UNLOGGED modifier, 153
unlogged tables, 16, 152
unnest function
    improved functionality, 18
    string_to_array function and, 103
    unnesting arrays into rows, 104, 113
    xpath function and, 128
\unset command, 62
untrusted languages, 205, 213
updatable setting, 258
UPDATE command, 39, 166, 175
UPDATE OF clause, 11, 203
updates
    conflict handling, 16
    lock failures, 17
    protecting against in views, 17
upper function, 173
UPSERT construct, 176
UTC (Coordinated Universal Time), 106

V

VACUUM ANALYZE command, 241
VALID UNTIL clause, 35
VALUES keyword, 173
values list, 173
varchar data type, 101, 148
variables
    configuration, 246
    environment, 59
    global, 36
    local, 210
    psql shortcuts and, 64
versions
    pgAdmin tool, 75
    pgAgent tool, 98
    pg_dump tool, 87
    pg_restore tool, 87
    PostgreSQL 10, 13
    PostgreSQL 9.4, 17-19

PostgreSQL 9.5, 16
PostgreSQL 9.6, 15
    upgrade recommendations, 13
views, 9
    (see also specific views)
    about, 9, 165
    avoiding SELECT * within, 231
    materialized, 17, 165, 169-171
    protecting against updates in, 17
    single table, 166
    updating with triggers, 167-169
views view, 11
VODKA index method type, 159
VOLATILITY setting, 201

W

WAL (write-ahead log), 246
\watch command, 65
WHEN trigger condition, 203
WHERE clause, 166
whitespace, trimiming, 102
window functions
    about, 184
    aggregate functions and, 204
    ORDER BY clause, 186-188
    PARTITION BY clause, 185
    writing in PL/V8, 218-220
Windows platform
    archive_command directive and, 250
    installing PostgreSQL, 265
    pgAgent versions and, 98
    psql tool and, 62
    restore_command directive and, 252
    retrieving command history, 65
window_object helper function, 218
WITH CHECK OPTION modifier, 17, 166
WITH clause, 11
WITH GRANT OPTION modifier, 43
WITH ORDINALITY clause, 129, 193-195
WITHIN GROUP modifier, 17, 183
work_mem network setting, 28
writable CTEs, 189
write-ahead log (WAL), 246
writing better queries
    about, 228
    avoiding SELECT *, 231
    CASE usage considerations, 232
    FILTER usage considerations, 233
    overusing subqueries in SELECT, 228-230

About the Authors

Regina Obe is a coprincipal of Paragon Corporation, a database consulting company based in Boston. She has more than 20 years of professional experience in various programming languages and database systems, with special focus on spatial databases. She is a member of the PostGIS steering committee and the PostGIS core development team as well as the pgRouting and GEOS development teams. Regina holds a BS degree in mechanical engineering from the Massachusetts Institute of Technology. She coauthored *PostGIS in Action* (Manning) and *pgRouting: A Practical Guide* (Locate Press).

Leo Hsu is a coprincipal of Paragon Corporation, a database consulting company based in Boston. He has more than 20 years of professional experience developing and thinking about databases for organizations large and small. Leo holds an MS degree in engineering of economic systems from Stanford University and BS degrees in mechanical engineering and economics from the Massachusetts Institute of Technology. He coauthored *PostGIS in Action* (Manning) and *pgRouting: A Practical Guide* (Locate Press).

Colophon

The animal on the cover of *PostgreSQL: Up and Running* is an elephant shrew (*Macroscelides proboscideus*), an insectivorous mammal native to Africa named for its lengthy trunk, which resembles that of an elephant. They are distributed across southern Africa in many types of habitat, from the Namib Desert to boulder-covered terrain in South Africa and thick forests.

The elephant shrew is small and quadrupedal; they resemble rodents and opossums with their scaly tails. Their legs are long for their size, allowing them to move around in a hopping fashion similar to a rabbit. The trunk varies in size depending on species, but are all able to twist around in search of food.

They are diurnal and active, though they are hardly seen due to being wary animals, which makes them difficult to trap. They are well camouflaged and quick at dashing away from threats.

Though elephant shrews are not very social, many of them live in monogamous pairs, sharing and defending their home territory. Female elephant shrews experience a menstrual cycle similar to that of human females; their mating period lasts for several days. Gestation lasts from 45 to 60 days, and the female gives birth to litters of one to three young, which are born fairly developed and remain in the nest for several days before venturing out. This can happen several times a year.

Five days after birth, young elephant shrews add mashed insects—which their mother collects and transports in her cheeks—to their milk diet. The young begin their migratory phase after about 15 days, lessening their dependency on the mother. They subsequently establish their own home range and become sexually active within 41 to 46 days.

Adult elephant shrews feed on invertebrates, such as insects, spiders, centipedes, millipedes, and earthworms. Eating larger prey can be somewhat messy. The elephant shrew must pin down the prey using its feet, then chews pieces with its cheek teeth, which can result in many dropped bits. The elephant shrew then uses its tongue to flick small food into its mouth, similar to an anteater. When available, some also eat small amounts of plant matter, such as new leaves, seeds, and small fruits.

Many of the animals on O'Reilly covers are endangered; all of them are important to the world. To learn more about how you can help, go to *animals.oreilly.com*.

The cover image is from *Meyers Kleines Lexicon*. The cover fonts are URW Typewriter and Guardian Sans. The text font is Adobe Minion Pro; the heading font is Adobe Myriad Condensed; and the code font is Dalton Maag's Ubuntu Mono.

Learn from experts.
Find the answers you need.

Sign up for a **10-day free trial** to get **unlimited access** to all of the content on Safari, including Learning Paths, interactive tutorials, and curated playlists that draw from thousands of ebooks and training videos on a wide range of topics, including data, design, DevOps, management, business—and much more.

Start your free trial at:

oreilly.com/safari

(No credit card required.)

Milton Keynes UK
Ingram Content Group UK Ltd.
UKHW050453240924
448772UK00005B/18